THE DEMOGRAPHY
OF RACIAL
AND ETHNIC GROUPS

STUDIES IN POPULATION

Under the Editorship of: H. H. WINSBOROUGH

Department of Sociology
University of Wisconsin
Madison, Wisconsin

Samuel H. Preston, Nathan Keyfitz, and Robert Schoen. **Causes of Death:** *Life* **Tables for National Populations.**

Otis Dudley Duncan, David L. Featherman, and Beverly Duncan. **Socioeconomic Background and Achievement.**

James A. Sweet. **Women in the Labor Force.**

Tertius Chandler and Gerald Fox. **3000 Years of Urban Growth.**

William H. Sewell and Robert M. Hauser. **Education, Occupation, and Earnings:** *Achievement in the Early Career.*

Otis Dudley Duncan. **Introduction to Structural Equation Models.**

William H. Sewell, Robert M. Hauser, and David L. Featherman (Eds.). **Schooling and Achievement in American Society.**

Henry Shryock, Jacob S. Siegel, and Associates. **The Methods and Materials of Demography.** *Condensed Edition by Edward Stockwell.*

Samuel H. Preston. **Mortality Patterns in National Populations:** *With Special Reference to Recorded Causes of Death.*

Robert M. Hauser and David L. Featherman. **The Process of Stratification:** *Trends and Analyses.*

Ronald R. Rindfuss and James A. Sweet. **Postwar Fertility Trends and Differentials in the United States.**

David L. Featherman and Robert M. Hauser. **Opportunity and Change.**

Karl E. Taeuber, Larry L. Bumpass, and James A. Sweet (Eds.). **Social Demography.**

Thomas J. Espenshade and William J. Serow (Eds.). **The Economic Consequences of Slowing Population Growth.**

Frank D. Bean and W. Parker Frisbie (Eds.). **The Demography of Racial and Ethnic Groups.**

In preparation

Maris A. Vinovskis (Ed.). **Studies in American Historical Demography.**

THE DEMOGRAPHY
OF RACIAL
AND ETHNIC GROUPS

Edited by

FRANK D. BEAN
W. PARKER FRISBIE
Population Research Center and the Department of Sociology
The University of Texas at Austin
Austin, Texas

 BIP-87

ACADEMIC PRESS   New York   San Francisco   London
A Subsidiary of Harcourt Brace Jovanovich, Publishers

ACADEMIC PRESS, INC.
111 Fifth Avenue, New York, New York 10003

United Kingdom Edition published by
ACADEMIC PRESS, INC. (LONDON) LTD.
24/28 Oval Road, London NW1 7DX

Library of Congress Cataloging in Publication Data
Main entry under title:

The Demography of racial and ethnic groups.

Based on papers presented at a conference held
in Austin, Tex. during the summer of 1977 in
conjunction with the 6th annual meeting of Directors
of Program Projects and Population Research Centers.
Includes bibliographies.
1. Minorities--United States--Social conditions
--Congresses. 2. Minorities--United States--
Economic conditions--Congresses. 3. United
States--Population--Congresses. 4. United States
--Race relations--Congresses. I. Bean, Frank D.
II. Frisbie, William Parker, Date.
E184.A1D35   301.45'0973   78-22040
ISBN 0-12-083650-5

PRINTED IN THE UNITED STATES OF AMERICA

78 79 80 81 82   9 8 7 6 5 4 3 2 1

Contents

Contents

List of Contributors

Numbers in parentheses indicate the pages on which the authors' contributions begin.

FRANK D. BEAN (1, 143, 189), Population Research Center and the Department of Sociology, The University of Texas at Austin, Austin, Texas 78712

BENJAMIN S. BRADSHAW (261), Population Studies Unit, School of Public Health, University of Texas Health Sciences Center, Houston, Texas 77025

ISAAC W. EBERSTEIN (143), Population Research Center, The University of Texas at Austin, Austin, Texas 78712

REYNOLDS FARLEY (15), Population Studies Center, University of Michigan, Ann Arbor, Michigan 48104

EDWIN FONNER, JR. (261), Population Studies Unit, School of Public Health, University of Texas Health Sciences Center, Houston, Texas 77025

WILLIAM H. FREY (79), Center for Demography and Ecology, University of Wisconsin, Madison, Wisconsin 53706

W. PARKER FRISBIE (1, 143), Population Research Center and the Department of Sociology, The University of Texas at Austin, Austin, Texas 78712

STANLEY LIEBERSON (119), Department of Sociology, University of Arizona, Tucson, Arizona 85721

JOHN P. MARCUM (189), Department of Sociology, University of Southern Illinois, Carbondale, Illinois 62901

ALBERTO PALLONI (283), Population Research Center, The University of Texas at Austin, Austin, Texas 78712

JOHN SHELTON REED (213), Department of Sociology, University of North Carolina, Chapel Hill, North Carolina 27514

RONALD R. RINDFUSS (213), Department of Sociology, University of North Carolina, Chapel Hill, North Carolina 27514

CRAIG ST. JOHN (213), Department of Sociology, University of North Carolina, Chapel Hill, North Carolina 27514

TERESA A. SULLIVAN (165), Population Research Center, The University of Chicago, Chicago, Illinois 60637

GORDON F. SUTTON (301), Department of Sociology, University of Massachusetts, Amherst, Massachusetts 01002

JAMES A. SWEET (221), Center for Demography and Ecology, University of Wisconsin, Madison, Wisconsin 53706

KARL E. TAEUBER (51), Center for Demography and Ecology, University of Wisconsin, Madison, Wisconsin 53706

FRANKLIN D. WILSON (51), Center for Demography and Ecology, University of Wisconsin, Madison, Wisconsin 53706

Preface

This volume is an outgrowth of a conference organized under the auspices of The University of Texas Population Research Center and held in Austin during the summer of 1977, in conjunction with the sixth annual meeting of directors of program projects and population research centers supported by the Center for Population Research of the National Institute of Child Health and Human Development. The theme chosen for the conference was "the demography of racial and ethnic groups." As the following chapters make clear, the demographic behavior of racial and ethnic groups raises issues that have significance in both theoretical and public policy areas. The demography of racial and ethnic groups is theoretically important because the understanding of subpopulation characteristics and processes is basic to any understanding of phenomena pertaining to larger populations. It has policy implications because racial and ethnic groups are often the targets of special social and economic programs, the implementation of which is difficult without demographic knowledge of the particular groups at which the programs are aimed.

When organizing the conference, we did not specify that each author or set of authors concentrate on a single racial or ethnic group. To have done so would have been to forgo at the outset the insights that only comparative analysis of two or more subpopulations can provide. Nor did we insist that all the topics of interest to demographers be covered (although most of these were, in fact, addressed in one or more of the works included). Rather, our intent and expectation was that the analyses be representative (but not necessarily all-inclusive) of current substantive, methodological, and theoretical investigations involving one or more racial–ethnic groups in the United States. We hope we have succeeded with respect to this criterion, although that judgment must ultimately be left to the reader.

A number of persons deserve special thanks for their efforts in bringing about the conference, this book, or both. Dr. William A. Sadler of the Center for Population Research at NICHD provided enthusiastic support for the conference at every opportunity. Harley Browning, at that time the director of the Population Research Center at The University of Texas at Austin, was a constant source of encouragement. Hal Winsborough of the University of Wisconsin has been extremely helpful in preparing the manuscript for publication. Shirley Agee helped arrange the conference, and Jeannie Taylor and Peggy Kelley typed portions of the manuscript. Without the assistance of all of these persons, as well as that of others who contributed in smaller but no less important ways, this book would not have been possible.

1

Some Issues
in the Demographic
Study of Racial
and Ethnic Populations

W. PARKER FRISBIE
FRANK D. BEAN

The study of demography is in many instances closely connected to the investigation of racial and ethnic populations. Our general comprehension of demographic characteristics and processes is enhanced by comparative investigations of particular subpopulations variously designated as racial, ethnic, and/or minority groups. Benefits of such analyses are not difficult to enumerate. Obviously, global demographic profiles and trends are composites that obscure the sometimes similar, but often divergent, structures and processes of subpopulations comprising the whole. To illustrate, only a short time ago a great deal of concern was manifested regarding rapid population growth in the United States in general and over the expansion of metropolitan populations in particular. With fertility now hovering near replacement level and with the surprising (to most) reversal of net migration trends in favor of nonmetropolitan areas, increasing attention is being given to the possible effects of a stable population, to the "graying of America," and to the

1

The Demography of Racial and Ethnic Groups.

"nonmetropolitanization" resulting from the recent shift in the direction of population redistribution.

However, not all segments of the American population have contributed proportionately to these changes. Completed fertility (i.e., children ever born per 1000 women aged 35–44) among blacks and the Spanish-surname population continues to be substantially above that of Anglos, although all three groups have experienced declining fertility since the peak attained in the late 1950s (Bradshaw and Bean, 1972, 1973). On the other hand, the completed fertility of other groups, such as Cubans and Japanese Americans, stands at a level considerably lower than that of the white (or Anglo) population (U.S. Bureau of the Census, 1971, 1973). Likewise, at least one large minority group, blacks, has apparently not shared in the nonmetropolitan net migration reversal (Zuiches and Brown, 1975). Thus, the initial and most clear-cut advantage of the comparative demographic study of racial and ethnic groups is the greater descriptive richness and precision that such analyses bring to demographic studies.

CULTURAL VERSUS STRUCTURAL EXPLANATIONS OF DEMOGRAPHIC DIFFERENCES AMONG SUBPOPULATIONS

The uncovering of differences across subpopulations leads directly to investigations of the causes and consequences of the observed variation. By *subpopulations* we mean groups more commonly referred to as racial, ethnic, or minority groups. In this chapter, a distinction is drawn between racial and ethnic groups on the one hand and minorities on the other. To be meaningful, research into the determinants of demographic variation by race, ethnicity, or minority group status must involve, at a minimum, some reasonable delimitation of the universe of variables that may be expected to afford some degree of explanatory power. Inevitably, it would seem, the decision as to where to look for explanation will be premised on some notion, however vague, of the nature of the subpopulations to be studied. In general, research in this area seems to have adopted one or both of two approaches, though one would be hard pressed to find a comprehensive theoretical statement of either.

One approach searches for determinants of demographic variation in the history and cultural traditions of different subpopulations. Underlying (usually implicitly) this perspective is a conceptualization of subpopulations that parallels rather closely Schermerhorn's (1970) definition of an ethnic group: "A collectivity within a larger society having real or putative common ancestry, memories of a shared historical past, and a cultural focus on one or more symbolic elements defined as the epitome of peoplehood [p. 12]." Examples of symbolic elements include kinship patterns, nationality, language, phenotypical features, and religious affiliation. Let us refer to the analytical strategy that relies primarily on explanations of this sort as the "cultural approach," since demographic differences among groups are attributed to cultural differences, or, in some cases, to varying degrees of cultural assimilation (acculturation).

A second approach seeks an explanation in the extent to which subpopulations have obtained access to and have been assimilated into the economic and political structures of the larger society. Taking some liberties with an already overworked term, we shall call research in this vein the "structural approach" because of its focus on structural assimilation. In this instance, our use of the term *assimilation* is not in any sense intended to be judgmental. It makes no assumption that distinctive racial or ethnic groups should or will lose their identity through amalgamation with some dominant group. By *structural assimilation*, we refer simply to the degree to which subpopulations have acquired the political and economic characteristics of the general population. Gordon (1964) has identified seven dimensions of assimilation and gives a meaning to the term structural assimilation quite different from the one offered here. With the possible exception of marital assimilation, all of Gordon's dimensions seem to be derivatives of cultural and structural assimilation, as just defined. Our own perspective is somewhat more closely akin (but is not identical) to van den Berghe's (1967) view of cultural versus social (structural) pluralism.

At times, the structural approach has seemed atheoretical in the sense that it appears to lack interest in the sources of structural differences (or inequalities) and, therefore, might better be seen as merely "compositional" in character. Yet by and large the underlying assumption (again, often implicit) is that the subpopulations constitute *minorities*, that is, groups "whose members experience a wide range of discriminatory behavior and frequently are relegated to positions low in the status hierarchy [Gittler, 1956:vii; quoted in Yetman and Steele, 1975:1–2]."[1]

[1] Definitions of a minority (e.g., Robin Williams, 1964) that emphasize hereditary membership and/or a high degree of endogamy seem much too restrictive (Yetman and Steele, 1975:1). For example, Mexican Americans and blacks who intermarry with Anglos may still be relegated to inferior positions in the status hierarchy and may perhaps be subjected to even more virulent forms of discrimination than those who marry endogamously. Furthermore, certain religious groups (e.g., Baptists in the Soviet Union) may be appropriately considered as minorities, yet their position is neither hereditary nor the result of endogamy.

To the extent that this emphasis predominates, the focus gains precision as the search for explanation is concentrated specifically on differentials in power and control of resources. The two approaches are necessarily not mutually exclusive and certainly are not contradictory, since in the United States, at least, cultural pluralism tends to parallel structural separation (Goldscheider and Uhlenberg, 1969:361; for a somewhat similar perspective, see van den Berghe, 1967:34–37). On the other hand, it is quite true that the "degree of acculturation and the desire for acculturation do not necessarily imply structural integration [Goldscheider and Uhlenberg, 1969:370]."

Although several of the subpopulations that have received attention from demographers are often described as racial groups, the concept of *race* per se does not play a definitive role in the two analytical approaches delineated in the preceding discussion. One conventional definition of race is "a human group that defines itself or is defined by others as different from other groups by virtue of innate and immutable characteristics [van den Berghe, 1967:9]." In other words, it is not the physical characteristics themselves but the *social definition* that is of relevance. If the social distinction is made in terms of differences in historical traditions, language, nationality, etc., the approach is cultural. If the emphasis is on compositional differences with little or no attention to the sources of the differences, the distinction can be viewed as the compositional variant of the structural approach. If physical differences are used as a rationale for discriminatory behavior and for limiting a group's power and control of resources, the minorities dimension of the structural approach comes into play.

An argument could perhaps be made that if, in addition to being an ethnic subpopulation as defined in the preceding discussion, a group also defines itself or is defined by others as being different by virtue of innate characteristics (however ill-founded the assumption), that ethnic group is also a racial group. However, the purpose here is not to derive and defend a given set of definitions but rather to distinguish and describe what appear to be the two principal approaches in research designed to account for differences observed in various subpopulations. It seems clear that even where the term race might be applied, both of the approaches depend basically on social definitions. Of course, it would be foolish to assert that biology plays no role in explaining demographic differences. One obvious example is the effect on mortality of certain diseases (such as sickle-cell anemia) that appear in some groups but rarely, or not at all, in others. Such phenomena are essentially outside the purview of this chapter (and of this volume).

An ethnic group may or may not be a minority. That is, maintenance of historic cultural distinctions does not mean that a group will necessarily exercise only a minimal degree of power and resource control. Furthermore, an ethnic group may be a minority at one point in time but not at another. At one stage of American history, for example, the Irish were clearly both an ethnic group and a minority, but currently they would not seem to constitute a minority as defined herein. To a large extent, much the same might be said of Japanese Americans who, after suffering severe restrictions on their ability to control resources from the early stages of immigration (e.g., proscriptive alien land laws) up to and including the World War II incarceration and the aftermath, have come to surpass the general population in areas such as educational achievement (Uhlenberg, 1972) and life expectancy (Kitagawa and Hauser, 1973:99–101). Although it is possible to quibble over the appropriateness of these illustrations, the general points should be clear.

The difference between the two approaches and the difficulties that beset them, separately and in combination, are illustrated in studies of the effects of minority group status on fertility. Examinations of the effects of minority group status on fertility (Goldscheider and Uhlenberg, 1969; Kennedy, 1973; Rindfuss and Sweet, 1977; Roberts and Lee, 1974; Sly, 1970) come closer than other types of research to making explicit the thrust of the two approaches. In general, two alternative explanations are juxtaposed: The "characteristics" or "assimilationist" hypothesis attributes fertility differentials to dissimilarities between groups in regard to various social, demographic, and economic characteristics. When such differences disappear, or are controlled statistically, "differences in fertility should be eliminated" or at least should converge to the point of insignificance (Goldscheider and Uhlenberg, 1969:361). The alternative proposition indicates that "even when groups are similar socially, demographically, and economically, minority group membership will continue to exert an effect on fertility [Rindfuss and Sweet, 1977:113]." Still another hypothesis is indicated by Goldscheider and Uhlenberg's (1969) finding that the fertility of high socioeconomic status members of some groups is lower than that of their majority counterparts, even though fertility for the group as a whole exceeds that of the majority group. Goldscheider and Uhlenberg explain this result in terms of the "insecurity" that accompanies minority group status (see Bean and Marcum, Chapter 8 of this volume). Whatever the adequacy of their explanation, the observed pattern suggests the possibility that group membership and social and economic characteristics interact in their effects on fertility.

Such interaction effects complicate the interpretation of fertility differentials in terms of the two approaches already discussed. To the degree that fertility differences are explained by reference to distinctive values, norms, and ideologies (e.g., see Goldscheider and Uhlenberg [1969:371] on divergent Catholic fertility)[2] the approach is clearly cultural, and the emphasis is on "ethnicity." If an attempt is made to account for variation in fertility in terms of divergent social, demographic, and economic characteristics, the approach is structural or compositional. If certain fertility patterns, such as differing relationships between social and economic variables and fertility, are attributed to the "insecurities of minority group status" (Goldscheider and Uhlenberg, 1969:370), the model corresponds rather closely to the perspective that views the group in question as a *minority*, that is, lacking in power and resource control.

Ambiguities persist because of the conceptual underdevelopment characterizing both general approaches. This underdevelopment may be partially explained by the lack of awareness on the part of researchers of the distinctions between the two perspectives and of the necessity for greater precision in their application. The structural approach fails to distinguish simple compositional effects from those stemming from inequalities in power and position in the stratification system. The cultural approach may be even more unsatisfying owing to the tendency to allocate variance unexplained after controls for socioeconomic characteristics to a broad residual category, "culture," without attempting to identify more specific explanations (for a critique, see Goldscheider and Uhlenberg, 1969).

It should not be inferred that these comments apply only to fertility analysis. For example, in the research by Frisbie *et al.* (Chapter 6 of this volume), several alternative hypotheses are identified that bear on the prevalence of marital instability among Mexican Americans, blacks, and Anglos. One, the "family structural" perspective, offers a cultural interpretation based on differences in norms and values regarding family life that purportedly distinguish the three groups. The second relies on demographic and socioeconomic characteristics for explanation, without making clear whether the decisive factor is background differences pure and simple or the fact that blacks and Chicanos are minority groups. Some argument is made in favor of an interaction effect involving differentials in resource control and specific norms associated with a familistic orientation, but the argument applies mainly to only one of the groups, Mexican Americans.

---

[2] However, the recent convergence of Catholic birth control practices to a point nearly identical to those of non-Catholics suggests that higher Catholic fertility may not maintain itself in the future (Westoff and Jones, 1977:203–207).

Resolving this conceptual vagueness would seem to be the first order of business for researchers engaged in comparative analysis of demographic differences, but other questions must eventually be addressed as well. For example, can the two approaches be expected to be equally useful in explaining both individual and aggregate differences? As Rindfuss and Sweet point out, arguing that group differences in fertility will converge as social, economic, and demographic characteristics become similar "is not the same thing as saying that, when an *individual* member of a minority group acquires [characteristics similar to those] of the dominant group, his or her fertility will resemble that of the majority group [1977:112, n. 2]." Fertility research has concentrated (although not exclusively) on group differences, whereas the marital instability research just mentioned takes individuals as the unit of analysis. Finally, it remains to be determined which, if either, of the two approaches is superior in accounting for changes in demographic characteristics as contrasted to cross-sectional differences.

TOPICS IN RACIAL–ETHNIC GROUP DEMOGRAPHY

Obviously, and inevitably, many issues of theoretical and practical significance have not been addressed in the present volume. Among the more prominent research themes not included is the subordination of minority populations with respect to income, education, and occupational status—a topic that seems more the province of studies in stratification or race and ethnic relations in general. This is not to say that demographically oriented research has made no contribution to the study of majority–minority inequality. In fact, certain stratification-related phenomena are dealt with by authors in this volume, including Farley (Chapter 2), Wilson and Taeuber (Chapter 3), and Frey (Chapter 4) on residential and school segregation and Sullivan (Chapter 7) on labor force participation.

However, other types of analyses of inequality that fit easily under the broad heading of "population studies" do not appear in this collection. Although it does not coincide with the emphasis of this volume, the significance of such research is made obvious by the nature of the findings forthcoming from it. Examples include the demonstration of: (a) both the high degree of socioeconomic inequality that separates majority and minority groups in the United States and the (usually slow) diminution of the gap over time (e.g., Farley, 1977; Farley and Hermalin, 1972; Grebler *et al.*, 1970); (b) the influence of such basic demographic variables as the absolute and relative size of minority populations (and their increase) on socioeconomic disparities (Blalock, 1956, 1957; Brown and Fuguitt, 1972; Frisbie and Neidert, 1977; Glenn, 1964, 1966) and on the resistance of minorities to perceived inequality (Downes, 1970; Spilerman, 1970, 1971); (c) the cost of being black or Mexican American (Poston and Alvírez, 1973; Poston et al., 1976; Siegel, 1965); and (d) the differences in minority patterns of social mobility (Duncan, 1968; Hauser and Featherman, 1974; Lieberson and Fuguitt, 1967).

Another area of research not represented in this volume documents differentials in wanted, desired, and expected family size and in contraceptive behavior (Bauman and Udry, 1973; Ryder and Westoff, 1971; Westoff, 1975; Westoff and Ryder, 1970). It has been shown, for example, that although black women want (and desire) fewer children than white women, they expect more births. The principal reason that analyses of this sort have not been included is that, although there are a large number of studies focusing on black–white and Catholic–non-Catholic differences, virtually no current research is available that involves other subpopulations. One exception from already published research can be seen in an examination carried out by the Austin Family Study of desired and expected family size and contraceptive use among Mexican Americans. In this study it was discovered that Mexican American females want more children than either black or Anglo women. However, they also have more children than they desire (Alvírez, 1973; Bradshaw and Bean, 1972). Unfortunately, little additional research has yet been forthcoming.

Yet another gap in our coverage has to do with migration and population redistribution. Included is the excellent historical study by Lieberson (Chapter 5) on selective black migration from the South (see also Lieberson and Wilkinson, 1976; Long and Heltman, 1975; Taeuber and Taeuber, 1965). Left out, however, is research documenting the gradual dispersion of other racial and ethnic groups, such as Mexican Americans from the Southwest (Grebler et al., 1970) and Japanese Americans from the West, including Hawaii (Kitano, 1969), and the adjustment of various groups of migrants at destination (Price, 1971; Shannon and Morgan, 1966; Shannon and Shannon, 1973).

The recent upsurge of demographic interest in family organization is reflected in the chapters by Sweet on family structure (Chapter 10) and by Frisbie et al. on marital instability (Chapter 6). However, the volume contains no research on intermarriage across racial or ethnic lines. Exogamy, of course, has important implications for both ethnic and minority status. Majority group resistance to intermarriage prevents "the

diffusion of power, authority and preferred status to persons not affili-
ated with [the] dominant group [Merton, 1941:368]." Moreover, "at the
limit, that is, where no barriers exist and contracting of marriages across
ethnic or racial lines is essentially a random event, one might reasonably
conclude that the assimilation of a minority, both cultural and structural, is virtually complete [Murguía and Frisbie, 1977:374; see also
Gordon, 1964]." A somewhat unusual situation exists in regard to recent
investigations of exogamy in that, unlike most other areas of comparative research, less attention has been devoted to blacks and more to
other subpopulations, notably Mexican Americans. Exogamy by blacks
has been and continues to be quite rare (Heer, 1966; Monahan, 1970),
whereas rates of intermarriage of other groups (e.g., Japanese Americans
and the Spanish-Surname population) are relatively high, especially
among female members of these groups (Bean and Bradshaw, 1970;
Mittelbach and Moore, 1968; Murguía and Frisbie, 1977; U.S. Bureau of
the Census, 1972; Vander Zanden, 1972).

Although not comprehensive, either in intent or fact, this volume
encompasses a very broad range of empirical questions. Each contribution to the volume is replete with important implications, not only for
the groups studied but also for the entire society. Few issues have more
bearing on the solidarity of American society or have evoked more
strident polemics than the debate over residential and school desegregation. Farley (Chapter 2) traces the social, legal, and political history of
this controversy as a necessary background for understanding recent
trends in the segregation of students and teachers. Frey's analysis
(Chapter 4) represents, to date, the only empirical examination of the
pace at which metropolitan-wide integration can be expected to proceed.
Wilson and Taeuber (Chapter 3) report on one of the very few studies of
school segregation in a triethnic situation and suggest that, in addition
to the usual concern over the role of residential segregation in preserving
school segregation, one must also acknowledge the reverse, namely "that
the racial–ethnic organization of schooling has had a continuing and
profound influence on population distribution." Addressing the issue
of the effects of population redistribution on a broader, society-wide
scale, Lieberson (Chapter 5) finds little support for the argument that
depicts a deterioration of the position of blacks in the North and the
West as a result of massive in-migration by southern blacks.

Indicators of the life chances and quality of life of populations are
numerous and varied, but none are more basic than mortality and cause
of death rates, which reflect disparities in exposure to risk of disease or
injury, quality of nutrition, and access to health care. Similarly, a

rather direct measure of access to the economic system is the rate of labor force participation. Differentials in these crucial indicators of well-being are analyzed, respectively, by Bradshaw and Fonner (Chapter 11), who focus particularly on comparisons of Mexican Americans with blacks and Anglos, and by Sullivan (Chapter 7), whose work encompasses ten racial or ethnic groups. Complementing Bradshaw and Fonner's analysis is the study by Palloni (Chapter 12), which outlines a new technique for estimating mortality, one that may prove especially useful in the case of certain racial–ethnic groups. Sutton (Chapter 13) is also concerned with mortality, and he studies the effects of mortality differentials on surviving family members and the extent to which the differences augment the disadvantage of the nonwhite population.

Social and economic well-being also depends on family structure and stability. Family composition affects not only consumption needs but also the ability to meet those needs. Likewise, marital dissolution tends to be disruptive of economic and social stability. Determinants of marital instability among Mexican Americans, blacks, and Anglos are examined by Frisbie et al. (Chapter 6), and Sweet (Chapter 10) delineates the familial structure characterizing over a dozen subpopulations.

Finally, reproductive behavior, which influences and is influenced by a group's ethnic status and position in the stratification system, is investigated by Bean and Marcum (Chapter 8) and by Rindfuss et al. (Chapter 9). The former authors summarize, criticize, and extend the growing literature on the minority group status explanation of fertility differences, and the latter offer an intriguing analysis of what may be a most unusual, unintended consequence for fertility rates of certain public policies.

Thus, although not fully covering the variety of research currently underway in the demography of racial and ethnic groups, the research reported in this volume substantially increases our knowledge of the area in both a theoretical and a policy-relevant sense.

A NOTE ON SEMANTICS

We have selected as the title for this volume *The Demography of Racial and Ethnic Groups*. All the research included in this collection compares groups that constitute racial or ethnic categories, but not all of these could be classified as minorities according to the distinctions drawn in this chapter. This raises the issue of semantics, an issue that is not regarded as crucial in and of itself. What is important is that authors make clear the conceptual approach guiding their analyses (whether it be one of the general ones outlined in this chapter, some variant of these, or yet another persepective not quite so apparent in the literature). Although some of the authors are much more concerned with the minority status of the groups investigated than with race or ethnicity, their approach is easily discerned and will occasion no difficulty from the reader's standpoint. Thus, *The Demography of Racial and Ethnic Groups* was selected as the most generally descriptive rubric under which to include these studies. In some respects, a title such as "The Demography of Subpopulations" might be more appropriate, but the unfamilarity of such terminology would likely create more ambiguity than it would eliminate.

REFERENCES

Alvirez, David
    1973   "The effects of formal church affiliation and religiosity on the fertility of Mexican-American Catholics." *Demography* 10:19–36.
Bauman, Karl E., and J. Richard Udry
    1973   "The difference in unwanted births between blacks and whites." *Demography* 10 (August):315–328.
Bean, Frank D., and Benjamin S. Bradshaw
    1970   "Intermarriage between persons of Spanish and non-Spanish surname: Changes from the mid-nineteenth to the mid-twentieth century." *Social Science Quarterly* 51:389–395.
Blalock, Hubert M. Jr.
    1956   "Economic discrimination and Negro increase." *American Journal of Sociology* 21:584–588.
    1957   "Percent nonwhite and discrimination in the South." *American Sociological Review* 22:677–682.
Bradshaw, Benjamin S., and Frank D. Bean
    1972   "Some aspects of the fertility of Mexican Americans." Pp. 140–164 in Charles F. Westoff and Robert Parke, Jr. (eds.), *Demographic and Social Aspects of Population Growth*, Research Reports, Vol. I, Commission on Population Growth and the American Future. Washington, D.C.: U.S. Government Printing Office.
    1973   "Trends in fertility of Mexican Americans, 1950–1970." *Social Science Quarterly* 53:688–696.
Brown, David L., and Glenn V. Fuguitt
    1972   "Percent nonwhite and racial disparity in nonmetropolitan cities in the South." *Social Science Quarterly* 53:573–582.
Downes, Bryan T.
    1970   "A critical reexamination of the social and political characteristics of riot cities." *Social Science Quarterly* 51:349–360.
Duncan, Otis Dudley
    1968   "Patterns of occupational mobility among Negro men." *Demography* 5:11–22.

Farley, Reynolds
    1977   "Trends in racial inequalities: Have the gains of the 1960's dis-
                appeared in the 1970's?" *American Sociological Review* 42 (April):
                189–208.
Farley, Reynolds, and Albert I. Hermalin
    1972   "The 1960's: A decade of progress for blacks?" *Demography* 9:353–
                370.
Frisbie, W. Parker, and Lisa Neidert
    1977   "Inequality and the relative size of minority populations: A com-
                parative analysis." *American Journal of Sociology* 82:1007–1030.
Gittler, Joseph B.
    1956   *Understanding Minority Groups.* New York: John Wiley and Sons.
Glenn, Norval D.
    1964   "The relative size of the Negro population and Negro occupational
                status." *Social Forces* 43:42–49.
    1966   "White gains from Negro subordination." *Social Problems* 14:149–
                178.
Goldscheider, Calvin, and Peter R. Uhlenberg
    1969   "Minority group status and fertility." *American Journal of Sociology*
                74 (January):361–372.
Gordon, Milton
    1964   *Assimilation in American Life.* New York: Oxford University Press.
Grebler, Leo, Joan W. Moore, and Ralph C. Guzman
    1970   *The Mexican American People.* New York: The Free Press.
Hauser, Robert, and David L. Featherman
    1974   "White–nonwhite differentials in occupational mobility among men
                in the United States, 1962–1972." *Demography* 11:247–266.
Heer, David
    1966   "Negro–white marriage in the United States." *Journal of Marriage
                and the Family* 28:262–273.
Kennedy, Robert E. Jr.
    1973   "Minority group status and fertility: The Irish." *American Sociologi-
                cal Review* 38 (February):85–96.
Kitagawa, Evelyn M., and Philip M. Hauser
    1973   *Differential Mortality in the United States: A Study in Socioeconomic
                Epidemiology.* Cambridge: Harvard University Press.
Kitano, Harry H. L.
    1969   *Japanese Americans.* Englewood Cliffs, N.J.: Prentice-Hall.
Lieberson, Stanley, and Glenn V. Fuguitt
    1967   "Negro–white occupational differences in the absence of discirimina-
                tion." *American Journal of Sociology* 73:188–200.
Lieberson, Stanley, and Christy A. Wilkinson
    1976   "A comparison between northern and southern Blacks residing in
                the North." *Demography* 13:199–224.
Long, Larry H., and Lynn R. Heltman
    1975   "Migration and income differences between black and white men in
                the North." *American Journal of Sociology* 80 (May):1391–1409.
Merton, Robert K.
    1941   "Intermarriage and the social structure: Fact and theory." *Psychiatry*
                4:361–374.

Mittelbach, Frank G., and Joan W. Moore
1968   "Ethnic endogamy: The case of Mexican Americans." *American Journal of Sociology* 74:50–62.
Monahan, Thomas P.
1970   "Interracial marriage: Data for Philadelphia and Pennsylvania." *Demography* 7:287–299.
Murguía, Edward, and W. Parker Frisbie
1977   "Trends in Mexican American intermarriage: Recent findings in perspective." *Social Science Quarterly* 58(3):374–389.
Poston, Dudley L. Jr., and David Alvírez
1973   "On the cost of being a Mexican American worker." *Social Science Quarterly* 53:695–709.
Poston, Dudley L. Jr., David Alvírez, and Marta Tienda
1976   "Earnings differences between Anglo and Mexican American male workers in 1960 and 1970: Changes in the 'cost' of being Mexican American." *Social Science Quarterly* 67:618–631.
Price, Daniel O.
1971   "Rural to urban migration of Mexicans, Negroes and Anglos." *International Migration Review* 5:281–291.
Rindfuss, Ronald R., and James A. Sweet
1977   *Postwar Fertility Trends and Differentials in the United States.* New York: Academic Press.
Roberts, Robert E., and Eun Sul Lee
1974   "Minority group status and fertility revisited." *American Journal of Sociology* 80 (September):503–523.
Ryder, Norman B., and Charles F. Westoff
1971   *Reproduction in the United States, 1965.* Princeton, New Jersey: Princeton University Press.
Schermerhorn, R. A.
1970   *Comparative Ethnic Relations: A Framework for Theory and Research.* New York: Random House.
Shannon, Lyle W., and Magdaline Shannon
1973   *Minority Migrants in the Urban Community: Mexican American and Negro Adjustment to Industrial Society.* Beverly Hills, California: Sage.
Shannon, Lyle W., and Patricia Morgan
1966   "The prediction of economic absorption and cultural integration among Mexican Americans, Negroes, and Anglos in a northern industrial community." *Human Organization* 25:154–162.
Siegel, Paul M.
1965   "On the cost of being a Negro." *Sociological Inquiry* 35:41–57.
Sly, David F.
1970   "Minority-group status and fertility: An extension of Goldscheider and Uhlenberg." *American Journal of Sociology* 76 (November): 433–459.
Spilerman, Seymour
1970   "The causes of racial disturbances: A comparison of alternative explanations." *American Sociological Review* 35:627–649.
1971   "The causes of racial disturbances: Tests of an explanation." *American Sociological Review* 36:427–442.

Taeuber, Karl E., and Alma F. Taeuber
   1965   "The changing character of Negro migration." *American Journal of Sociology* 70:374–382.
Uhlenberg, Peter
   1972   "Demographic correlates of group achievement: Contrasting patterns of Mexican-Americans and Japanese-Americans." *Demography* 9:119–128.
U.S. Bureau of the Census
   1971   "Fertility variations by ethnic origin: November, 1969." Current Population Reports, Series P-20, no. 226. Washington, D.C.: U.S. Government Printing Office.
   1972   "Marital status." Subject Reports, PC (2)–4C. Washington, D.C.: U.S. Government Printing Office.
   1973   "Women by number of children ever born." Subject Reports, PC(2)–3A. Washington, D.C.: U.S. Government Printing Office.
van den Berghe, Pierre L.
   1967   *Race and Racism: A Comparative Perspective.* New York: John Wiley and Sons.
Vander Zanden, James W.
   1972   *American Minority Relations* (3rd Edition). New York: The Ronald Press.
Westhoff, Charles F.
   1975   "The yield of the imperfect: The 1970 national fertility survey." *Demography* 12:573–580.
Westoff, Charles F., and E. F. Jones
   1977   "The secularization of U.S. Catholic birth control practices." *Family Planning Perspectives* 9:203–207.
Westoff, Charles F., and Norman B. Ryder
   1970   "Contraceptive practice among urban blacks in the U.S., 1965." *Milbank Memorial Fund Quarterly* 48:215–233.
Williams, Robin M. Jr.
   1964   *Strangers Next Door: Ethnic Relations in American Communities.* Englewood Cliffs, New Jersey: Prentice-Hall.
Yetman, N. R., and C. H. Steele
   1975   *Majority and Minority: The Dynamics of Racial and Ethnic Relations* (2nd Edition). Boston, Massachusetts: Allyn and Bacon.
Zuiches, James J., and David L. Brown
   1975   "The changing character of the rural population." Paper presented at the annual meetings of the Rural Sociological Society, San Francisco, August.

2

School Integration
in the United States[1]

REYNOLDS FARLEY

THE SOCIAL, LEGAL, AND POLITICAL CONTEXT
OF SCHOOL INTEGRATION

When we review the history of attempts to integrate schools, we discern a common pattern. Black parents recognize that their children attend less adequate schools than white children and then they seek—often with the aid of civil rights groups—improved or integrated

[1] The author thanks Clarence Wurdock, who assembled many of the data reported in this paper, Lynda Swanson, who analyzed residential segregation data, and Karlin Richardson. This investigation was supported in part by a grant from the National Institute of Education, NIE G-76-0036, which helped result in "Does the Racial Integration of Public Schools Produce White Flight?"; a grant from the National Institute of Mental Health, R03MH27639, which facilitated the writing of "Recent Trends in Racial Segregation in Public Schools"; and by a grant from the National Science Foundation, SOC76-0078, which helped produce "The Causes of Racial Residential Segregation in the Detroit Area."

schools. Typically, elected school boards refuse to make substantial changes in the black schools or to mix white and black students. Obtaining no redress from school officials, black plaintiffs, with the assistance of those civil rights groups that possess the resources to do so, initiate litigation. I believe the major variable has been the decision that a court renders in a school desegregation case. If one is to account for fluctuations in the history of school integration, I believe one must explain why courts have given their rulings. To do this, it is necessary to consider both constitutional principles and the social and political thought of the day.

Early Efforts to Integrate Schools

The first widely cited court decision concerning segregated schools was given by the Massachusetts Supreme Court in 1849 (*Roberts* v. *City of Boston*, 5 Cushing Reports, 201, 1849). Although abolitionists removed many barriers to civil liberties in New England, Boston school authorities refused to admit blacks to their white schools. Benjamin Roberts, whose daughter had to walk past several white schools to get to her black school, filed suit, but the court sustained the segregationist practices of the Boston School Committee and, in doing so, it established principles that guided judicial decisions for the next century. The court argued, first, that local authorities had great autonomy in operating their schools, including the prerogative of segregating students, and, second, that segregation in the schools did not create or perpetuate either racial prejudice or the inferior status of blacks. The court additionally argued that racial prejudices could not be altered by judicial decree (Kluger, 1976:75–77; Wineberg, 1967:10).

The Civil War led to the passage of constitutional amendments and civil rights laws that in the long run—but definitely not in the short run—fostered integrated schools. President Johnson's original reconstruction program rapidly readmitted the southern states and permitted the white supremacists to adopt severe "black codes." Republicans in Congress recognized that these states were replacing slavery with involuntary servitude and agreed that they should be readmitted only if they ratified the Fourteenth Amendment with its due process clause that guaranteed the citizenship rights of blacks (Franklin, 1967:Ch. XVIII; Stampp, 1967:Ch. 4 and 5). Later, Congress facilitated passage of the Fifteenth Amendment and the Civil Rights Acts of 1866, 1870, and 1875. These protected the rights of blacks to vote, to serve jury duty, and to be served in places of public accommodation. In addition, these civil rights specified that civil rights violations were to be tried in the federal, not the state, courts.

Despite these seemingly strong guarantees, by the end of the nineteenth century all but a handful of southern blacks were unable to vote. Most southern states mandated segregation in public places, and racially separate schools operated with the explicit approval of the courts. The political influence of blacks was greatly limited; indeed, it was hardly greater than during the days of slavery (DuBois, 1964:Ch. XVI; Myrdal, 1944:578–592; Woodward, 1957).

This came about because of Supreme Court interpretations of the constitutional amendments that led them to overturn the Civil Rights Acts. The Supreme Court placed great emphasis upon the responsibilities of states and correspondingly minimized the significance of federal laws. Thus, when mobs of whites in New Orleans harassed black voters (*U.S.* v. *Cruikshank*, 92 U.S. 542, 1876), when mobs of whites in Tennessee took custody of blacks from a sheriff (*U.S.* v. *Harris*, 106 U.S. 629, 1883), and when a voting registrar in Lexington, Kentucky turned away a potential black voter (*U.S.* v. *Reese*, 92 U.S. 214, 1876), the Supreme Court argued that the state's rights of blacks—not their federal rights—were being violated and that the only appropriate prosecution was at the state level.

In 1883, the Supreme Court overturned those portions of the Civil Rights Act of 1875 that banned discrimination in public accommodations by arguing that such discriminatory practices were individual actions and not state actions (*Civil Rights Cases*, 109 U.S. 31, 1883). The judges went further and suggested that racial distinctions in the public sphere were not necessarily invidious.

Court decisions with regard to racial discrimination culminated in the 1896 *Plessy* ruling in which the court decided that states could insist upon racial segregation so long as separate but equal facilities were provided. They justified their view by arguing that courts were powerless to alter long-standing racial differences.

> We consider the underlying fallacy of the plaintiff's argument to consist in the assumption that the enforced segregation of the two races stamps the colored race with a badge of inferiority.... Legislation is powerless to eradicate racial instincts or to abolish distinctions based upon physical differences and the attempt to do so can only result in accentuation of the difficulties of the present situation [*Plessy* v. *Ferguson*, 163 U.S. 537, 1896].

The *Plessy* decision involved railroad transportation, but the justices were cognizant of its implications for schools; indeed, the *Roberts* ruling was cited as precedent. Two subsequent decisions made it even more difficult for blacks to obtain equal educational opportunities. In the first case, the separate but equal principle was compromised. The school board in Richmond County, Georgia closed a secondary school for blacks but maintained one for whites. Black plaintiffs won an injunction in Georgia courts against this apparent discrimination, but the Federal Supreme Court overturned the injunction and permitted the closing of the black school (*Cumming* v. *Richmond*, 175 U.S. 528, 1899). The most liberal of the justices, Justice Harlan, argued that federal authority should not interfere with the management of local schools. The second decision restricted private integrated education. Kentucky enacted legislation that prevented schools from simultaneously training blacks and whites on the same campus. A private integrated college—Berea College—challenged this law, but in 1908 the Supreme Court let the Kentucky legislation stand (*Berea College* v. *Kentucky*, 211 U.S. 45, 1908).

In the 35 years following the Civil War, the courts adopted three principles that had great impact for school integration. First, they argued in several cases—particularly in the *Civil Right Cases* and *Plessy*—that racial distinctions did not necessarily affect blacks adversely. Second, they consistently upheld the prerogatives of states and individuals, including the right to discriminate racially. Third, they stressed that governmental actions could not alter racial distinctions or racial prejudices.

It is likely that, rather than being based upon legal principles, these decisions reflected the social thought and popular sentiments of the day. The evolutionary model of society—which was frequently espoused—contended that governmental actions could not change social processes and defended the reality of racial and ethnic distinctions. The Supreme Court's comments about the inability of legislation to alter racial prejudice could have been written by William Graham Sumner or many of the other leading social thinkers of the late nineteenth century (Hofstader, 1959). The notion of racial differences was propounded not only by Caucasians of that day but was also suggested by Booker T. Washington—the most popular spokesman for blacks in the pre-World War I era. In his Atlanta Exposition speech, he observed that the masses of blacks were to live by the productions of their hands and that there was just as much dignity in tilling a field as there was in writing a book (1965:145–157).

After the turn of the century, southern states operated segregated schools and faced few pressures to provide equal facilities for blacks. In many of these states, racial discrepancies in education widened (Bond,

1934:Ch. XIII; Bullock, 1973:179–182; Myrdal, 1944:Ch. 40). In the North, there probably were integrated schools in most cities, but, as the volume of black migration to these places increased, segregation and identifiably black schools became common (Chicago Commission on Race Relations, 1922:234–271; Kusmer, 1976:182–184). Evidence presented in recent school litigation in such cities as Columbus (*Penick* v. *Columbus Board of Education*, 429 F. Supp. 235, 1977) and Indianapolis (*U.S.* v. *Board of School Commissioners, Indianapolis*, 386 F. Supp. 1199, 1974) reveals the very long history of racial segregation on the part of school administrators. In northern states, where laws seemed to prohibit segregated schools, numerous suits were filed, but the plaintiffs lost as frequently as they won (Weinberg, 1967).

Overturning the Plessy Decision

To integrate schools, plaintiffs had to challenge the social assumptions underlying the *Plessy* ruling before they could overturn the separate but equal doctrine. This was accomplished not through the passage of new constitutional amendments or civil rights laws but, rather, by persistent litigation, the history of which is thoroughly described in Kluger's *Simple Justice* (1976).

Those interested in school desegregation addressed three issues. First, they demonstrated that separate facilities were not equal and that blacks were disadvantaged because of the schools they attended. Litigants did this effectively by focusing attention upon an area judges knew well—legal training. A 1935 case in Maryland stressed the advantages a Baltimore lawyer would have if he or she attended the state university's law school, and the courts eventually admitted blacks to that school (Kluger, 1976:192–193). Three years later, the Federal Supreme Court ordered that blacks be admitted to the law school of the University of Missouri (*Missouri ex rel. Gaines* v. *Canada*, 305 U.S. 337, 1938), and, shortly after World War II, Supreme Court decisions led to the admission of blacks to a graduate school in Oklahoma (*McLaurin* v. *Oklahoma State Regents for Higher Education*, 339 U.S. 637, 1950) and a state law school in Texas (*Sweatt* v. *Painter*, 339 U.S. 629, 1950).

Second, federal courts had to recognize limitations on the discriminatory actions of both state authorities and individuals; that is, the doctrine of states' rights had to be challenged. This occurred very slowly. Southern states employed many ruses, such as grandfather clauses, to disenfranchise black voters, and federal courts moved lethargically to overturn these. For instance, the definition of the Democratic Party as a private club for whites only was overturned in 1944 (*Smith* v. *Allwright*, 321 U.S. 649), and 4 years later the court ruled that contracts restricting the sale of housing to whites could not be enforced (*Shelly* v. *Kramer*, 334 U.S. 1, 1948). By the late 1940s, the Supreme Court was restricting some of the most blatant discriminatory practices.

Third, the litigants showed that state actions were responsible, in part, for racial distinctions and racial prejudice and that change in state policies could mitigate racial differences. Rather than being a legal issue, the nature of the causes of racial differences is in the area of social science research. In the law school cases and in many other educational suits that preceded the 1954 *Brown* ruling, plaintiffs stressed the inadequacy of educational facilities for blacks and the lasting effects of such deficiencies. Litigants in the *Brown* case, for example, made extensive use of Kenneth Clark's evidence, which implied that black children in segregated schools had low self-esteem. (For a detailed history, see Friedman, 1969, and Kluger, 1976:Ch. 14).

We shall never determine the extent to which the 1954 school integration decision was based upon the social thought of its time (Rosen, 1972: Chap. 7). However, the social thinking was very different than it was 60 years earlier. In the 1950s, those who wrote about the sociology of race relations were much more likely to quote Gunnar Myrdal, whose massive study carefully documented the discrepancy between the ideal of equal opportunity and the actual status of blacks, than William Graham Sumner, Lester Ward, E. A. Ross, or other social Darwinists. World War II demonstrated that millions of individuals could be rapidly trained by the government for productive tasks and that their attitudes could be changed. Furthermore, that war underlined the principles of the American Constitution and the folly of German policy, which magnified racial and ethnic distinctions. In brief, by the early 1950s the evolutionary model of society was dead, and the notion of innate racial or ethnic distinctions was seriously questioned.

I suspect that social science evidence itself did not move the Supreme Court to make their 1954 decision. Rather, there was probably consensus that state-imposed racial discrimination in public education was inconsistent with fundamental American values and violated constitutional guarantees. The social science findings served to justify the opinion of the Supreme Court. Thus, it cited the studies of Gunnar Myrdal, Kenneth Clark, and Franklin Frazier and concluded that separating children solely on the basis of race generated feelings of inadequacy that permanently affected their hearts and minds, and that this impact was heightened because it had the sanction of law (*Brown* v. *Board of Education*, 347 U.S. 483, 1954).

Reactions to the Brown Decision

The *Brown* decision and its corollary a year later, which assigned to district federal courts the task of ordering school integration (*Brown* v. *Board of Education*, 349 U.S. 294, 1955), were greeted differently throughout the South. In some border states, laws requiring segregated schools were voided, and a few cities (including Baltimore, Louisville, St. Louis, and Washington) switched from dual systems to neighborhood schools, but residential segregation isolated blacks in these cities (Crain, 1968:15,72). Within the Deep South, there was massive opposition, and southern states passed literally hundreds of laws to prevent racial mixing (Orfield, 1969:18). Civil rights workers and plaintiffs in desegregation cases were frequently harassed (Peltason 1971:Ch. 5).

To integrate schools in southern cities, it was necessary to exhaust all possible local or state remedies and then to convince a federal judge that the schools were segregated. This was an extremely complex, costly, and time-consuming process, since states often altered their school laws and school boards appealed endlessly. Federal judges were political appointees. Many of them disagreed with the *Brown* ruling and defended the right of states to segregate (Peltason, 1971). However, certain aspects of the Supreme Court's 1954 decision were unambiguous, and by the early 1960s courts were ordering southern districts to adopt freedom of choice plans, which permitted some blacks to enroll in formerly white schools. This involved a small number of students, since, in 1960, no more than one-sixth of 1% of the black students in the states of the Confederacy attended schools that enrolled whites (Carter, 1969:70).

More Recent Efforts to Integrate Schools

Another turning point in civil rights occurred in the early 1960s. I believe that there was agreement that the time for delay was over and that federal powers should be used to ensure the elemental civil rights of blacks in southern states. Martin Luther King and his followers peacefully but dramatically demonstrated that, 100 years after the Civil War, most southern blacks could not vote, could not hold public office, were not tried by their peers, and could not eat at the same lunch counter as whites. The jailing of Dr. King and the violent reactions of some whites, which included the firebombing of black churches in Alabama and the slayings of Chaney, Goodman, and Schwerner in Mississippi, focused even more attention upon the civil rights grievances of blacks (Franklin, 1967:Ch. 31). However, studies of white attitudes about blacks reveal that during this time whites came much more to accept the idea that blacks should not be kept out of white neighborhoods or white schools and should not be segregated into the back of the bus (Hyman and Sheatsley, 1964; Sheatsley, 1966). In 1964, this nation adopted the Twenty-Fourth Amendment, which sought, once again, to guarantee blacks their right to vote by banning the poll tax in federal elections, and, in the same year, Congress enacted the most comprehensive civil rights legislation in the nation's history. The Civil Rights Act of 1964 included provisions to prevent discrimination in public accommodations and in hiring and promotions and permitted the Justice Department to initiate litigation in the field of civil rights. In his account of the history of this law, Orfield suggests that there was no strong Congressional desire to force localities to integrate their schools (1969:Ch. 2). The law, however, called for a study of racial inequalities in education—(the Coleman Report)—and provided federal assistance for school districts undergoing desegregation.

Title VI of the Civil Rights Act was not specifically designed to influence schools, but it stated that federal funding should be terminated if it were allocated in a racially discriminatory way. In 1964, there were only modest amounts of federal monies going to local schools, but this changed with the enactment of the Elementary and Secondary Education Act of 1965. Southern school districts, since they were relatively poor, qualified for large sums of federal monies, and the Department of Health, Education, and Welfare (HEW) was obligated to enunciate school integration guidelines.

The provisions of the 1964 Civil Rights Act and the school integration requirements certainly put additional pressures upon school districts to integrate. However, court decisions have been more responsible than have HEW guidelines for the desegregation of schools that has been accomplished in the last decade. HEW administrators, for example, are more subject to political pressures than are the federal courts. In 1965, blacks from Chicago convinced HEW officials that local school officials were using federal funds in a discriminatory manner, and the spending was terminated. However, the funds were almost immediately restored following a meeting of Mayor Daley with President Johnson (Orfield, 1969:Ch. 4). Between 1969 and 1976, HEW made very limited use of the fund termination provisions, apparently the result of an administration decision to go slow on school desegregation (Center for National Policy Review, 1974; U.S. Commission on Civil Rights, 1973:208–215).

Given the history of legally segregated schools in the South and racial residential segregation in northern cities, integration could be achieved only if black and white children were assigned to the same schools, a procedure that necessitated substantial changes in the organizations of schools or the busing of many pupils. Despite the 1954 ruling, elected school boards seldom effectively integrated their facilities, and therefore black parents and civil rights groups had to file suits.

Between 1968 and 1973, the Supreme Court and federal district courts issued numerous rulings that hastened the integration of schools. Four especially impactful decisions will be outlined in the following discussion. (For more detailed studies, see Bolner and Shanley, 1974:Ch. 1; Read, 1975.)

Green v. *New Kent County* (391 U.S. 430, 1968). Because of HEW pressures, this Virginia county adopted a freedom of choice plan, and some black children opted for the previously white school at the opposite end of the county, but no whites enrolled in the black school. The Supreme Court ended reliance upon ineffective freedom of choice plans by declaring that the plans were acceptable only if they achieved actual integration of schools. If they failed to do that, district federal courts were obligated to order more effective programs.

Alexander v. *Holmes* (396 U.S. 19, 1969). Thirty Mississippi school systems were ordered to integrate at the beginning of the fall term of 1969. They appealed for a delay, and the Secretary of HEW and the Attorney General—in an unusual move—supported their request. This request was granted by the Fifth Circuit Court of Appeals, but the Supreme Court unanimously overturned the stay and stated that the principle of integration "with all deliberate speed" was no longer constitutionally permissible. They ruled that school districts must terminate dual systems (i.e., racially identifiable schools) *at once* and operate only unitary schools—then and thereafter.

Swann v. *Charlotte–Mecklenburg* (402 U.S. 1, 1971). In the mid-1960s, court orders forced Charlotte to modify its school system and reduce segregation, but the city continued to operate some racially identifiable schools. Furthermore, litigation led the district judge to require that the ratio of black to white students be about the same at all schools and that children be bused to achieve this. The Supreme Court unanimously upheld this integration order and thereby legitimized the use of busing and racial ratios as a means of achieving integration.

Keyes v. *School District No. 1, Denver* (396 U.S. 1215, 1973). The *Brown* decision dealt with states where school segregation was legally mandated. Litigants outside the South had a more difficult time obtaining favorable court rulings. In the mid-1960s, suits in Cincinnati (*Deal* v. *Cincinnati Board of Education,* 224 F. Supp. 572, 1965); Gary (*Bell* v. *School City of Gary,* 213 F. Supp. 819, 1963), and Kansas City (*Downs* v. *Board of Education* 366 F. 2d. 988, 1964) failed to produce integration orders because the courts believed that school segregation resulted primarily from residential patterns. Plaintiffs eventually convinced courts that northern school boards segregated black students by gerrymandering attendance zones, by permitting whites to transfer away from black schools, and by the selective construction of new schools. In 1973, the Supreme Court extended the principle of school integration to the North when they ruled that, because school administrators were partly responsible for the segregation of blacks in the northeast section of Denver, a city-wide busing program was an appropriate remedy. This decision served as precedent for numerous other integration orders in northern and western cities such as Boston, Dayton, Detroit, Milwaukee, Minneapolis, and Omaha.

It is interesting to speculate about whether the court rulings between 1968 and 1973 represent a new appreciation of judicial principles, better efforts by plaintiffs, or improved understanding by the courts of the social and political processes that surround school integration. I believe that litigants became more proficient in demonstrating segregation, especially outside the South, and they had a history of favorable rulings to buttress their efforts. However, it seems likely that the growing awareness of civil rights violations affected the courts, and, by the late 1960s, judges realized that, during the 15 years that followed *Brown*, most southern and northern school boards resisted efforts to mix white and black students. Recognizing that local administrators would seldom integrate schools and that the adverse effects of segregation were as substantial in the North, where segregation had a de facto origin, as in the South, where it had a de jure origin, courts gradually moved the nation toward school integration.

SCHOOL INTEGRATION IN THE NATION'S LARGEST METROPOLISES

Data for the Analysis of Segregation Trends

Few court-induced social changes can be monitored as thoroughly as school desegregation. Title VI of the Civil Rights Act of 1964 authorized the Office for Civil Rights (OCR) within HEW to conduct periodic racial–ethnic surveys of the nation's public schools. Beginning in the fall of 1967, studies were conducted to determine the racial composition of individual schools in the nation's larger school districts. The most recent data in this series pertain to 1974.

The analysis reported in this chapter deals with the 100 largest metropolitan areas (as of 1970) in the conterminous United States. Since blacks are much more likely to live in central cities than in suburbs and because most integration efforts involve large cities, we shall first analyze data for the nation's largest central cities.

Some metropolitan areas contain 2 or more central cities, and thus the nation's 100 largest metropolises include 134 cities. We desired to study racial integration, and so we eliminated 15 cities in which public school enrollments were less than 3% black in 1970.[2] Two cities—Phoenix, Arizona and Orange, Texas—failed to submit usable data, and two other central cities—Fort Lauderdale and Hollywood, Florida—are in the countywide Broward school district. This meant that school segregation trends from 1967 to 1974 were studied for 116 central city school districts. These 116 central city districts include large places such as New York, where the schools enroll more than one million students, and small towns such as Holyoke, Massachusetts and High Point, North Carolina, where the schools enroll fewer than 10,000 students.

In the North and West, school districts are generally coterminous with the corporate limits of a central city, whereas in the South they are often coterminous with county or parish lines. Exceptions are numerous. In Indianapolis and in Kansas City, for example, the central city school districts do not include the entire city (U.S. Office of Education, 1974: xiii). Atlanta, Birmingham, and Richmond are southern cities, but their school districts are not countywide.

The Racial Segregation of Students

Table 2.1 presents data about racial composition and student segregation in the 15 largest central city school districts in the South and in other regions. It is important to use this regional distinction because the legal history and timing of desegregation are not the same in the North and South.

Looking at the first columns of Table 2.1, we find that black students are heavily represented in big city school systems. Nationally, blacks comprised about 15% of the public elementary and secondary school enrollment in 1967, but, in the typical southern central city, about one-third of the students were black, and, in northern cities, one-quarter were black. For the entire nation, the proportion of black students remained at

[2] The cities we eliminated were Anaheim, Garden Grove, Ontario, San Jose, and Ventura in California; Moline, Illinois; Chicopee, Massachusetts; Clifton, New Jersey; Albuquerque, New Mexico; Bethlehem and Hazelton, Pennsylvania; Pawtucket and Warwick, Rhode Island; Everett, Washington; and Salt Lake City, Utah.

TABLE 2.1

Racial Composition of Large Central City School Districts and Indicators of Racial Segregation of Students, 1967 and 1974

	Proportion of black students (%)			Average proportion black for white students (%)			Average proportion white for black students (%)			Index of dissimilarity for students		
	1967	1974	Change	1967	1974	Change	1967	1974	Change	1967	1974	Change
South												
Houston [a]	33	42	+9	5	15	+10	7	14	+7	92	79	−13
Baltimore	64	72	+8	18	28	+10	10	11	+1	82	76	−6
Dallas [a]	31	43	+12	3	15	+12	7	16	+9	94	78	−16
Washington	92	96	+4	44	47	+3	4	2	−2	75	84	+9
San Antonio	15	16	+1	7	23	+16	14	24	+10	86	67	−19
Memphis	52	70	+18	4	50	+46	4	21	+17	95	51	−44
New Orleans	66	79	+13	17	37	+20	9	9	—	85	76	−9
Jacksonville [b]	28	33	+5	3	26	+23	7	52	+45	92	37	−55
Atlanta	59	85	+26	7	49	+42	5	9	+4	94	75	−19
Nashville [b]	24	29	+5	6	23	+15	19	57	+38	83	41	−42
Fort Worth	25	33	+8	3	26	+23	8	44	+36	92	45	−47
Oklahoma City	21	28	+7	2	28	+26	7	65	+58	94	24	−70
Louisville	45	54	+9	17	16	−1	20	14	−6	74	79	+5
Miami [b]	24	26	+2	5	19	+14	13	31	+18	87	64	−13
Tulsa	12	17	+5	2	9	+7	13	42	+29	91	73	−18
Average for 40 southern districts	36	43	+7	9	30	+21	14	40	+26	84	47	−37

North and West

New York [c]	30	37	+7	20	23	+3	32	22	−10	62	69	+7
Chicago	52	58	+6	8	9	+1	7	4	−3	90	92	+2
Los Angeles	21	25	+4	5	9	+4	11	15	+4	90	83	−7
Philadelphia	58	62	+4	22	11	−11	15	15	—	75	82	+7
Detroit [d]	58	72	+14	21	30	+9	15	11	−4	75	75	—
Cleveland	56	57	+1	9	8	−1	7	6	−1	89	91	+2
Indianapolis	32	43	+11	10	29	+19	22	38	+16	78	48	−30
Milwaukee	24	33	+9	6	10	+4	18	20	+2	86	79	−7
San Francisco	24	30	+6	22	46	+24	39	43	+4	54	25	−29
San Diego	11	14	+3	5	9	+4	30	45	+15	80	61	−19
Boston	26	37	+11	12	26	+14	33	36	+3	71	52	−19
St. Louis	63	70	+7	11	11	—	7	5	−2	89	91	+2
Columbus	26	31	+5	10	14	+4	29	32	+3	73	68	−5
Seattle	11	16	+5	6	11	+5	50	52	+2	67	62	−5
Pittsburgh	39	43	+4	16	21	+5	25	28	+3	70	62	−8
Average for 76 northern and western districts	24	31	+7	13	19	+6	44	44	—	63	55	−8

Source: U.S. National Center for Education Statistics, Directory of Public School in Large Districts with Enrollment and Staff by Race, Fall, 1967; U. S. Office for Civil Rights, Tape files of Directory of Public Elementary and Secondary Schools in Selected Districts, Enrollment and Staff by Racial/Ethnic Groups, 1968 to 1974.

[a] Data for these cities refer to 1968 and 1974.
[b] These school districts include an entire county.
[c] Data refer to 1967 and 1973.
[d] Data refer to 1966 and 1974.

15% from 1967 to 1974, but, because of the out-migration of whites from central cities and other demographic changes, the proportion of black students went up by seven percentage points in the central cities of both regions.

A variety of measures have been suggested to assess whether black and white children attend the same or separate schools (Zoloth, 1976). One indicator is the average proportion of black students in the school the typical white student attends. Indexes of this nature are shown in the central columns of Table 2.1. In making these calculations, we define *the white population* to include all students who are not blacks, Orientals, American Indians, or of Spanish heritage. In most cities, almost all students are either black or white, as we defined it, but in New York, Los Angeles, San Antonio, and Miami there are many Spanish-heritage students and, in San Francisco, numerous Orientals.

Data in Table 2.1 suggest that by 1967 most southern cities made progress in dismantling their dual school systems because the typical white was going to a school where about 9% of the students were black. In certain cities where there were early integration efforts and large black enrollments—Baltimore, Louisville, New Orleans, and Washington—whites went to school with relatively many blacks.

Between 1967 and 1974, the racial composition of the schools that southern whites attended changed substantially. This change reflected both federal court orders and demographic changes. By the latter year, the typical white in a southern central city went to a school where almost one-third of the pupils were black.

Reductions in racial isolation were smaller outside the South. In 1967, students in northern cities were going to schools with a higher proportion of blacks than were white students in the South, but changes in the ensuing 7-year span were less in the North, and, in 1974, white students in northern and western cities went to schools in which about one-fifth of the students were black.

The OCR data may also be used to determine the average proportion of whites in the school of the typical black student. In 1967, blacks in many southern cities attended schools that enrolled whites, and the average proportion of white for black students was considerably higher than the average proportion of black for white students. This occurred because of the strategies school boards used to comply with integration demands. That is, there was much less opposition to busing some black children into formerly white schools than to busing white children into black schools. Following 1967, the average proportion of white for black students increased sharply in the South as the court orders and HEW pressures took effect, but outside that region there was no increase in the proportion of whites in the school the typical black student attended.

The measure we have described is an accurate index of potential racial contact within a school system, but it is not very useful if one wishes to compare racial segregation in many different cities, because this measure is strongly influenced by the racial composition of the school district. If a court ordered Washington to integrate its schools by randomly assigning students, the typical white student would attend a school that was 96% black. In San Diego, a similar random assignment would result in an average proportion of 14% black.

The index of dissimilarity is a measure of segregation that is independent of the racial composition of the school district. It takes on its maximum value of 100 if all blacks and all whites attend racially homogeneous schools, and it equals zero if every school has the same racial composition, an ideal that several judges described in their integration rulings. The index of dissimilarity succinctly assesses whether black and white children attend the same schools, and its numerical value indicates the proportion of students of either race who would have to be shifted from one school to another to eliminate segregation, that is, bring about an index of zero (Taeuber and Taeuber, 1965:Appendix 1, 1976). The final columns of Table 2.1 present indexes of dissimilarity for students.

Changes in school segregation may be readily summarized. In many southern cities and some cities in the North, federal court orders and HEW pressures led districts to integrate. Usually, busing was substantially increased in the large cities, attendance zones were redrawn, and other major changes were effected. Between 1967 and 1974, great reductions in student segregation were recorded in Memphis, where the index fell from 95 to 51, and in Jacksonville, Nashville, Fort Worth, and Oklahoma City. Among the northern cities shown in Table 2.1, the biggest changes occurred where the courts mandated integration— Indianapolis and San Francisco. We might consider a drop of 20 or more in the index of dissimilarity as indicative of a major integration effort. Such efforts were more common in the South than elsewhere, and we find that 63% of the southern central cities and roughly one-quarter of the northern cities experienced this much school integration.

A large number of districts show modest declines in segregation. Presumably, these districts closed some exclusively black schools, redrew attendance zones, established magnet schools, or bused modest numbers of students. If we use declines in the index of dissimilarity of 6 to 19 points to classify such places, we find that about one-quarter of the southern and one-third of the northern cities are in this category.

Many northern and a few southern cities made little progress in eliminating segregation. Central city school districts might be placed in this category if their index of student segregation either increased or decreased by fewer than six points. Using this criterion, 10% of the southern and 40% of the northern cities had schools that were as segregated in 1974 as they were years earlier. Although school segregation was generally declining, 17 northern cities, including Chicago, Cincinnati, Cleveland, New York, Newark, Philadelphia, and St. Louis, had schools that actually were more highly segregated by race in 1974 than in 1967.

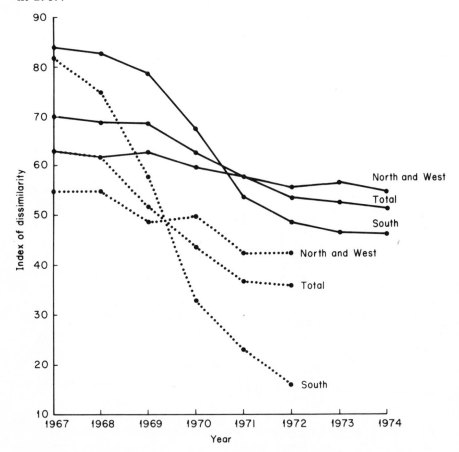

Figure 2.1 Average values of indexes of racial segregation in central city school districts. (Data from Tables 2.1 and 2.2.) ...... = Index of dissimilarity for instructional staff; ——— = Index of dissimilarity for students.

Figure 2.1 summarizes trends in student segregation by indicating average values of the index of dissimilarity. In 1967, segregation was much greater in the South than in the North—the mean difference being 20 points on this measure. Declines were more common and more extensive in the South, and by 1971 segregation levels were similar in cities of the two regions. Although progress in desegregation seems less rapid after 1971 than before, more change occurred in the South, and by 1974 schools in southern cities were less segregated than those in northern or western cities.

Racial Integration of Instructional Staffs

Eliminating segregation in schools meant integrating teaching staffs as well as mixing students. When southern school districts faced pressures to integrate in the early 1960s, some of them fired black instructors or switched black teachers to janitorial jobs, hoping thereby to lessen support for desegregation among blacks. At the insistence of President Johnson, HEW revised its integration guidelines in 1965 to prohibit the selective dismissal of black teachers (Orfield, 1969:106–108).

The federal courts played a major role in protecting black teachers and in integrating them with whites. In 1967, district judge Frank Johnson ordered Montgomery school officials to assign teachers so that the ratio of white to black would be the same at all schools in the district (*Carr* v. *Montgomery County Board of Education*, 289 F. Supp. 654, 1967), and 2 years later the Supreme Court unanimously upheld this mandate (*U.S.* v. *Montgomery County Board of Education*, 395 U.S. 236, 1969). Following this decision and the explicit *Alexander* v. *Holmes* ruling, which called for the immediate operation of unitary schools, federal courts throughout the South prohibited the firing of black teachers and ordered that no school be racially identifiable either because of its student body or its staff (*Singleton* v. *Jackson Municipal Separate School District*, 419 F. 2d. 1211, 1970).

From 1967 through 1972, OCR tabulated data about the racial composition of the instructional staff of each school in their sample of districts. Some caution is needed in interpreting these data since, in 1967, the instructional staff included all professionals assigned to a school (U.S. National Center for Educational Statistics, 1969:3), but, by 1972, the data were restricted to full-time classroom teachers (U.S. Office for Civil Rights, 1974:iii).

Table 2.2 presents information about instructional staffs for the same

TABLE 2.2

Proportion of Black Teachers, Index of Dissimilarity for Teachers, and Proportion of Students of Each Race with Teachers of Other Race: 1967 and 1972

	Proportion of black teachers (%)			Index of dissimilarity for teachers			Proportion of white students with black teachers (%)			Proportion of black students with white teachers (%)		
	1967	1972	Change	1967	1972	Change	1967	1972	Change	1967	1972	Change
South												
Houston [a]	31	36	+5	82	13	−69	5	33	+28	21	57	+36
Baltimore	53	59	+6	66	48	−18	18	31	+13	27	28	+1
Dallas [a]	24	28	+4	94	15	−79	1	26	+25	26	65	+39
Washington	79	85	+6	51	39	−12	38	62	+24	16	13	−3
San Antonio	12	16	+4	79	20	−59	1	14	+13	38	68	+30
Memphis	44	43	−1	90	12	−78	2	40	+38	16	54	+38
New Orleans	52	57	+5	96	14	−82	2	54	+52	17	40	+23
Jacksonville [c]	28	30	+2	96	33	−63	1	27	+26	8	55	+47
Atlanta	52	62	+10	92	24	−68	3	48	+45	11	33	+22
Nashville [b]	20	23	+3	85	9	−76	3	23	+20	30	77	+47
Fort Worth	22	23	+1	94	19	−75	1	7	+6	15	71	+56
Oklahoma City	18	23	+5	86	15	−71	2	22	+20	30	25	−5
Louisville	31	36	+5	70	33	−37	8	23	+15	43	50	+7
Miami [b]	19	22	+3	74	19	−55	4	26	+22	38	81	+43
Tulsa	11	11	—	82	17	−65	2	11	+9	32	84	+52
Average for 40 southern districts	32	33	+1	83	21	−62	6	29	+23	26	62	+36

North and West

New York [c]	9	9	—	48	49	+1	3	3	—	78	84	+6
Chicago	33	38	+5	69	42	−27	4	16	+12	41	47	+6
Los Angeles	14	15	+1	67	68	+1	2	2	—	52	53	+1
Philadelphia	30	34	+4	43	35	−8	13	20	+7	59	58	−1
Detroit [d]	35	46	+11	43	33	−10	18	29	+11	53	45	−8
Cleveland	38	40	+2	60	57	−3	10	10	—	39	38	−1
Indianapolis	22	24	+2	78	19	−59	5	22	+17	41	71	+30
Milwaukee	13	15	+2	69	60	−9	3	2	−1	61	69	+8
San Francisco	6	10	+4	40	33	−7	4	9	+5	83	76	−8
San Diego	4	6	+2	52	59	+7	2	1	−1	87	79	−8
Boston	5	7	+2	53	50	−3	2	3	+1	89	86	−3
St. Louis	53	54	+1	79	68	−11	8	6	−2	19	27	+8
Columbus	13	15	+2	56	50	−6	5	7	+2	71	69	−2
Seattle	4	6	+2	53	58	+5	3	5	+2	84	76	−8
Pittsburgh	11	16	+5	50	37	−13	5	9	+4	79	77	−2
Average for 76 northern and western districts	11	14	+3	55	45	+10	5	8	+3	79	77	−2

Source: See Table 2.1.

[a] Data for these cities refer to 1968 and 1974.
[b] These school districts include an entire county.
[c] Data refer to 1967 and 1973.
[d] Data refer to 1966 and 1974.

cities shown in Table 2.1. The first columns indicate the proportion of black teachers, and we observe that blacks were more represented on southern faculties than on northern ones. Furthermore, the racial composition of teachers and students was more alike in the South than in the North. That is, in 1967 about 36% of the students in southern central cities and one-third of the teachers were black. Outside that region, about one-quarter of the students but only one-tenth of the teachers were black.

Between 1967 and 1972, the representation of blacks on instructional staffs did not decline. Because of the changing definitions used by the OCR, we cannot accurately determine whether blacks were shifted into or out of classroom teaching or administrative roles at the time of desegregation. However, in all but two of the cities for which data are shown in Table 2.2, the proportion of the instructional staff that was black increased during the 5-year span following 1967.

The index of dissimilarity assesses whether blacks and whites teach at the same schools. If all schools in a district had racially homogeneous teaching staffs, the index would equal 100, but if the ratio of black to white instructors was the same in all schools, it would equal 0. The value of this index lies in its reporting of the proportion of either black or white teachers who would have to be shifted from one school to another to eliminate the racial segregation of teachers.

Data in Table 2.2 reveal that, in 1967, teachers were much more highly segregated by race in the South than elsewhere, but more progress was made in reducing this segregation in the South. In a variety of southern cities, court orders and HEW pressures led to reductions of 60, 70, or 80 points in this index. Changes of this magnitude were rare outside the South, although the racial segregation of teachers declined in both regions.

Figure 2.1 also shows average levels of segregation for instructional staffs. Among both teachers and students, reductions in segregation after 1967 were greater in the South than elsewhere, and, in both regions, decreases in the racial isolation of instructors between 1967 and 1972 were much larger than declines in student segregation in the same time-span.

Well into the 1960s, white students in southern cities had white teachers, but recent integration efforts have also changed this. If we assume that teachers and students are randomly assigned within individual schools, we can estimate the proportion of white students in a school district who had black teachers and the proportion of black students who had white teachers. Data concerning this aspect of school segregation are presented in the left-hand columns of Table 2.2. In 1967, in 11 of the 15 largest cities of the South, fewer than 5% of the white students had black teachers, and, overall, the average proportion with black teachers was only 6%. Substantial changes occurred, and, by 1972, the average proportion of white students with a black teacher reached about 30% in southern central cities. In 1967, it was not uncommon for white teachers to be assigned to schools with black students in southern cities, but the integration of the subsequent period greatly increased the probability that a black student would have a white teacher.

Outside the South, fewer changes were registered in the proportion of students of one race who had a teacher of the other. Because of the sparse representation of blacks on instructional staffs in the North and because of persistently high levels of faculty segregation in northern cities, it is still rather unusual for white students in these cities to be taught by blacks. The vast majority of black students, on the other hand, have white teachers.

The Racial Segregation of Students at the Metropolitan Level

Within many metropolises, a great proportion of blacks live within the central city, whereas the suburban ring contains a largely white population. We have reported that court orders led to the integration of schools in numerous southern and in some northern cities. However, if such efforts are restricted to central cities, they may fail to integrate effectively schools at the metropolitan level, since almost all blacks will go to central city schools and all whites to suburban schools.

Segregation at the metropolitan level can be assessed at only three dates. Many suburban school districts have small enrollments, and the only OCR surveys to include such school districts were those conducted in 1968, 1970, and 1972. We use the term *suburban* to mean the entire area outside the central city or cities but within the Standard Metropolitan Statistical Area (SMSA) as defined by the U.S. Bureau of the Census in 1970 (1971:Table 32). We will again describe the 100 largest metropolitan areas, but 4 of them—Albuquerque, Phoenix, Salt Lake City, and San Jose—were eliminated either because data were not available or because there were few black students.

Five conclusions should be drawn about metropolitan school segregation. First, patterns of school organization differ greatly from state to state. Many of the southern metropolises contain only one or two school districts; thus, they frequently enroll both city and suburban children,

TABLE 2.3
Information about Schools and Enrollment in Metropolitan Areas

| | Number of suburban school districts (1) | Proportion black in 1972 (%) | | | | Perentage of students in suburban schools 1972 | |
| | | Central city | | Suburbs | | | |
		Students (2)	Teachers (3)	Students (4)	Teachers (5)	White students (6)	Black students (7)
South							
Houston	38	39	9	11	9	68	25
Baltimore	6	69	59	8	8	82	14
Dallás	34	39	28	9	6	67	21
Washington	8	95	85	13	10	99	32
San Antonio	13	16	16	3	4	84	29
Memphis	6	58	43	38	34	27	14
New Orleans	3	75	37	19	17	76	20
Jacksonville		(Entire metropolis in one school district)					
Atlanta	8	77	62	6	6	91	21
Nashville	4	28	23	10	8	27	10
Fort Worth	16	30	23	2	< 1	64	6
Oklahoma City	13	26	23	3	1	63	15
Louisville	5	51	36	4	3	83	18
Miami ·		(Entire metropolis in one school district)					
Tulsa	13	15	11	3	2	31	8
Average for 34 southern metropolises	7	41	33	13	11	59	21
North and West							
New York	130	36	9	7	3	64	12
Chicago	204	57	38	6	3	80	12
Los Angeles [a]	75	25	14	9	6	59	28
Philadelphia	111	61	34	10	6	83	23
Detroit	76	68	46	5	4	88	14
Cleveland	47	58	40	6	2	81	15
Indianapolis	36	39	24	2	< 1	71	6
Milwaukee	33	30	15	< 1	< 1	65	1
San Francisco [a]	58	31	10	8	4	90	35
San Diego	23	13	6	2	1	61	14
Boston	73	33	7	2	1	88	18
St. Louis	72	69	54	12	8	91	38
Columbus	19	29	15	1	1	55	4
Seattle [a]	25	14	7	1	< 1	75	12
Pittsurgh	81	42	16	5	1	90	38
Average for 62 northern and western metropolises	35	28	14	3	2	73	19

Source: See Table 2.1.

[a] In these metropolises, city data refer to the largest central city: Los Angeles, San Francisco, and Seattle.

whereas the typical nonsouthern central city is surrounded by numerous small enrollment suburban districts. Information about school organization in the 15 largest metropolises in each region is contained in Table 2.3. Column 1 reports that the Chicago suburban ring includes more than 200 suburban districts, and, around Philadelphia and New York, there are in excess of 100 suburban districts. If white parents oppose the integration of a central city's schools, they generally have more opportunities to move into suburban white enclaves in the North than in the South. If litigation to integrate schools must proceed on a district by district basis, the possibilities for delay are greater outside the South.

Second, central city and suburban school districts differ in racial composition, but the city-ring difference is greater in the North than in the South. Columns 2–5 of Table 2.3 report the proportions of black students and teachers in 1972 in central cities and in their suburban rings. In 1972, 6 of the 15 largest southern cities had majority black enrollments; however, schools in southern suburban rings enrolled more than token numbers of blacks. For example, in Memphis the proportion of blacks in suburban schools was 38%; in New Orleans, 19%; and in Washington, 13%. In the North, 5 of the 15 largest cities had majority black enrollments, but blacks generally do not live in northern suburbs. Within most of these suburban rings, there are a large number of school districts that enroll no more than a few blacks and several districts that are predominantly black (i.e., suburban black enclaves). Of the 204 suburban districts surrounding Chicago in 1972, 53 had no black students, and another 93 had enrollments that were less than 1% black. Four of Chicago's suburban districts had majority black enrollments.

Third, white enrollments in central cities are declinging rapidly. In part this reflects trends in fertility, since the number of white births in 1976 was only about 70% as great as the number of white births in 1957 (U.S. National Center for Health Statistics, 1970:Table 1–1; 1976: Table 1; 1977, 1). The change in white enrollment also reflects the outmigration of whites. Several years ago, Coleman et al. (1975) suggested that current strategies for integrating central city schools were ineffective, since they encouraged whites to withdraw their children from city public schools. Several other investigators have analyzed data on that topic, and there is consensus that white enrollments are falling rapidly both in cities whose schools were integrated and in cities whose schools remain segregated (Cataldo et al., 1975; Farley, 1975; Giles, 1977; Jackson, 1975; Lord, 1975; Lord and Catau, 1976; Pettigrew and Green, 1976; Rossell, 1975, 1975–1976; Wegmann, 1975).

There is also tentative agreement that school integration is related to the loss of white students in the largest cities. Based upon 1967 to 1974 trends, it appears that a major integration order—one that reduced the index of dissimilarity by 20 points in a city of at least 300,000 where one-third of the students are black—produced an incremental loss of white students equal to one year's normal loss of whites (Farley, 1977a).

High rates of white loss in central cities and modest increases in suburban white enrollment are found in most metropolises of both regions. As a result, a much higher fraction of white than of black students attend suburban schools. The final columns of Table 2.3 indicate the proportion of metropolitan area students attending suburban schools in 1972. In the typical northern metropolis, about three-quarters of the white but less than one-fifth of the black students went to suburban schools. An extreme case is Milwaukee, where 65% of the metropolitan whites but only 1% of the blacks attended suburban schools. In the typical southern metropolis, about 60% of the white as compared to 21% of the black students enrolled in suburban schools.

Fourth, between 1968 and 1972, the segregation of black students from whites declined at the metropolitan level but by a smaller amount than in central cities. Information about this is presented in Table 2.4. The first three columns refer to all schools within a metropolitan area. If all schools in the entire metropolis had identical racial compositions, this index of dissimilarity would equal zero. The next three columns of Table 2.4 show similar measures of student segregation for the 1968 to 1972 interval for the central city of the metropolis.

In Dallas, for example, the index of dissimilarity for students in the entire metropolis decreased 11 points, from 88 to 77. The decline in student segregation within the central city was somewhat greater, from 94 to 80. On the average, the level of student segregation—as assessed by the index of dissimilarity—fell 34 points in southern central cities and 25 points at the metropolitan level. The changes were smaller within the North, but the same pattern appeared; there was an average decrease of three points in student segregation at the metropolitan level and six points at the central city level.

Fifth, school integration policies that are restricted to specific school districts will be, at best, moderately effective. Present strategies strive to eliminate the segregation of blacks from whites within particular school districts, but they generally do not minimize city–suburban differences in the racial composition of school districts. We can hypothesize that current policies are completely effective and eradicate segregation within individual school districts but do not alter the racial composition of the districts. We can then determine what the index of student segregation for a metropolis would be and compare it to the current segregation. In making these calculations, we are assuming that every school within a

TABLE 2.4

Information about Student Segregation in Metropolitan Areas

	Indexes of dissimilarity measuring student segregation						Between district segregation score
	Metropolitan area			Central city			
	1968 (1)	1972 (2)	Change (3)	1968 (4)	1972 (5)	Change (6)	1972 (7)
South							
Houston	86	79	−7	92	82	−10	52
Baltimore	80	79	−1	82	82	0	68
Dallas	88	77	−11	94	80	−14	55
Washington	84	80	−4	79	79	0	67
San Antonio	82	72	−10	84	70	−14	64
Memphis	95	78	−17	95	86	−9	15
New Orleans	85	70	−15	83	78	−5	56
Jacksonville [a]	87	33	−54				
Atlanta	88	82	−6	91	81	−10	72
Nashville	80	42	−38	82	38	−44	17
Fort Worth	86	77	−9	89	71	−18	58
Oklahoma City	91	59	−32	89	28	−61	57
Louisville	79	80	+1	76	80	+4	66
Miami [a]	85	63	−22				
Tulsa	83	74	−9	89	74	−15	24
Average for 34 southern metropolises	83	58	−25	83	49	−34	40
North and West							
New York	70	72	+2	64	69	+5	55
Chicago	90	90	—	90	91	+1	71
Los Angeles [b]	89	84	−5	90	86	−4	54
Philadelphia	79	80	+1	75	79	+4	68
Detroit	89	89	—	77	76	−1	83
Cleveland	91	91	—	90	91	+1	75
Indianapolis	84	81	−3	77	72	−5	65
Milwaukee	90	88	−2	85	82	−3	64
San Francisco [b]	78	75	−3	58	27	−31	71
San Diego	79	71	−8	77	68	−9	49
Boston	79	78	−1	73	74	+1	73
St. Louis	87	87	—	88	90	+2	77
Columbus	80	79	−1	74	71	−3	51
Seattle [b]	76	71	−5	64	59	−5	67
Pittsburgh	74	72	−2	71	66	−5	67
Average for 62 northern and western metropolises	76	73	−3	62	56	−6	62

Source: See Table 2.1.

[a] In these places, one school district contains the entire metropolis.

[b] Figures are for the largest central city in these metropolitan areas: Los Angeles, San Francisco, and Seattle.

specific school district has the same racial composition but that district-to-district variations in racial composition are not changed. This is equivalent to calculating an index of dissimilarity for a metropolis using entire school districts as the units of analysis. We shall call these measures between-school-district segregation scores, and they are displayed in the final columns of Table 2.4.

In many metropolises, these indexes are only a little smaller than actual segregation scores. In Atlanta, for instance, the actual segregation was 82, but the between-school district score was 72. That is, if every district in the Atlanta area eliminated segregation within its schools, the segregation index for the entire metropolis would decline only ten points because of racial differences in the composition of school districts. Approximately 90% of the Atlanta area's black students attend the central city's schools, as compared to only 10% of the white. In Philadelphia, the actual level of segregation would be lowered 12 points, from 80 to 68, if all schools within each district had the same racial composition but district-to-district variations in racial composition were left unchanged.

When all northern metropolises are considered, we find that they actually have an average index of dissimilarity of 73. If there had been no within-district segregation of black students from white, the average score would have been 62. In the South, school districts are organized quite differently, and many suburban schools enroll blacks. There, a program of complete within-district integration would have a greater effect upon segregation at the metropolitan level, and the average index for a metropolitan area would have declined from 58 to 40.

PROSPECTS FOR FURTHER INTEGRATION OF SCHOOLS

The late 1960s and early 1970s were unusually favorable years for school integration, but persistent racial residential segregation and the movement of whites to suburbs means that there are still many exclusively black or exclusively white schools. Will the trend toward integration continue? An answer to this question may be framed around several topics.

Social and Political Attitudes

Since the end of the depression, racial prejudice in the United States has decreased. I believe that we as a nation have confronted the dilemma posed by Myrdal (1944) and have accorded blacks civil rights. Attitude surveys, for example, suggest that whites are much more tolerant of integration now than they were in the 1940s, and this liberalization was not halted by the racial riots of the late 1960s (Greeley and Sheatsley, 1971; Hyman and Sheatsley, 1964; Sheatsley, 1966). Behavioral changes are even more meaningful. Throughout the nation, blacks now work at jobs that were once restricted to whites (Farley, 1977b:196–198; Garfinkle, 1975; Levitan *et al.*, 1975:44–63), and issues that provoked violent controversies 20 years ago—such as the right of blacks to ride buses with whites, to serve on juries, or to vote—have been resolved. In the political sphere, blacks have been elected to office in all southern states and (U.S. Bureau of the Census, 1975; Table 100) have served as mayors in predominantly white cities and as politicians in all sections of the country. Therefore, it is no longer possible to run racist campaigns on the principle of states' rights.

Turning to attitudes about desegregated schooling, we discover that whites overwhelmingly endorse the ideal of integrated education. In 1976, 85% of a national sample of whites said that blacks and whites should go to the same schools, an increase from 39% in 1942 (Greeley and Sheatsley, 1971:14; National Opinion Research Center, 1976:Item 92). Within the South, the change in the proportion of whites giving their assent to integrated schools rose from about 1% in 1942 to 69% in 1976. Concomitant changes in behavior are evident. In the late 1950s and early 1960s, when token numbers of blacks were admitted to white schools in Little Rock or New Orleans, for example, black children were taunted by whites, who often boycotted the schools, and violence was not rare (Crain, 1968:Pt. 3; Peltason, 1971:Ch. 5). With the dramatic exception of Boston, we have moved on to a more peaceful acceptance of school integration throughout the nation.

Although whites approve of integrated schools in the abstract, they strongly oppose the most effective means of desegregating schools—busing—and have misgivings about enrolling their children in predominantly black schools. In a study we conducted in the Detroit area a year ago, we discovered that 85% of the whites felt that black and white children should go to the same schools. However, 93% of those who approved such integration said that they disapproved of busing. We pursued this and asked those respondents who endorsed integration but opposed busing how they thought schools were to be integrated. The majority of whites did not propose any strategies for integrating schools; instead, they reiterated their opposition to busing and their support for neighborhood schools. It is interesting to note that about one-quarter of these whites observed that integrated neighborhoods would lead to integrated schools.

In summary, there is much more white support for integrated education now than there was two decades ago, and black parents or civil rights groups no longer face intransigent white opposition. Nevertheless, the apprehensions whites have about sending their children to majority black schools and their feelings about busing children away from their own neighborhoods to achieve integration suggest that elected school boards and state officials will oppose most effective efforts to desegregate schools.

Demographic Trends

On the optimistic side, we have consistent evidence that racial residential segregation has slowly declined. An analysis of 109 central cities from 1940 to 1970 implies that residential segregation decreased outside the South after 1950 and within the South since 1960 (Sørensen et al., 1975:132). The study of Van Valey et al. (1977:Table 2) dealt with all central cities and metropolises from 1960 to 1970 and corroborated these findings. Particularly large declines in segregation were recorded in smaller cities and in those having relatively few black residents.

Data about racial residential segregation are ordinarily available only from the decennial censuses, but 13 cities of 50,000 or more conducted special censuses after 1973. Table 2.5 presents information about recent changes in segregation in these locations. This information is similar to Table 2.1 and indicates the proportion of the black population; the average proportion of black residents in the census tract of the typical white; the average proportion of whites in the census tract of the typical black; and the index of racial residential dissimilarity calculated from census tract data. We find that in most cities the indicators of potential interracial contact at the tract level have increased, and, in 11 of the 13 cities, the indexes of dissimilarity fell. Although it is impossible to generalize on the basis of this selection of cities, the declining values of the indexes of residential segregation imply that the trends seen in the investigations of Taeuber, Roof, and their collaborators have continued into this decade. It may be that changing racial attitudes of whites, particularly their increasing willingness to tolerate a black neighbor, and the Civil Rights Act of 1968, which banned discrimination in the marketing of most housing, permit a few persistent and financially capable blacks to enter residential areas once closed to them.

On the pessimistic side, I suspect that the basic tendency toward a concentration of blacks in central cities and whites in suburbs has not been, and will not soon be, altered. Between 1970 and 1974, about 7.7 million whites moved from central cities to suburbs, as compared to

TABLE 2.5

Indicators of Racial Residential Segregation in Cities Conducting Special Census in the Mid-1970s

City	Proportion (%) of population black		Average percentage black in census tract in typical white		Average percentage white in census tract in typical black		Index of dissimilarity		Date of special census
	1970	Mid-1970s	1970	Mid-1970s	1970	Mid-1970s	1970	Mid-1970s	
Austin, TX [a]	11	11	6	7	47	59	72	61	4/20/76
Davenport, IW	4	5	3	4	77	78	74	63	2/14/75
Elgin, IL	3	5	4	5	88	87	44	49	8/11/76
Ft. Smith, AK	7	7	5	5	66	69	75	71	7/13/75
Greenville, SC	31	34	19	23	43	44	59	51	9/13/76
Little Rock, AK	25	29	9	11	28	28	77	75	8/16/74
Milwaukee, WS	15	19	4	6	25	25	87	81	3/3/75
North Little Rock, AK	16	16	6	6	31	32	74	74	4/28/76
Phoenix, AZ	5	5	3	3	54	62	80	67	10/15/75
St. Petersburg, FL	14	15	2	4	12	10	94	88	1/30/76
San Bernadino, CA	13	14	8	9	45	56	72	62	4/1/75
Tucson, AZ	3	4	3	3	80	88	59	41	10/20/75
Waukegan, IL	13	15	9	11	57	63	62	54	1/9/75
Average for thirteen cities	12	14	6	7	50	54	71	64	

Sources: U.S. Bureau of the Census, Census of Population: 1970, PHC(1)-Numbers 17, 43, 53, 72, 84, 115, 131, 160, 187, 212, and 218. Current Population Reports, Series P-28, Numbers 1506,1513, 1514, 1521, 1524, 1527, 1538, 1541, 1542, 1543, 1548, 1550, and 1551.

[a] Data refer to entire Travis County.

about 3.3 million moving from the suburbs to central cities. In other words, the suburbs gained more than one million whites each year, primarily at the expense of the central cities (U.S. Bureau of the Census, 1974:Table 1). By the fall of 1975, two-thirds of the white students in metropolitan areas went to suburban schools, but only 30% of the metropolitan area black students attended such schools (U.S. Bureau of the Census, 1977:Table 2). Within many metropolises, this demographic shift of whites to the suburbs is the major barrier to school integration, and, in a few locations, such as Washington, D.C., it may produce schools that are almost as extensively segregated as southern schools prior to the *Brown* decision.

Legal Principles

Between 1968 and 1973, the Supreme Court enunciated legal principles that accelerated school integration. The rulings established precedents that led district federal courts to order integration in many cities, and it is likely that segregation levels in 1977 were lower than those reported in Tables 2.1 and 2.2 of this chapter. That is, since 1974, court-ordered integration went into effect or was expanded in Baltimore, Boston, Detroit, Houston, Louisville, and Milwaukee. Federal courts in Cleveland and Columbus and state courts in Los Angeles and San Diego have found those districts responsible for racial segregation, and some type of integration orders will eventually be issued.

There are clear indications that, since 1973, the Supreme Court has been much more reluctant to order effective school desegregation, and plaintiffs may now face more difficulties than they did in the years preceeding 1973. The next major breakthrough will involve pooling central city black and suburban white students to achieve integration. It is unrealistic to believe that state legislatures or elected bodies will redraw school district lines to facilitate the integration of central city blacks, and thus city–suburban mergers are likely to occur only if courts act. Litigants in Richmond (*Bradley* v. *School Board of Richmond,* 338 F. Supp. 67, 1972) and Detroit (*Bradley* v. *Milliken,* 345 F. Supp. 914, 1972) convinced federal judges that states bore responsibility for metropolitan school segregation, and the judges called for the pooling of the city and suburban students. The Supreme Court, however, was unconvinced, and these integration orders were never implemented (*Bradley* v. *School Board of Richmond,* 94 S. Ct. 31, 1973; *Milliken* v. *Bradley,* 418 U.S. 717, 1974).

In 1976, the Supreme Court began to argue that plaintiffs in discrimination cases must prove intent. That is, in Washington, D.C. the police department screened officer candidates with a verbal ability test, and many more blacks than whites failed the test. In Arlington Heights, Illinois—a Chicago suburb—city officials refused to rezone an area so that moderate income housing could be built. The effect of course, was to make it more difficult for blacks to enter the suburb. Plaintiffs in both cases demonstrated that the actions had unusually adverse effects upon blacks and requested that the courts overturn the verbal ability test and mandate rezoning.

The Supreme Court recognized the adverse consequences of the test and the zoning ordinance for blacks but argued that this was not sufficient to have them declared unconstitutional. Rather, the plaintiffs would have to demonstrate that those who selected the test or refused to alter the zoning intended to discriminate racially (*Village of Arlington Heights* v. *Metropolitan Housing Development Corporation*, 97 S. Ct. 555, 1977; *Washington* v. *Davis*, 96 S. Ct. 2040, 1976).

Since these decisions were rendered, the Supreme Court has dealt with school integration in four cities, and, each time, it has raised questions about whether or not large-scale busing programs were needed in light of the principles developed in *Washington* v. *Davis* and in *Village of Arlington Heights* v. *Metropolitan Housing Development Corporation*. The Fifth Circuit Court ordered an extensive busing program for Austin, Texas, but the Supreme Court suggested that the remedy was probably more extensive than the violations and called for more hearings, particularly on the issue of intent to segregate (*Austin Independent School District* v. *United States*, 76–200 U.S. S. Ct., 1976). In Dayton, a busing program reduced segregation, and the Supreme Court let it continue. It did, however, call for more hearings to ascertain whether or not school administrators intended to violate the rights of blacks when they took actions that separated blacks from whites (*Dayton Board of Education* v. *Brinkman*, 53 L. Ed., 2d., 851, 1977). Similarly, integration programs for Omaha (*School District of Omaha* v. *United States*, 53 L. Ed. 2d., 1039, 1977) and Indianapolis (*Board of School Commissioners* v. *Buckley*, 76–520 97 S. Ct., 1977) were vacated until further hearings could determine the intent of school officials.

At the start, we indicated that if there is a constant factor in the struggle to integrate education, it is the attempt of black parents and civil rights groups to secure equal opportunities. Plaintiffs in Austin, Dayton, Indianapolis, and Omaha will endeavor to convince courts that school administrators deliberately segregated children and that encom-

passing integration programs are needed. The variable factor in school integration has been the decision a court renders in such suits. We have no prescience about whether courts will now move slowly and tolerate high levels of segregation or will again issue the orders that—as reported in Tables 2.1 and 2.2—reduced segregation in many cities.

REFERENCES

Alexander v. *Holmes*
    1969   396 U.S. 19.
Austin Independent School District v. *United States*
    1976   97 S. Ct. 517.
Bell v. *Schools, City of Gary*
    1963   213 F. Supp. 819.
Berea College v. *Kentucky*
    1908   211 U.S. 45.
Board of School Commissioners v. *Buckley*
    1977   76–520 S. Ct. 97.
Bolner, James, and Robert Shanley
    1974   *Busing: The Political and Judicial Process.* New York: Praeger.
Bond, Horace Mann
    1934   *The Education of the Negro in the American Social Order.* New York: Prentice-Hall.
Bradley v. *Milliken*
    1972   345 F. Supp. 914.
Bradley v. *School Board of Richmond*
    1972   338 F. Supp. 67.
    1973   94 S. Ct. 31.
Brown v. *Board of Education*
    1954   347 U.S. 483.
    1955   349 U.S. 294.
Bullock, Henry Allen
    1973   *A History of Negro Education in the South.* Cambridge, Massachusetts: Harvard University Press.
Carr v. *Montgomery County Board of Education*
    1968   289 F. Supp. 647.
Carter, Robert L.
    1969   "Equal educational opportunity for Negroes—Abstractions or reality." In John H. McCord (ed.), *With All Deliberate Speed: Civil Rights Theory and Reality.* Urbana, Illinois: University of Illinois Press.
Cataldo, Everett, Michael Giles, Deborah Athos, and Douglas Galtin
    1975   "Desegregation and white flight." *Integrated Education* 13:3–5.
Center for National Policy Review
    1974   *Justice Delayed and Denied.* Washington, D.C.: Center for National Policy Review, School of Law, Catholic University of America.

Chicago Commission on Race Relations
    1922   *The Negro in Chicago.* Chicago, Illinois: University of Chicago
            Press.
Civil Rights Cases
    1883   109 U.S. 31.
Coleman, James S., Sara D. Kelly, and John A. Moore
    1975   *Trends in School Segregation, 1968–73.* Washington, D.C.: The
            Urban Institute. (Paper 722–03–01)
Crain, Robert L.
    1968   *The Politics of School Desegregation.* Chicago, Illinois: Aldine Pub-
            lishing Company.
Cumming v. *Richmond County Board of Education*
    1899   175 U.S. 528.
Dayton Board of Education v. *Brinkman*
    1977   53 L. Ed. 2d. 851.
Deal v. *Cincinnati Board of Education*
    1965   244 F. Supp. 572.
Downs v. *Board of Education*
    1964   366 F. 2d. 988.
DuBois, W. E. B.
    1964   *Black Reconstruction in America.* Cleveland, Ohio: World.
Farley, Reynolds
    1975   "Racial integration in the public schools, 1967 to 1972: Assessing
            the effect of governmental policies." *Sociological Focus* 8:3–26.
    1977a   "Can governmental policies integrate schools?" Unpublished manu-
            script.
    1977b   "Trends in racial inequalities: Have the gains of the 1960s dis-
            appeared in the 1970s?" *American Sociological Review* 42, no. 2
            (April):189–208.
Franklin, John Hope
    1967   *From Slavery to Freedom.* New York: Knopf.
Friedman, Leon (ed.)
    1969   *Argument.* New York: Chelsea House.
Garfinkle, Stuart H.
    1975   "Occupations of women and black voters, 1962–72." *Monthly Labor
            Review* 98, no. 11 (November):25–35.
Giles, Michael W.
    1977   "Racial stability and urban school desegregation." *Urban Affairs
            Quarterly* 12 (4):499–510.
Greeley, Andrew M., and Paul B. Sheatsley
    1971   "Attitudes toward racial integration." *Scientific American* 225 (6):
            13–20.
Green v. *New Kent County*
    1968   391 U.S. 430.
Hofstadter, Richard
    1959   *Social Darwinism in American Thought.* (Revised Edition). New
            York: George Braziller.
Hyman, Herbert H., and Paul B. Sheatsley
    1964   "Attitudes toward desegregation." *Scientific American* 211 (July):
            2–9.

Jackson, Gregg
  1975   "Reanalysis of Coleman's 'Recent Trends in School Desegregation'."
            Educational Researcher 4 (November):21–25.
Keyes v. School District No. 1, Denver
  1973   396 U.S. 1215.
Kluger, Richard
  1976   Simple Justice. New York: Knopf.
Kusmer, Kenneth L.
  1976   A Ghetto Takes Shape; Black Cleveland, 1870–1930. Urbana: Uni-
            versity of Illinois Press.
Levitan, Sam A., William B. Johnston, and Robert B. Taggart
  1975   Still a Dream: The Changing Status of Blacks Since 1960. Cam-
            bridge, Massachusetts: Harvard University Press.
Lord, G. Dennis
  1975   "School busing and white abandonment of public schools." South-
            eastern Geographer 15 (2):81–92.
Lord, J. Dennis, and John C. Catau
  1976   "School desegregation, busing and suburban migration." Urban
            Education 11 (3):275–294.
McLaurin v. Oklahoma State Regents for Higher Education
  1950   339 U.S. 637.
Milliken v. Bradley
  1974   418 U.S. 717.
Missouri ex rel. Gaines v. Canada
  1938   305 U.S. 337.
Myrdal, Gunnar
  1944   An American Dilemma. New York: McGraw-Hill.
National Opinion Research Center
  1976   National Data Program for the Social Sciences, Spring 1976: General
            Social Survey. Chicago, Illinois: National Opinion Research Center.
Orfield, Gary
  1969   The Reconstruction of Southern Education. New York: Wiley and
            Sons.
Peltason, J. W.
  1971   Fifty Eight Lonely Men. Urbana, Illinois: University of Illinois Press.
Penick v. Columbus Board of Education
  1977   429 F. Supp. 229.
Pettigrew, Thomas F., and Robert L. Green
  1976   "School desegregation in large cities: A critique of the Coleman
            'white flight' thesis." Harvard Educational Review 46:1–53.
Plessy v. Ferguson
  1896   163 U.S. 537.
Read, Frank T.
  1975   "Judicial evolution of the law of school integration since Brown v.
            Board of Education." Law and Contemporary Problems 39 (1):7–49.
Roberts v. City of Boston
  1849   5 Cushing Reports. 198.
Rosen, Paul L.
  1972   The Supreme Court and Social Science. Urbana, Illinois: University
            of Illinois Press.

Rossell, Christine H.
    1975   "White flight." *Integrated Education* 12:3–10.
    1975-76 "School desegregation and white flight." *Political Science Quarterly* 90:675–695.
School District of Omaha v. United States
    1977   53 L. Ed. 2d. 1039.
Sheatsley, Paul B.
    1966   "White attitudes toward the Negro." *Daedulus* 95 (1):217–238.
Shelly v. Kramer
    1948   334 U.S. 1.
Singleton v. Jackson Municipal Separate School District
    1970   414 F. 2d. 1211.
Sipuel v. Oklahoma State Board of Regents
    1948   332 U.S. 631.
Smith v. Allwright
    1944   321 U.S. 649.
Sørensen, Annenette, Karl E. Taeuber, and Leslie J. Hollingsworth, Jr.
    1975   "Indexes of racial residential segregation for 109 cities in the United States, 1940 to 1970." *Sociological Focus* 8, 2 (April):125–142.
Stampp, Kenneth M.
    1967   *The Era of Reconstruction: 1865–1877.* New York: Vintage Books.
Swann v. Charlotte–Mecklenburg
    1971   402 U.S. 1.
Sweatt v. Painter
    1950   339 U.S. 629.
Taeuber, Karl E., and Alma F. Taeuber
    1965   *Negroes in Cities.* Chicago, Illinois: Aldine Publishing Company.
    1976   "A practitioner's perspective on the index of dissimilarity." *American Sociological Review* 41 no. 5 (October):884–889.
U.S. Bureau of the Census
    1971   Census of Population: 1970. PC(1)-A1.
    1974   Current Population Reports, Series P-20, no. 262
    1975   Current Population Reports, Series P-23, no. 54.
    1977   Current Population Reports, Series P-20, no. 309.
U.S. Commission on Civil Rights
    1973   The Federal Civil Rights Enforcement Effort–A Reassessment.
U.S. National Center for Educational Statistics
    1969   Directory, Public Schools in Large Districts with Enrollment and Staff by Race, Fall, 1967.
U.S. National Center for Health Statistics
    1970   Vital Statistics of the United States, 1968.
    1976   Monthly Vital Statistics Report. Vol. 25, no. 10, Supplement.
    1977   Monthly Vital Statistics Report. Vol. 25, no. 12.
U.S. Office for Civil Rights
    1974   Directory of Public Elementary and Secondary Schools in Selected Districts, Enrollment and Staff by Racial–Ethnic Groups, 1972.
U.S. Office of Education
    1974   Education Directory: 1973–74. Public School System.
U.S. v. Board of School Commissioners, Indianapolis
    1974   386 F. Supp. 1199.

U.S. v. *Cruikshank*
    1876   92 U.S. 542.
U.S. v. *Harris*
    1883   106 U.S. 629.
U.S. v. *Montgomery County Board of Education*
    1969   395 U.S. 236.
U.S. v. *Reese*
    1876   92 U.S. 214.
Van Valey, Thomas L., Wade Clark Roof, and Jerome E. Wilcox
    1977   "Trends in residential segregation: 1960–1970." *American Journal of
                Sociology 82.* 4 (January):826–844.
Village of Arlington Heights v. *Metropolitan Housing Development Corporation*
    1977   97 S. Ct. 555.
Washington, Booker T.
    1965   "The Atlanta exposition address." In John Hope Franklin and Isidore
                Starr (eds.), *The Negro in Twentieth Century America.* New York:
                Random House.
Washington v. *Davis*
    1976   96 S. Ct. 2040.
Wegmann, Robert D.
    1975   "Neighborhoods and schools in racial transition." *Growth and
                Change.* 6:3–8.
Weinberg, Meyer
    1967   *Race and Place.* Washington, D.C.: Government Printing Office.
Woodward, Vann C.
    1957   *The Strange Career of Jim Crow.* New York: Oxford.
Zoloth, Barbara S.
    1976   "Alternative measures of school segregation." *Land Economics* 52
                (3): 278–298.

3

Residential and School Segregation: Some Tests of Their Association[1]

FRANKLIN D. WILSON
KARL E. TAEUBER

Correspondence between the racial composition of schools and residential neighborhoods is widely accepted as factual, educationally sound, and morally proper. Two of these three beliefs have been the subject of much recent investigation and controversy. The history of "neighborhood schools" and their place in contemporary educational administration are being reexamined by educational researchers (Weinberg, 1968, 1977). The propriety of allowing school racial segregation to be linked

[1] This chapter is one in a series, "Studies in Racial Segregation," supported by funds granted to the Institute for Research on Poverty at the University of Wisconsin by the Department of Health, Education, and Welfare pursuant to the provisions of the Economic Opportunity Act of 1964. Additional support was provided by Contract No. HEW-100-76-0196 from the Assistant Secretary for Planning and Evaluation, DHEW, and by Grant No. 5 RO1 MH 27880-02 from the Center for Studies of Metropolitan Problems, NIMH. Data acquisition and processing were supported in part by Population Research Center Grant No. 5 PO1-HD-O-5876 awarded to the Center for Population Research of the National Institute for Child

The Demography of Racial and Ethnic Groups.

to residential racial segregation is reflected in the controversy over de facto versus de jure school segregation and has been examined and reexamined by legislative, executive, and judicial branches of government (see in particular United States Supreme Court, 1971, 1976a,b).

The factual character of the link between residential and school segregation has been taken for granted. It is a commonplace that the high levels of racial segregation observed in northern and western school districts (and in many southern districts after "desegregation") result from the residential separation of whites and minorities (Farley, 1975; Wolf, 1976). It seems tautological that if the attendance zones of schools are drawn to embrace contiguous areas surrounding the schools, school segregation will be a simple reflection of residential segregation. Because the relation seems obvious, it has been regarded as true without the benefit of careful conceptualization or systematic empirical testing. A search of the sociological literature reveals no logical arguments or empirical results that justify the acceptance of this purported association as a sociological fact.

Empirical studies of racial residential segregation indicate persisting high levels of separation between whites and racial minorities in the nation's metropolitan areas (de Leeuw et al., 1976; Sørensen et al., 1975; Van Valey et al., 1977). Empirical studies of racial school segregation report high levels of separation between white and minority pupils in those school districts that have not implemented extensive desegregation programs (Coleman et al., 1975; Farley, 1976; Farley and Taeuber, 1974). The few studies that report on the association between residential and school segregation indicate that less than 50% of the variance is attributable to the correlation (Dye, 1968; Farley, 1975; Farley and Taeuber, 1974). A correlation of this magnitude does not justify the elaborate interpretive structure that has been built on the base of a direct one-to-one association of schools with neighborhood residents.

The magnitude of the correlation reported between residential and school segregation has been influenced by a number of methodological problems, some of which can be controlled more effectively. Indices of residential segregation in these studies were computed over the entire residential population rather than over persons of school age or persons enrolled in school. Because of racial differences in fertility, family composition, migration, and housing consumption patterns, the percentage

Health and Human Development. Mark Day and Jay Goldstein assisted with data processing. The special California data set was made available by Millicent Cox of the Rand Corporation. Conclusions and interpretations are the sole responsibility of the authors.

of blacks in the total population of a residential area is often well below the percentage of blacks among school-age children (Farley, 1975:169–174). This finding should tend to depress the correlation. Among the large cities included in these studies, it is not always the case that a single city school district serves the city but no other territory. Municipal and school district boundaries often differ, and this fact should also tend to depress the correlation between city residential segregation indices and school district pupil segregation indices. Still another distortion of the correlation arises from the use of residential indices calculated from decennial census data (for April 1) and school indices calculated from fall enrollment data for another year.

A fundamental weakness of these studies is the lack of coincidence between the neighborhood units over which indices of residential segregation have been computed and the attendance zones from which schools draw their pupils. Neither of the two areal systems readily available from decennial census data—census tracts and city blocks—corresponds to school attendance zones. It is a well-known property of residential segregation indices that their magnitude is affected by the size of the areal unit and the system used for determining areal unit boundaries. Failure to use school attendance zones for the measurement of residential segregation could thus be a major source of attenuation of the correlation.

If these methodological problems are overcome, a more readily interpreted correlation coefficient can be calculated to measure the association between school segregation and residential segregation. This is the first task we shall undertake, using a special set of data for selected school districts in California. The small number of districts included in this data set limits the generality of the analysis we can undertake, but the California locale provides the opportunity to pay attention to school and residential segregation patterns among three racial and ethnic groups rather than simply two.

Establishing the magnitude of the correlation between indices of school and residential segregation provides only a partial and indirect answer to the original question: Is there a perfect correspondence between the racial composition of residential neighborhoods and that of schools? Three types of disturbances to the association may be identified as those having to do with school administration, those having to do with the utilization of public schooling by residents, and those having to do with residential responses.

School attendance policies in most school districts do not rely exclusively on one-to-one matching of residential locations and schools. Optional attendance zones, voluntary transfer programs, magnet schools, and special education programs all tend to loosen the link between residential location and school assignment. School desegregation litigation in both southern and northern districts has proven that administrative devices such as these have commonly been manipulated to enhance racial isolation in the schools. Indeed, the drawing and modification of school attendance zones, the selection of sites for new schools, and the designation of feeder-patterns from primary to secondary schools have been used directly for racial segregation. We do not provide evidence in this chapter on such practices, but we shall refer to them later to indicate that the causal link between residential racial patterns and school racial patterns is not unidirectional.

Just as school administrators may be responsive to residential patterns, so may residents be responsive to school patterns. Residents with school-age children may choose not to use the assigned public school. Unless the district permits transfers to other schools, their alternatives are to send children to private schools, move elsewhere within the district, or move to another district. Each of these choices entails social and economic considerations. We shall examine whether the racial composition of schools is associated with racial and ethnic disparities in socioeconomic characteristics.

Residential choice is affected by many other considerations besides the racial composition of neighborhood schools. Housing cost, location with respect to jobs and amenities, neighborhood quality, taxes, and numerous other factors enter into a household's choice of location. Some of these factors have a differential racial impact and account in part for the prevailing racial residential segregation. In assessing the link between school racial composition and residential racial composition, it is appropriate to take into account these general residential determinants. With some of the determinants, particularly those most directly related to patterns of white avoidance of minority neighbors, there is a conceptual problem in identifying causality. The process of racial turnover in residential areas tends to occur simultaneously with racial turnover in the schools. White persons' perceptions of the inevitability of complete racial transition are affected by perceptions of the quality of public services (including educational services) and by what happens to that quality during racial transition. The racial transition often proceeds more rapidly in local elementary schools than in housing, and this also contributes to the residential change. White utilization of private schooling for class, religious, or educational purposes is hard to disentangle completely from "white flight" from minority contact. This is particularly true in changing neighborhoods (see Orfield, 1975). In any case, the greater the white withdrawal from public schools for whatever reasons, the more likely that the public school racial transition will lead the neighborhood transition and become a contributing part of the self-fulfilling prophecy that culminates in nearly total racial separation. We cannot control fully for all of the determinants of housing location choice, nor can we resolve the conceptual complexities in the limited data analysis that follows. Our analysis should be regarded as illustrative, and our interpretations shall be cautious.

DATA

For selected California school districts, attendance zone boundaries for individual schools were plotted on census tract maps. Data from the 1970 census tapes for census tracts (fourth count) were then reassembled to provide estimated census characteristics for the attendance zones. Enrollment by race for each school was obtained from a tape report of the fall survey of public school enrollments (1970), conducted by the Office for Civil Rights (OCR) of the Department of Health, Education, and Welfare. Thus, it is possible to associate the racial composition of each public school with the racial, socioeconomic, and housing characteristics of the people residing within the school attendance zone.

For our analysis, we utilize a maximum of nine urban school districts for which the special data are available and which contain substantial numbers of minority pupils. Summary data on the schools and the school attendance zones are presented in Table 3.1. The OCR survey identifies five racial and ethnic categories: American Indian, Oriental, Spanish-surnamed American, Negro, and Other. We use the last three categories and designate them as Hispanic, black, and Anglo. From the census data, we obtained roughly similar categories by selecting Negro and white. Subtracting from the white those of Spanish heritage yields Hispanic and Anglo figures. The census definition of *Spanish heritage* in California is "persons of Spanish language or Spanish surname." OCR categories and procedures are not strictly comparable with census categories and procedures, but we believe that, in practice, most children in the three categories we use were classified the same in both sources.

Elementary schools in all districts included grades K–6. In Pasadena, under terms of a desegregation plan, elementary education was split into two systems, one for grades K–3 and one for grades 4–6. We utilize the lower grade system for this analysis. Census data are presented for the age group 5–13 years. Not all children aged 5–13 on April 1, 1970, or children in grades K–6 in fall, 1970, would be expected to be in school, but this is the closest match we could make. The count of children aged

TABLE 3.1
Characteristics of Elementary Schools and Attendance Zones for Selected School Districts: 1970

| School | Selected characteristics of schools | | | | Selected characteristics of school attendance zones | | | | |
| | Enrollment | | | Number of schools | Population aged 5–13 Yr | | | | |
	Total	Percentage black	Percentage Hispanic		Total	Percentage black	Percentage Hispanic	Percentage enrolled in grades 1–8	Anglos in grades 1–8: Percentage in private schools
Compton	18,844	80.9	12.7	21	23,831	76.2	13.5	89.5	7.5
Fresno	30,724	9.5	22.0	51	38,878	8.0	25.9	91.6	3.5
Long Beach	35,163	10.1	7.1	51	47,845	7.7	9.9	89.9	10.2
Los Angeles	341,282	26.7	24.8	429	505,568	23.7	27.2	88.7	13.5
Oakland	32,266	61.9	8.9	57	41,772	55.5	11.9	92.9	19.3
Pasadena	7,906	38.0	10.1	14	21,449	29.2	13.6	90.1	23.6
Pomona	12,936	20.4	18.6	20	18,154	16.8	19.5	86.6	9.6
San Jose	19,721	1.6	26.2	31	24,891	1.3	28.0	90.0	6.7
Santa Clara	11,217	1.7	16.0	21	16,325	.5	20.3	91.9	6.8

5–13 also exceeds the number of children enrolled in public schools in grades K–6 because the former includes private school children, those in special education or not attending, and public school children in grades 7 and 8.

RESIDENTIAL AND SCHOOL RACIAL SEGREGATION

Indices of racial segregation were calculated for three population groupings—the total population, the population aged 5–13 years residing within attendance zones, and the population enrolled in public elementary schools. The index of dissimilarity is used to measure segregation (Farley and Taeuber, 1974). We seek to determine whether the magnitude of segregation observed for each paired comparison of blacks, Anglos, and Hispanics differs according to which population grouping is examined. Indices for the nine California school districts are exhibited in Table 3.2.

The residential and school indices for Pasadena, presented in Table 3.2, were lowered by the school desegregation program implemented in fall, 1970. The effect on school indices is straightforward. Noncontiguous geographic attendance zones were drawn for each K–3 elementary school for the specific purpose of reducing black-Anglo and Hispanic-Anglo school segregation. The residential indices are also reduced far below what they otherwise would have been. Persons residing in each of the noncontiguous portions of a school attendance zone are treated (for the purpose of evaluating residential segregation) as residents of a single zone. Socially, the only contact between, for example, Anglos resident on the east side of Pasadena and blacks and Hispanics resident in the central and southern parts of the city may occur through their children and at school functions. Nevertheless, these persons are residents of the same attendance zone, and, for the purpose of our analysis, they do represent the residential base population that is affected by that school.

There are many comparisons that can be made among the rows and columns of Table 3.2, but only a few require emphasis. The residential segregation of children aged 5–13 is usually greater than the residential segregation of the total population. Specifying school-age children thus seems to be a useful methodological strategy. But the school-age residential indices are not uniformly closer to the school indices than are the all-age residential indices.

The correlation coefficient between the school segregation index and the residential segregation index for children aged 5–13 is .87 (for the

TABLE 3.2

Indices of Racial Segregation for Elementary Schools and Attendance Zones for Selected School Districts: 1970

School district	Blacks versus Anglos			Hispanics versus Anglos			Blacks versus Hispanics		
	Residential		Schools	Residential		Schools	Residential		Schools
	Total	5–13 Yr		Total	5–13 Yr		Total	5–13 Yr	
Compton	67	67	71	49	56	55	44	41	52
Fresno	84	90	77	36	42	51	71	74	65
Long Beach	79	81	77	21	28	35	64	64	55
Los Angeles	89	93	92	53	60	65	82	83	80
Oakland	63	70	70	38	53	54	44	43	54
Pasadena	23	21	09	16	21	20	27	29	32
Pomona	67	72	72	28	37	44	53	58	60
San Jose	67	73	60	38	52	66	40	52	31
Santa Clara	56	56	47	24	24	31	48	50	60

black-Anglo comparison for eight districts, excluding Pasadena). This coefficient is considerably larger than the coefficients reported in previous literature, but the relationship between school and residential segregation is still imperfect. The explained variance (the square of the correlation coefficient) is 76%, and there may be other systematic factors that account for the remaining 24%. Of course, this particular result is based on too few districts for us to give much weight to the specific measures of association, and, we cannot know in what way this result is affected by being limited to black–Anglo segregation in California.

Information on residential and school segregation between Hispanics and Anglos and between blacks and Hispanics is also included in Table 3.2. The general pattern conforms to that observed in other studies (Grebler et al., 1970; Taeuber and Taeuber, 1965), black-Anglo segregation being the greatest, followed by black–Hispanic segregation, and a lower but still substantial Hispanic–Anglo segregation. The intricacies of triethnic segregation complicate the school desegregation process. Note that after desegregation Pasadena's remarkably low school segregation index for blacks–Anglos is accompanied by a low index for Hispanics–Anglos and a not-so-low index for blacks–Hispanics.

SOCIOECONOMIC RESIDENTIAL SEGREGATION

Racial residential segregation in the United States tends to occur for reasons other than the sizable socioeconomic racial disparities (Taeuber, 1968; Erbe, 1975; Farley, 1977; Schnare, 1977; Taeuber and Taeuber, 1965). Between blacks and whites of the same income, occupation, or educational level high levels of racial residential segregation occur. Thus, racial segregation and class segregation are distinguishable phenomena, despite the frequency with which they are considered inseparable in discussions of metropolitan population redistribution or of the educational needs of the disadvantaged in central cities. In this section of our analysis, we seek to assess whether the racial composition of school attendance zones is associated with racial and ethnic disparities in socioeconomic status.

The procedure employed is first to partition the total amount of race–ethnic residential variation in the population of a school district into components reflecting (a) within-attendance-zone variability in racial composition; (b) racial differences in socioeconomic status; and (c) racial residential segregation within socioeconomic status levels. Let $T_{..}$, $T_{i.}$, and T_{ij} be the total population of the district, the ith status level, and the ith $(i = 1, \ldots , k)$ status level within the jth $(j = 1, \ldots , n)$ attendance zone, respectively, and $P_{..}$, $P_{i.}$, and P_{ij} be the proportion of blacks (or Hispanics) in the total population of the district, the ith status level, and the ith status level within the jth attendance zone. Then

$$T_{ss} = T_{..} P_{..} (1 - P_{..}),$$

and

$$B_{ss} = \left[\sum_{i=1}^{k} \sum_{j=1}^{n} T_{ij}(P_{ij} - P_{..})^2 \right] / T_{ss},$$

$$W_{ss} = \left[\sum_{i=1}^{k} \sum_{j=1}^{n} T_{ij}P_{ij}(1 - P_{ij}) \right] / T_{ss}$$

where T_{ss} is the total racial variation in the population of a district, B_{ss} is the proportion of total variation in race that can be attributed to residential and socioeconomic segregation, and W_{ss} is the proportion of total variation in race that can be attributed to variation in racial composition within attendance zones and socioeconomic categories. Readers familiar with analysis of variance techniques will recognize T_{ss} as the total sums of squares, the numerator of B_{ss} as the between sums of squares, and the numerator of W_{ss} as the within sums of squares.

Our primary interest is in the residential–socioeconomic component (B_{ss}). This can be decomposed as follows:

$$B_{ss\ (i.)} = \left[\sum_{i=1}^{k} T_{i.}(P_{i.} - P_{..})^2 \right] / T_{ss}$$

and

$$B_{ss\ (ij)} = \left[\sum_{i=1}^{k} \sum_{j=1}^{n} T_{ij}(P_{ij} - P_{i.})^2 \right] / T_{ss},$$

where $B_{ss(i)}$ is the proportion of total variation in race that can be attributed to racial differences in socioeconomic status levels, and $B_{ss(ij)}$ is the proportion of total variation in race that can be attributed to racial residential segregation within socioeconomic status levels.

These three components may be computed for any socioeconomic characteristic that is included in the special census data tabulated by school attendance zones. We have prepared illustrative results using four characteristics, income (15 categories), poverty ratio (8 categories), occupation (10 categories), and education (10 categories). Three districts within the Los Angeles metropolitan area were chosen for presentation in Table 3.3. For each district, the decomposition was performed separately for each of the three pairwise racial–ethnic comparisons.

TABLE 3.3
Indices of Racial, Socioeconomic, and Residential Segregation for Three School Districts

Socioeconomic characteristic and district	Blacks versus Anglos			Hispanics versus Anglos			Blacks versus Hispanics		
	Total residential-socioeconomic segregation	Racial inequality in socioeconomic status	Racial residential segregation within status levels	Total residential-socioeconomic segregation	Racial inequality in socioeconomic status	Racial residential segregation within status levels	Total residential-socioeconomic segregation	Racial inequality in socioeconomic status	Racial residential segregation within status levels
Income									
Los Angeles	.827	.079	.748	.412	.062	.349	.752	.008	.745
Long Beach	.355	.020	.335	.071	.066	.004	.544	.059	.485
Pasadena	.162	.069	.093	.061	.015	.045	.207	.030	.177
Occupation									
Los Angeles	.816	.080	.735	.385	.103	.282	.739	.045	.694
Long Beach	.365	.022	.344	.057	.005	.052	.524	.062	.461
Pasadena	.186	.105	.081	.101	.034	.066	.222	.058	.164
Education									
Los Angeles	.768	.032	.736	.365	.128	.237	.727	.058	.669
Long Beach	.294	.007	.286	.054	.009	.045	.521	.019	.512
Pasadena	.111	.040	.071	.058	.035	.023	.159	.020	.139
Poverty ratio									
Los Angeles	.825	.104	.721	.406	.096	.311	.741	.007	.734
Long Beach	.350	.029	.321	.057	.027	.029	.158	.022	.136
Pasadena	.180	.104	.076	.057	.027	.030	.158	.022	.136

For Los Angeles, the first three columns of the first row of Table 3.3 assess the distribution of blacks and Anglos among elementary school attendance zones, using income as the socioeconomic characteristic. The first figure, .827 (computed from the formula for B_{ss}), indicates that 83% of the total racial variation in Los Angeles can be attributed to differing racial proportions in the various income categories and attendance zones. This is the total residential and socioeconomic component. It can be divided into two additive components. The component representing racial inequality in income (computed from the formula for $B_{ss(i.)}$) is rather small (.079). The component representing racial residential segregation within income levels (computed from the formula for $B_{ss(ij)}$) is much larger (.748). Thus, income differences between blacks and Anglos account for only a small proportion of the total, and residential segregation between blacks and Anglos at each income level accounts for most of the racial differentiation among school attendance zones. Similar results obtain for Los Angeles for each of the socioeconomic characteristics and for each of the racial–ethnic comparisons. The total component is lower for Hispanics versus Anglos than for the other comparisons; this is in a sense an alternative indication of the residential segregation pattern revealed in Table 3.2. Even for these groups, though, the residential segregation component is much greater than the socioeconomic inequality component.

The components for Pasadena in Table 3.3 reveal the substantial racial–ethnic and socioeconomic homogenization of attendance zones that was effected by the delineation of noncontiguous zones. The components for Long Beach are considerably lower than those for Los Angeles. Long Beach has a very low degree of socioeconomic differentiation among its racial–ethnic groups, and this may reflect its niche as an old industrial enclave within the densely settled part of the urbanized area.

The general finding that school attendance zones in these districts display a substantial degree of racial–ethnic segregation beyond that attributable to socioeconomic differentiation prompts us to undertake a further specification. Within socioeconomic categories, there is pronounced racial–ethnic segregation, but is that segregation greater at one end of the status scale than at the other? Are high-status blacks and Anglos more or less segregated from one another than are low-status blacks and Anglos? To perform a further decomposition of the $B_{ss(ij)}$ component requires a large data set, and we present in Table 3.4 the results of one illustrative computation, using income levels for Los Angeles. Ignoring the highest income categories, which include very small numbers of families, racial–ethnic residential segregation within

TABLE 3.4

The Decomposition of Racial Residential Segregation within Income Levels, Los Angeles, 1970

Income Level	Blacks versus Anglos	Hispanics versus Whites	Blacks versus Hispanics
Under $1,000	3.98	4.14	4.31
$ 1,000– 1,999	4.11	3.90	4.14
$ 2,000– 2,999	6.09	5.82	5.72
$ 3,000– 3,999	6.64	6.47	6.62
$ 4,000– 4,999	6.71	7.30	7.01
$ 5,000– 5,999	7.11	7.83	7.46
$ 6,000– 6,999	7.46	8.42	7.72
$ 7,000– 7,999	7.68	8.54	8.16
$ 8,000– 8,999	7.28	7.02	7.35
$ 9,000– 9,999	6.44	7.91	6.51
$10,000–11,999	11.85	11.98	11.43
$12,000–14,999	11.95	10.36	11.02
$15,000–24,999	11.07	9.05	10.68
$25,000–49,999	1.46	1.02	1.56
$50,000 and over	.22	.28	.30
Total	100% (.748)	100% (.349)	100% (.745)

school attendance zones is an increasing function of income level. This extension of our decomposition technique is an alternate methodological approach to the calculation of indices of dissimilarity for each income level (Farley, 1977; Taeuber, 1968). Neither technique has received much use, yet the specification of socioeconomic status differentials in racial–ethnic segregation seems, from these few examples, to be a promising topic for further analysis.

WHITE AVOIDANCE

In this section of our analysis, we examine directly the relationship between characteristics of the population residing in a school's attendance zone and the racial composition of the school. The analyses in previous sections were more indirect. Segregation indices summarize features of the residential distribution and features of the school distribution. The correlation between residential and school segregation indices thus relates aggregate measures and provides a test of similarities in patterns. The assessment of socioeconomic and residential segregation also utilized summary measures (of the variation of distributions). The regression models to which we now turn evaluate the zone-by-zone correspondence between residential and school composition.

The "white flight" notion may be translated into a hypothesis that the greater the percentage of blacks among the pupils in a public school, the greater the tendency of white parents in the attendance zone to place their children in private schools or to move out of the zone. The current controversy revolves around the existence, magnitude, and consequences of such white flight when the racial composition of schools is altered as a result of deliberate desegregation programs. Desegregation programs are of recent vintage, and many large cities have not yet undertaken them; nevertheless, as emphasized in our introductory discussion, the issues of racial turnover in schools and neighborhoods have been with us for decades.

One way to search for evidence on the residence–school link in the more general process of white "avoidance" of racially mixed housing and schools is to analyze school systems that have not undergone extensive school desegregation. What evidence can we find in such districts of the influence of racial minorities on the utilization of public schools by white Anglos?

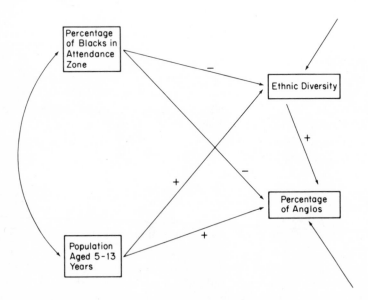

Figure 3.1 Determinants of the representation of Anglos in public elementary schools (with expected signs for each path).

An elementary model of the determinants of Anglo presence in public schools is portrayed in Figure 3.1. This model is simply a step toward a more complex analysis. The basic relationship is between the percentage that blacks compose of the school-age population of an attendance zone and the percentage that Anglo pupils compose of the enrollment in a public elementary school.

In the eight California districts (Pasadena is excluded) for which we shall evaluate this model, the presence of Hispanic residents and pupils and a small number of persons of other racial–ethnic groups confounds the simple white-avoidance-of-blacks model. We include a measure of ethnic diversity in the model. The index is computed as follows (Theil, 1972:6): Let there be k minority groups, each of which represents a certain proportion (P_i) of the minority population of a school or attendance area; then

$$H = \left[\sum_{i=1}^{k} (P_i) \log(1/P_i) \right] /k.$$

This index measures the concentration of members of three racial–ethnic categories (blacks, Hispanics, and other nonwhite races) in attendance zones. If only one of these groups resides in an attendance zone, the index value is zero; if all three groups are equally represented, the index value is one. Our hypothesis is that greater diversity among the racial–ethnic population is conducive to Anglos' utilization of the public schools. Anglo numerical and social dominance is presumably less threatened by a mélange of minority persons than by an equivalent number drawn all from one group. We also include the size of the school-age population in the zone and expect that a larger Anglo group of children will be less likely to withdraw from a particular percentage of blacks than would a smaller group.

Standardized regression coefficients for the three direct paths in this model are presented in Table 3.5. For each of the eight school districts, the coefficient for the percentage of blacks among the school-age population in the attendance zone is negative, as expected. The coefficient for the size of the school-age population has the expected positive sign for seven of the districts, but the magnitude of the coefficients is small. The coefficients for the index of racial diversity are varied in sign and magnitude. To the difficulty in obtaining a clear conceptual understanding of this index we can now add a difficulty in understanding the empirical outcome.

TABLE 3.5

Standardized Regression Coefficients Indicating the Effects of Selected Variables on the Percentage of Public Elementary School Pupils Who Are Anglo

Variables	Compton	Fresno	Long Beach	Los Angeles	Oakland	Pomona	San Jose	Santa Clara
Percentage of blacks among school-age population in attendance zone	−.955 [a]	−.813 [a]	−.860 [a]	−.688 [a]	−1.032 [a]	−.835 [a]	−.635 [a]	−.387 [a]
Total school-age population in attendance zone (log)	.054	.180 [a]	.048	.054	.032	−.019	.187	.372 [a]
Index of racial diversity	−1.663 [a]	.208	−.109	.077 [a]	−.164	−.119	.450 [a]	.643 [a]
School percentage of Anglos								
Mean	4.98	66.35	82.65	51.68	35.89	63.20	69.05	79.69
Standard deviation	9.52	29.30	20.39	38.11	32.28	29.30	28.71	14.88
Intercept	74.65	−34.53	78.07	23.33	79.86	94.64	−25.22	−32.56
R^2 (adjusted for df)	.764	.655	.800	.467	.800	.635	.514	.352
Number of observations	23	51	51	429	57	20	31	21

[a] Indicates that the regression coefficient is at least twice the size of its standard error.

The results obtained evaluating the elementary model are consistent with the hypothesis of Anglo avoidance of public schools in black and racially mixed neighborhoods. There is also an inescapable tautological element to this finding. In a two-race universe and looking solely at zone residents (or at school pupils), the percentage of blacks is a linear complement of the percentage of whites. Because our data refer to a multi-ethnic situation and we are relating percentages of blacks among zone residents to percentages of Anglos among school pupils, the strict tautology is removed, but only bizarre patterns could obviate a strong positive association between the two percentages.

A revised and elaborated model of the association between attendance zone population and Anglo school utilization is portrayed in Figure 3.2. If many Anglo parents seek to avoid sending their children to schools in which the potential for contact with black pupils is great (or that are perceived to be poor schools because of the presence of black pupils), then we should find evidence of one or both of the following: (a) enhanced Anglo enrollment in private schools; or (b) enhanced rates of out-migration of Anglo families with school-age children from the affected attendance zones. These are the direct indicators of white avoidance, and the school racial composition affects and is affected by these behaviors.

In a cross-section model with a delimited set of variables, we cannot specify fully the temporal processes. We can include several factors that describe the residential area; most of these factors tend to change only slowly, even in the face of out-migration and population turnover. The out-migration itself is to be inferred in this model from a smaller-than-expected percentage of school-age children in the Anglo population. If out-migration leads to racial residential turnover, there is a further confounding of causal paths. We include measures of housing type and price to control partially for the attractiveness of the residential area to black families (see Aldrich, 1975). A measure of the residential stability of black families living in the area in 1970 is included to identify areas of rapid black influx.

The model portrayed in Figure 3.2 treats Anglo out-migration, Anglo utilization of private schooling, and the percentage of Anglos in the public school as endogenous variables affected by the racial, social, economic, and housing characteristics of the population living within the attendance zone. The variables appearing in Figure 3.2 are defined in Table 3.6; note that three variables (education, occupation, and income) are used to measure socioeconomic status. Some of the directional arrows have been omitted from Figure 3.2 because the model is already complex. We do not seek to evaluate the full model but to estimate the

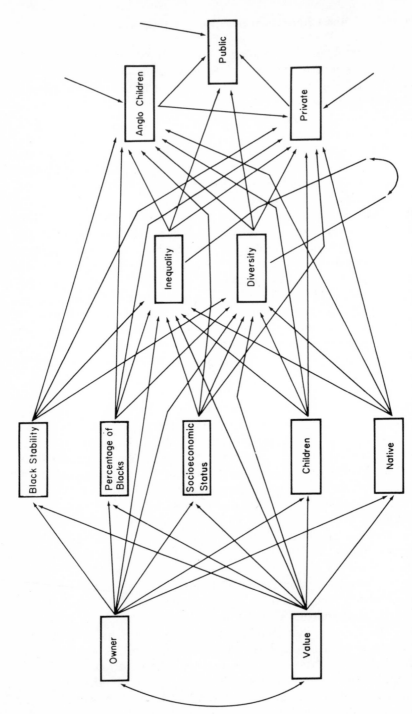

Figure 3.2 Revised model of the representation of Anglos in public elementary schools.

TABLE 3.6

Definition of Variables in Figure 3.2 and Equations (1)–(3)

Anglo children	Percentage of the Anglo population aged 5–13 years
Private	Percentage of Anglo elementary school children who are enrolled in private schools
Public	Percentage of pupils in the public elementary school who are Anglo
Inequality	Gini index of the similarity of the income distributions of black and Anglo families
Diversity	Index of racial diversity (defined in text)
Black stability	Percentage of the 1970 black population living in same house in 1965
Percentage of blacks	Percentage of the population aged 5–13 years who are black
Education	Percentage of the Anglo population with at least one year of college
Occupation	Percentage of Anglos employed in white-collar occupations
Income	Log of median family income of Anglo population
Children	Log of the total attendance zone population aged 5–13 years
Native	Percentage of Anglos native and of native parentage
Owner	Percentage of housing units that are owner-occupied

parameters of the following equations for the three primary endogenous variables:

$$
\begin{aligned}
\text{Anglo Children} = {} & B_i \text{ (owner)} + B_2 \text{ (value)} + B_3 \text{ (black stability)} \\
& + B_4 \text{ (percentage of blacks)} + B_5 \text{ (education)} \\
& + B_6 \text{ (occupation)} + B_7 \text{ (income)} + B_8 \text{ (children)} \\
& + B_9 \text{ (native)} + B_{10} \text{ (inequality)} + B_{11} \text{ (diversity)} \\
& + e_1.
\end{aligned}
\tag{1}
$$

$$
\begin{aligned}
\text{Private} = {} & B_1 \text{ (owner)} + B_2 \text{ (value)} + B_3 \text{ (black stability)} \\
& + B_4 \text{ (percentage of blacks)} + B_5 \text{ (education)} \\
& + B_6 \text{ (occupation)} + B_7 \text{ (income)} + B_8 \text{ (children)} \\
& + B_9 \text{ (native)} + B_{10} \text{ (inequality)} + B_{11} \text{ (diversity)} \\
& + B_{12} \text{ (Anglo children)} + e_2.
\end{aligned}
\tag{2}
$$

$$
\begin{aligned}
\text{Public} = {} & B_1 \text{ (owner)} + B_2 \text{ (value} + B_3 \text{ (black stability)} \\
& + B_4 \text{ (percentage of blacks)} + B_5 \text{ (education)} \\
& + B_6 \text{ (occupation)} + B_7 \text{ (income)} + B_8 \text{ (children)} \\
& + B_9 \text{ (native)} + B_{10} \text{ (inequality)} + B_{11} \text{ (diversity)} \\
& + B_{12} \text{ (Anglo children)} + B_{13} \text{ (private)} + e_3.
\end{aligned}
\tag{3}
$$

Equations (1)–(3) were estimated with data for the Los Angeles school district. The number of schools and attendance zones in the other Cali-

TABLE 3.7.

Standardized Regression Coefficients Indicating the Effects of Variables on Measures of Anglo Migration and Schooling, Los Angeles, 1970

Variables [a]	Equation (1) dependent variable: Anglo children	Equation (2) dependent variable: private	Equation (3) dependent variable: public
Owner	.728 [b]	.275 [b]	.070
Value	.154 [b]	.002	.145 [b]
Black stability	−.062 [b]	.034	−.021 [b]
Percentage of blacks	−.304 [b]	.251 [b]	−.345 [b]
Occupation	−.239 [b]	.205 [b]	.158 [b]
Education	−.008	.082	−.026
Income	−.193 [b]	−.086	.235 [b]
Children	.047	.180 [b]	−.024
Native	.064	.149 [b]	−.024
Inequality	.097 [b]	−.056	.071 [b]
Diversity	.065 [b]	−.012	−.008
Anglo children	—	−.422 [b]	.212 [b]
Private	—	—	−.007
Intercept	28.49	−6.09	−173.96
Dependent variable			
Mean	12.76	18.92	51.68
Standard deviation	7.37	22.53	38.11
R^2 (adjusted for df)	.614	.239	.722
Number of observations	429	429	429

[a] Variables are defined in Table 3.6.

[b] Indicates that the regression coefficient is twice the size of its standard error.

fornia districts is too small to permit useful estimation of these equations. The standardized regression coefficients are presented in Table 3.7.

In Eq. (1) the dependent variable indicates the ratio of children to total zone residents for the Anglo population. This variable is intended to represent recent out-migration of Anglo families with school-age children. Eight of the 11 explanatory variables in the equation have large standardized regression coefficients (at least twice the standard error; see Table 3.7). All 8 have the expected sign. An attendance zone's retention of Anglo children is positively associated with its proportion of owner–occupied housing and of high-priced housing, income inequality, and the racial diversity of the zone's non–Anglo residents. A zone's out-migration of Anglo children is associated with the percentage of blacks among its residents, stability of the black population, and higher occupational and income levels among Anglo residents. A summary interpretation of these coefficients is that attendance zones with expensive single–family homes attract Anglo families with children, but the presence of blacks repels them, and Anglo families of higher socioeconomic status are the quickest to move. No cross-sectional areal regression can fully sustain such interpretation, but this is the kind of pattern we hypothesized, and the empirical results are not inconsistent with it.

The dependent variable for Eq. (2) indicates the degree to which Anglo elementary school children attend private schools. Only 6 of the 12 variables have large standardized regression coefficients (Table 3.7). Greater recourse by Anglos to private schools occurs in public school attendance zones that have higher proportions of black residents, that have a lot of owner-occupied housing and an Anglo population of high socioeconomic status, that have a large number of school-age children, and that have fewer "white ethnics" among the Anglo population. The sign on this last variable (Native) surprises us, for we included it as an indicator of Catholic population and proclivity to attend parochial schools. The migration variable (Anglo children) that was the dependent variable of Eq. (1) appears as a strong independent variable in Eq. (2). Greater out-migration of Anglo families is associated with greater utilization of private schools by those Anglo families with children still residing in the zone. Although not all of the variables included in Eq. (1) and (2) proved to be empirically important, the general conclusion from both equations is that many Anglos in predesegregation Los Angeles avoided sending their children to public school with blacks by moving or by using private schools.

The third equation for which results are presented in Table 3.7 is an elaborated version of the equation presented for several school districts in Table 3.5. The dependent variable is the percentage of Anglos among public school pupils, and we are still confronted with a degree of circularity because we use the percentage of blacks among attendance zone residents as one of the independent variables. There are 12 other independent variables in Eq. (3), and 6 of them have large standardized regression coefficients. All of these coefficients have the sign expected from our avoidance hypothesis. Our interest centers on the coefficients for the final two variables in the list, the migration and private school measures that were dependent variables for Eq. (1) and (2). The positive sign for Anglo children is expected; those attendance zones that have retained more Anglo children (lost fewer to out-migration) have public schools with greater proportions of Anglo pupils. In this final equation, the private school utilization measure does not have a sizable relationship to the percentage of Anglos in the public school. A speculative interpretation of why the private school response emerges clearly in Eq. (2) but not in Eq. (3) centers on the presence of the migration variable in Eq. (3). Many Anglo families may resort to private schools as a temporary response to the black presence in the local public school until they are financially able to move without sacrificing general residential amenities.

To assess further the effects of socioeconomic status on the white avoidance response, we estimated the three equations for subsets of Los Angeles zones, defining the subsets by average income levels. To simplify, we present only the standardized partial regression coefficient for the percentage of blacks from each equation (Table 3.8).

The coefficient for the effect of the percentage of blacks in an attendance zone on the measure of migration of Anglo children is stronger for the low income zones than for the middle and higher income zones. Our prior assumption had been that the effect should be strongest for the middle income zones, for these persons are better able to afford to move than are lower income persons but are less able to sustain the continued annual costs of private schooling than are higher income persons. One factor contributing to the size of the coefficient for low income zones is evident from the last two columns of Table 3.8. The percentage of blacks has a much higher mean and variance in low income zones than in middle and high income zones. This same factor may be more important than income interpretations in explaining the coefficients for the other two dependent variables. In each case, the coefficient for percentage of blacks is greatest in magnitude for the low income attendance zones.

Our analyses of selected California school districts were introduced as illustrative, and we have concluded the analysis section with an illustration of the complexities that the real world intrudes upon our schemes to array empirical proof of parsimonious hypotheses about white flight.

TABLE 3.8.

Standardized Partial Regression Coefficients Indicating the Effect of the Percentage of Blacks on Measures of Anglo Migration and Schooling, Los Angeles, 1970 [a]

Average Anglo income level	Dependent variables			Percentage of Blacks	
	Anglo children	Private	Public	Mean	Standard deviation
Less than $10,000	−.387 [b]	.389 [b]	−1.057 [b]	36.87	41.17
$10,000–12,499	−331 [b]	.171	−.601 [b]	8.66	23.55
$12,500 or more	−.119 [b]	.093	−.821 [b]	5.65	18.12

[a] These estimates were obtained from equations that included all of the variables listed in Table 3.8.

[b] Indicates that the regression coefficient is twice the size of its standard error.

DISCUSSION

We have been examining the factual character of the link between residential and school segregation. In this section of the paper, we shall review the results of the three analytic sections and discuss some of the implications for research and policy. All three sections utilized a special data set that linked 1970 census data for the population resident in school attendance zones with racial–ethnic enrollment data for the corresponding public elementary schools. This data set permits novel analyses, but it covers only a few school districts in California. Our analyses illustrate the potential of the approach taken without providing empirical results that can safely be generalized.

The first analytic effort was to secure an improved estimate of the association between residential racial–ethnic segregation and school racial–ethnic segregation. There is a strong but imperfect association. Using a more appropriate data base probably increased the correlations, with the major effect coming from the use of school attendance zones and little benefit apparent from the use of school-age population.

The second analytic effort focused on the degree to which the level of racial–ethnic residential segregation among school attendance zones— and, by implication, the level of racial–ethnic school segregation— reflects racial–ethnic differentials in socioeconomic measures. The empirical results for the California school districts demonstrate clearly that racial–ethnic socioeconomic inequalities do not account directly for residential (or school) segregation. A variance decomposition technique applied to data for Los Angeles seemed to be a promising means for uncovering the pattern of relationship between socioeconomic level and residential segregation. In this school district, racial–ethnic segregation was greater the higher the income.

The third analytic effort was to determine whether the presence of minority residents in school attendance zones invokes avoidance responses among Anglos and to identify the two modes of avoidance, out-migration and private schooling. Using data that predate the current school desegregation controversy, evidence of both modes of avoidance was found for Los Angeles.

The linkage between residential and school segregation is indeed factual, but an unavoidable lesson from our illustrative analyses is that the character of the link is quite complex. There is no reason for demographic researchers to pretend otherwise. Three varieties of complexity emerged from our work. First, we have to show that many variables affect the residence–school link, even in the absence of explicit school desegregation efforts. Many social scientists who have commented on the contemporary shrill public debate about "white flight" have called for a broader conceptual and empirical analysis of urban demographic change. On the basis of our work, we repeat that call.

A second broadening lesson from these analyses is a fortuitous result of the accident that the necessary data source was available for selected California school districts. We were compelled to recognize a triethnic situation, and even that is a simplification of the true multiethnic situation. The black–white terms of the public debate are too narrow to be adopted unquestioningly by researchers.

A third lesson for researchers is that the usual data sources and analytic techniques are inadequate. The continuing demographic trend in the United States toward racial separation into black cities and white suburbs has been the subject of much study, and ingenious analyses of traditional data (censuses and national surveys) continue to be informative. To examine the further questions that arise when that trend is to be related to the confusing implementation of school desegregation programs challenges the capacity of demographic research.

The implications of these analyses for the national debate over school desegregation policy are suggestive rather than prescriptive and are necessarily hedged by academic qualifications. We have not examined any evidence nor reached any conclusions on the role of racial and ethnic discrimination or other unconstitutional actions on school or residential patterns. Neither conceptually nor analytically were we able to disentangle the mutual causality underlying the association between housing segregation and school segregation. We are worried that our use of the language of ordinary correlation and regression analysis and the terms "independent" and "dependent" variables will be taken as confirmation of the simplistic view that sees residential segregation as prior and school segregation as merely a reflection. The actual historical development of school segregation and housing segregation in each school district must be the subject of inquiry before specific conclusions are drawn for that district and before specific policy recommendations can be judiciously drawn. In one recent court case over school desegregation, the judge heard social science testimony about the school and housing linkages. Writing after the recent Supreme Court decisions calling for renewed caution in attributing responsibility to school officials (U.S. Supreme Court, 1976a,b), District Judge Duncan wrote

> School authorities do not *control* the housing segregation in Columbus, but the Court also finds that the actions of the school authorities have had a significant impact upon the housing patterns. The interaction of housing and the schools operates to promote segregation in each. . . . I do not suggest that any reasonable action by the school authorities could have fully cured the evils of resi-

dential segregation. . . . I do believe . . . that the Columbus defendants could and should have acted to break the segregation snowball created by their interaction with housing. (*Penick* v. *Columbus Board of Education, 1977*)

The multiethnic reality in many school districts has confused those who wish to devise school desegregation policy on the basis of the language of the original *Brown* decision of the U.S. Supreme Court (1954). We believe it is insufficient to generalize that decision simply by grouping together Negroes, Hispanics, Chinese Americans, Native Americans, etc. into a single category. In the California districts we examined, there are varying patterns of segregation in housing and schooling among Anglos, blacks, and Hispanics. Good policy could not be made on the basis of a consideration of "whites" versus "minorities." Nor can good policy consider Anglos and blacks without attention to the other citizens.

Socioeconomic aspects of segregation are of importance in understanding the causes and consequences of residential and school segregation, separately and in terms of their linkages. In our analyses, socioeconomic measures were available only for the residential population and not for the school pupils. Yet, it is these unexamined socioeconomic and racial–ethnic linkages that pose one of the most difficult current issues in federal educational policy. What is the potential conflict in methods and aims between desegregation actions designed to disperse pupils, educational assistance programs aimed at schools with concentrations of disadvantaged children, and programs developed to meet the special needs of non-English-speaking children and others of minority ethnic identification?

The United States has lacked a coherent population distribution policy, but federal, state, and local governments have many programs that affect distribution. Area redevelopment and urban renewal are obvious examples of programs with an intended distributional effect. Highway programs are recognized as having had a major impact on population distribution even within urban areas, although that was not their explicit justification. Public housing programs, although nominally planned to serve existing local needs, have in reality exerted a strong racially segregative influence on metropolitan residential patterns.

To these examples (from a long list) a number of commentators have recently added school desegregation programs. Such programs have been cited as profoundly influencing residential mobility within metropolitan America. We have already indicated our concern about the demographic narrowness of the empirical basis for such conclusions; more extensive criticisms have been published elsewhere (Taeuber and Wilson, 1978; see also Orfield, 1977). The conclusion we wish to stress here is the need for demographers to include more of the social institutional structure within their analytic domain. Traditional demographic research on migration and population distribution has taken many personal characteristics into account. Economic demographers have brought employment and earnings into the research domain, along with many other economic factors. From the human ecology tradition have come measures of community location in a hierarchical and functionally specialized system. From geography, an eclectic discipline, have come concerns with climate and with perceptions of amenities and distances. Schools are only occasionally mentioned in the extensive migration research literature, and then only as an aspect of the perceived quality of neighborhood and its influence on in- or out-movement. The organization of schooling has not in itself been brought directly into the domain. Historically, the organization of schooling has been neither static nor uniform throughout the nation, and it is time that more attention be given to assessing changing patterns of schooling on population distribution. To cite an example outside the purview of our analyses, consider the school district consolidation movement and its relationship to the population concentration process.

Our analyses lead us to suggest that the racial–ethnic organization of schooling has had a continuing and profound influence on population distribution. This influence predates the current school desegregation and busing controversies. The racial–ethnic organization of schooling has interacted with many other forces to create and sustain a pervasive pattern of residential and institutional racial–ethnic segregation. The conceptual approach for which social demographers should strive in their efforts to study such complex social facts is captured by Myrdal's (1944, Appendix 3) "principle of cumulation." Our data resources and methodological tools may not be up to the task, but that is no excuse for conceptual slovenliness.

REFERENCES

Aldrich, Howard
        1975   "Ecological succession in racially changing neighborhoods: A review
                  of the Literature."
Brown v. Board of Education
        1954   349 U.S. 294 Urban Affairs Quarterly, 10:327–348.
Coleman, James S., Sara D. Kelly, and John A. Moore
        1975   Trends in School Segregation, 1968–73, Washington, D.C.: Urban
                  Institute Paper 722–03–01.

de Leeuw, Frank, A., B. Schnare, and R. J. Struyk
  1976   "Housing." Pp. 119–178 in William Gorham and Nathan Glazer
           (eds.), The Urban Predicament. Washington, D.C.: The Urban Insti-
           tute.
Dye, Thomas R.
  1968   "Urban school segregation." Urban Affairs Quarterly 4:141–165.
Erbe, Brigitte Mach
  1975   "Race and socioeconomic segregation." American Sociological Review
           40 (December):801–812.
Farley, Reynolds
  1975   "Residential segregation and its implications for school integration."
           Law and Contemporary Problems 39 (Winter):164–193.
  1976   "Can governmental policies integrate public schools?" Paper pre-
           sented at the annual meeting of the American Sociological Associa-
           tion, New York City, September 1.
  1977   "Residential segregation in urbanized areas of the United States in
           1970: An analysis of social class and racial differences." Demography
           14 (November):497–518.
Farley, Reynolds, and Alma F. Taeuber
  1974   "Racial segregation in public schools." American Journal of Sociology
           79 (January):888–905.
Grebler, Leo, Joan W. Moore, and Ralph C. Guzman
  1970   The Mexican–American People. New York: The Free Press.
Myrdal, Gunnar
  1944   An American Dilemma: The Negro Problem and Modern Democracy.
           New York: Harper and Row.
Orfield, Gary
  1975   "White flight research: Its importance, perplexities and policy im-
           plications." Pp. 44–68 in Gary Orfield (ed.), Symposium on School
           Desegregation and White Flight. Notre Dame, Indiana: Center for
           Civil Rights.
  1977   "If wishes were houses then busing could stop: Demographic trends
           and desegregation policy." In School Desegregation in Metropolitan
           Areas: Choices and Prospects. Washington, D.C.: National Institute
           of Education.
Penick v. Columbus Board of Education
  1977   429 F. Supp. 229 (S. D. Ohio).
Schnare, Ann B.
  1977   Residential Segregation by Race in U.S. Metropolitan Areas: An
           Analysis across Cities and over Time. Washington, D.C.: The Urban
           Institute, Contract Report No. 246–2.
Sørensen, Annemette, Karl E. Taeuber, and Leslie J. Hollingsworth, Jr.
  1975   "Indexes of racial residential segregation for 109 cities in the
           United States, 1940 to 1970." Sociological Focus 8, no. 2 (April):
           125–142.
Taeuber, Karl E.
  1968   "The effect of income redistribution on racial residential segrega-
           tion." Urban Affairs Quarterly 4 (September):5–14.
Taeuber, Karl E., and Alma F. Taeuber
  1965   Negroes in Cities. Chicago, Illinois: Aldine Publishing Company.

Taeuber, Karl E., and Franklin D. Wilson
    1978   "The impact of desegregation policies on population redistribution
              in metropolitan areas." In Michael Kraft and Mark Schneider (eds.),
              Population Policy Analysis: Issues in American Politics. Lexington,
              Massachusetts: Lexington Books (forthcoming).
Theil, Henri
    1972   *Statistical Decompositional Analysis*. New York: American Elsevier
              Publishing Company.
U.S. Supreme Court
    1954   *Brown* v. *Board of Education*, 347 U.S. 483.
    1971   *Swann* v. *Charlotte–Mecklenburg*, 402 U.S. 1.
    1976a   *Pasadena City Board of Education* v. *Spangler*, 427 U.S. 424, 96 S. Ct.
              2697.
    1976b   *Texas Education Agency* v. *U.S.*, ___ U.S. ___, 97 S. Ct. 517.
Van Valey, Thomas, L., Wade Clark Roof, and Jerome E. Wilcox
    1977   "Trends in residential segregation: 1960–1970." *American Journal of
              Sociology* 82, no. 4 (January):826–844.
Weinberg, Meyer
    1968   *Race and Place: A Legal History of the Neighborhood School*.
              Evanston, Illinois: Integrated Education Associates.
    1977   *A Chance to Learn. A History of Race and Education in the United
              States*. Cambridge, Massachusetts: Cambridge University Press.
Wolf, Eleanor P.
    1976   "Do school violations cause school segregation? Can metropolitan
              busing correct it?" Paper presented at the annual meeting of the
              American Sociological Association, New York City, September 1.

4

Black Movement to the Suburbs:
Potentials and Prospects
for Metropolitan-Wide Integration[1]

WILLIAM H. FREY

INTRODUCTION

The link between black and white movement patterns and the achievement of residential integration is a crucial one both in the formulation of policy goals and in the strategies taken to implement such goals. In issuing its warning that the nation is headed on a course toward "two separate societies"—a white society located primarily in the suburbs and a black society concentrated within large central cities—the 1968 Kerner Commission sought to emphasize its commitment to policies aimed at

[1] This chapter arose from a paper presented at the conference on "The Demography of Racial and Ethnic Groups" held at the Population Research Center, University of Texas at Austin, August 19–20, 1977. This research is supported by a grant from the Center for Population Research of the National Institute of Child Health and Human Development, No. 1 RO1 HD-1-666-01, on "Migration and Redistribution: SMSA Determinants."

bringing about racial integration in large metropolitan areas (National Advisory Commission on Civil Disorders, 1968). Based on a review of available evidence, it concluded that the continued concentration of poor blacks in the central city, coupled with the outward movement of jobs and housing in a metropolitan context made up of fragmented local government structures, would result in even further polarization between the races. The commission therefore recommended that programs be implemented that would integrate "substantial numbers" of blacks into the society outside the ghetto. It was felt that this increased residential integration would, in addition to improving race relations in the society, materially aid minorities in terms of lowering unemployment, allowing access to better housing, and improving the education of their children.

Despite its belief that residential integration should be the ultimate goal of its recommendations, the Kerner Commission recognized that more immediate, interim measures would be necessary. These measures or "enrichment programs" would be aimed at improving the economic positions of central city minorities and the quality of their existing living environments until more widespread integration could be accomplished. As the commission stated:

> Enrichment must be an important adjunct to any integration course. No matter how ambitious or energetic such a program may be, relatively few Negroes now living in central-city ghettos would be quickly integrated. In the meantime, significant improvement in their present environment is essential [National Advisory Commission on Civil Disorders, 1968:406].

The benefits to be gained by ghetto dispersal or "open suburbs" have subsequently been enumerated by urban analysts. Downs (1973), in emphasizing the opening of suburbs to the poor rather than just to the black poor, has quantified specific policy objectives in terms of numbers of suburban dwelling units to be constructed and the volume of city-to-suburb movement needed. Urban economists have noted that, aside from benefiting minorities in a material sense, the dispersal of central city ghettos would lead to a greater investment in and development of declining central cities (Kain and Persky, 1969).[2] Arguments in favor of

---

[2] Advocates of "opening up" the suburbs are not without their critics. Glazer (1974) feels that residential integration of middle class blacks is currently taking place and that greater emphasis should be given to materially aiding poor, unstable black families in the central core. Harrison (1974) argues that dispersal will not contribute significantly to blacks' ability to secure employment, but that present levels of minority unemployment might be more closely linked to discrimination. Still others see the concentration of blacks in the central city as a means of consolidating their political power. Among those espousing the latter views, ghetto enrichment programs represent more than "interim" measures.

the metropolitan-wide residential desegregation of the races have been applied to school desegregation strategies as well (Farley, 1975). However, proposed area-wide school desegregation mechanisms, such as cross-district busing programs, must, in themselves, be thought of as interim policy measures aimed at achieving a greater level of interracial contact until more widespread residential integration can be brought about.

The degree to which metropolitan-wide residential integration can be counted on to achieve the goals of greater interracial unity in the society, material gains for minorities, and economically more viable central cities depends in large measure on the *pace* with which such integration can be accomplished. This was implicit in the Kerner Commission's dual recommendations favoring dispersal *and* enrichment. One obvious barrier to such integration must be linked to the greater incidence of poverty and the relatively lower economic status of blacks—a situation that, to some extent, prevents their moving to more desirable housing and neighborhoods outside the ghetto. Nevertheless, it has been demonstrated that most of the residential segregation existing between blacks and whites across urban neighborhoods cannot be attributed to income disparities between the races (Taeuber and Taeuber, 1965). The bulk of this segregation, it has been argued, must be associated with past and present racially discriminatory practices on the part of both public and private institutions. These have limited the residential choices of blacks and have served to channel them away from moving into all-white neighborhoods (Foley, 1973; Taeuber, 1975).

Given this situation, it is tempting to suggest that massive and sustained efforts aimed toward the elimination of racially discriminatory housing practices could lead to a corresponding elimination of the racial segregation that exists now between cities and suburbs and across neighborhoods within metropolitan areas. Indeed, it has been argued that, as a result of recent gains, blacks now possess the economic potential that would permit a high degree of residential integration to take place at the metropolitan level (Hermalin and Farley, 1973). Although persuasive, such arguments often fail to take into account the population dynamics of residential change.

In the present study, we utilize migration and redistribution data from 24 large metropolitan areas in order to evaluate empirically just how effective the lowering of institutional barriers to equal housing choice might be in achieving metropolitan-wide integration in the short term. We focus specifically on the redistributional impact such efforts would exert on increasing black representation in the suburbs, since increases in city–suburb racial integration are a prerequisite to metropolitan-wide integration at the neighborhood level. This analysis should shed light on the pace with which widespread residential desegregation can be brought about and the degree to which more interim measures need to be relied upon in order to achieve stated policy objectives.

Black Suburbanization: The Potential for Change

The recent history of black suburbanization in the United States does not portend a great deal of optimism for immediate metropolitan-wide racial integration. An examination of post-World War II change patterns with regard to the percentage of the total suburban population that is black, the economic status of suburban blacks, and the level of neighborhood integration that exists in the suburbs indicates that black suburbanization has been occurring at a painfully slow pace.[3] Despite these patterns, a study by Hermalin and Farley (1973) reports that the conditions are now ripe for an upturn in black suburbanization. Using aggregate population figures from the 1970 census and a time series of attitudinal survey data, the authors have sought to demonstrate that both the economic potential on the part of blacks and the attitudinal receptivity on the part of whites and blacks now exist for widespread residential integration to take place between metropolitan cities and suburbs and at the neighborhood level.

In order to illustrate black economic potential for residential integration, "expected" levels of black suburban representation were computed for each of 29 urbanized areas, based on the assumption that black families at each income level achieve the same level of surburban representation as white families at each income level. (Similar computations were also made standardizing on housing value rather than income.) The findings convincingly demonstrate that, under such conditions, black suburban representation would increase substantially in comparison to actual levels. In the 29 areas studied, the actual black suburbanization rate in 1970 was 17%, whereas the expected rate—when standardized by income—was computed to be 55%.

The authors' claim of increased receptivity to residential integration on the part of both races is based on a review of nationwide attitudinal surveys, going back to 1942, of respondents' feelings toward both resi-

[3] In most Northern metropolitan areas, the percentage of the suburban population that is black hovers around 5%, a figure that has changed only slightly over a period of four decades (Schnore et al., 1976). Recent patterns of black suburbanization in SMSAs are reviewed in Clay (1975), Connally (1973), Farley (1970, 1976), Grier (1973), and Rose (1976).

dential and school desegregation. According to this review, four out of five whites in 1972 would be receptive to having a black family with the same education and income move into their block—as opposed to 68% in 1965, 51% in 1956, and 35% in 1942. In addition, evidence is cited showing that most blacks in 1970 would prefer to live in racially mixed neighborhoods. Summarizing their results, Hermalin and Farley write:

> Economic factors account for little of the concentration of Blacks within central cities, their absence from suburbia or the residential segregation of Blacks from whites in either cities or suburbs.
>
> The attitudinal receptivity and economic potential exist for extensive residential integration . . . [1973:595].

This finding represents good news for those who see metropolitan-wide residential integration as a major route to achieving greater interracial unity and a better quality of life for blacks. It suggests that, if sustained progress can be made in the elimination of those formal and informal mechanisms that have, in the past, constrained the residential choices of blacks, then substantial gains in residential integration will be imminent.

Migration, Redistribution, and the Prospects for Short-Run Change

There is no doubt that significant gains in black suburbanization and metropolitan-wide integration could be brought about by "opening up" to blacks those homes and neighborhoods to which they have previously been denied residence. However, in order to choose among alternative long-run strategies, the question must be raised as to how soon an immediate reduction in discriminatory housing practices can effect a greater degree of residential integration in the aggregate? The expected or potential measures of black suburban representation computed by Hermalin and Farley (1973) are based on the assumption that the entire resident black population in the metropolitan area could be redistributed in a manner consistent with the existing resident white population. Although these measures serve to illustrate the high degree of present-day segregation that can be attributed to racial discrimination, which persisted through each metropolitan area's development history, the literature on migration and redistribution suggests that it would be unrealistic to anticipate any short-run convergence to the expected levels—even if the suburbs could immediately be opened to blacks.

It is well documented, for example, that only about one-fifth of

Americans change residence in a single year, and less than one-half change residence over a 5-year period. These figures remain fairly constant over time (Long and Boertlein, 1976), a phenomenon that might best be explained by the close correspondence between mobility incidence and major life-cycle stages. Moreover, residential mobility studies in central cities of large metropolitan areas show that about one-half of all moves take place within the same city neighborhood (Speare et al., 1975: Ch. 4; Zimmer, 1973). In short, the massive redistribution of blacks and whites that would need to be associated with short-run widespread integration at the metropolitan level is not consistent with existing data on population movement.

The present study addresses this issue empirically by evaluating the aggregate demographic impact that black and white movement patterns are likely to exert on suburban racial change under different sets of circumstances. It makes use of actual migration data reported in the 1960 and 1970 U.S. censuses for individual metropolitan areas. In the first part of the analysis, I contrast the city–suburb destination choices of both white and black movers in the late 1960s with those in the late 1950s. This sheds light on the progress that has been made in achieving a more balanced redistribution of the races in metropolitan areas over the 10-year period. It is followed up by an analysis of the aggregate impact these destination choice patterns exerted on the racial compositions of suburbs over the course of a migration interval. In the final portion of the study I simulate a redistribution process in each metropolitan area for which all racial differences in movers' city–suburb destination choices are eliminated. This analysis provides insights into how soon an "open" allocation of movers among metropolitan destinations will contribute to a racially integrated city–suburb residential pattern.

METROPOLITAN AREAS TO BE STUDIED

This study focuses on migration and redistribution patterns of individual metropolitan areas. In it, we utilize the only available census source that tabulates migration and residential mobility streams leading into metropolitan cities and suburbs by race and socioeconomic status— the *Mobility for Metropolitan Areas* subject reports in the 1960 and 1970 U.S. Censuses (U.S. Bureau of the Census, 1963, 1973). Because of our reliance on these reports, we are forced to use different measures and variables than appear in the Hermalin and Farley (1973) study, such that: (a) the *suburbs* focused upon here will include the non-central city portion of the Standard Metropolitan Statistical Area (SMSA) rather than the non-central city portion of the urbanized area (or the "urban fringe"); (b) the aggregate migration and redistribution patterns will pertain to individuals rather than to households; and (c) our measure of status will be number of years of schooling rather than income level or value of housing. (Although the *Mobility for Metropolitan Areas* subject reports (1973) provide income tabulations, these tabulations are not disaggregated by race in 1960.)

The 24 SMSAs selected for this study include metropolitan areas with 1970 populations of 500,000 or more in which blacks made up more than 10% of the central city population. Of the 47 SMSAs that were eligible under this criterion, 23 were eliminated because (a) central cities were not defined comparably in 1960 and 1970 (for example, the central city portion of the Seattle–Everett SMSA in 1970 included only Seattle in 1960); (b) a substantial amount of central city annexation took place between 1960 and 1970; (c) the SMSA contained a large military population; or (d) there were a substantial number of individuals whose migration status could not be ascertained (although such individuals were allocated for those SMSAs that were selected). Of the 24 SMSAs in the study, 12 are located in the North (northeast or north central census regions), 10 are in the South, and 2 are in the West.

In Table 4.1 I present 1960–1970 measures of metropolitan, central city, and suburban racial change that were obtained from various census sources.[4] For 20 of the 24 SMSAs, the black share of the metropolitan population increased during the 1960s. In all of these except one (Pittsburgh), both the black and white population grew during the period, but the former population grew at a greater rate. The four SMSAs that exhibited declines in black population percentage were in the South, and only one of these (Birmingham) registered an absolute loss of blacks. For most metropolitan areas, levels of increase in the black share of the population were small. In contrast to metropolitan-wide patterns, the central cities of *all* SMSAs registered 1960–1970 increases in their black population percentages. These increases, in every case, were greater than

---

[4] Throughout this chapter I continually refer to "blacks" and "whites" for convenience, whereas, in most instances, our data are actually separated according to white–non-white and non-black–black distinctions. In Table 4.1, the figures actually do pertain to blacks and whites; however, in the remainder of the tables and figures, data taken from the 1960 migration report (U.S. Bureau of the Census, 1963) pertain to whites and non-whites, whereas data taken from the 1970 report (U.S. Bureau of the Census, 1973) pertain to non-blacks and blacks.

TABLE 4.1
Measures of Racial Composition and 1960–1970 Population Change for 24 Selected SMSAs

SMSAs [a]	SMSA				City		Suburb	
	Percentage of blacks 1970	Change in percentage of blacks 1960–1970 [b]	White population: Percentage of change 1960–1970 [c]	Black population: Percentage of change 1960–1970 [d]	Percentage of blacks 1970	Change in percentage of blacks 1960–1970 [b]	Percentage of blacks 1970	Change in percentage of blacks 1960–1970 [b]
North								
Detroit	18.0	3.1	7.0	35.5	43.7	14.8	3.6	−.1
Gary–Hammond–East Chicago	17.7	2.5	6.8	28.7	33.4	8.9	.6	−.2
Chicago	17.6	3.3	7.0	38.3	32.7	9.8	3.6	.7
Philadelphia	17.5	2.0	7.7	25.8	33.6	7.2	6.6	.5
Cleveland	16.1	2.5	4.5	28.5	38.3	9.7	3.4	2.6
St. Louis	16.0	2.0	9.4	28.2	40.9	12.3	7.2	1.2
Columbus	11.6	.7	20.0	29.9	18.5	2.1	1.8	.1
Cincinnati	11.0	.7	8.1	16.8	27.6	6.0	2.9	.1
Youngstown–Warren	9.4	.2	4.7	8.4	21.7	4.7	2.0	−.9
Buffalo	8.1	1.8	1.1	31.2	20.4	7.1	1.6	0
Pittsburgh	7.1	.4	−.8	5.2	20.2	3.5	3.5	.1
Syracuse	3.7	1.5	10.7	90.4	10.8	5.6	.5	.2

South								
New Orleans	31.0	.4	14.4	16.5	45.0	7.8	12.5	−3.4
Birmingham	29.5	−2.6	6.2	− 5.8	42.0	2.4	20.9	−4.4
Baltimore	23.7	2.3	11.0	27.0	46.4	11.7	6.0	−1.0
Atlanta	22.3	− .5	37.1	34.2	51.3	13.0	6.2	−2.3
Houston	19.3	− .2	39.4	38.5	25.7	2.8	8.9	−4.0
Dallas	15.9	1.1	36.2	50.0	24.9	5.9	5.2	−3.1
Louisville	12.3	.8	12.8	21.7	23.8	5.9	3.3	− .6
Fort Worth	10.9	.3	31.8	37.2	19.9	4.1	1.3	− .7
Tampa–St. Petersburg	10.8	− .7	31.7	23.5	17.5	2.1	4.4	−1.4
Oklahoma City	8.5	.5	23.2	32.6	13.7	2.1	1.6	− .3
West								
Los Angeles–Long Beach	10.8	3.2	10.1	65.3	16.5	4.3	6.2	2.6
San Francisco–Oakland	10.6	2.1	11.0	46.1	20.5	6.2	5.4	1.6

Source: U.S. Bureau of the Census, 1971. Census of Population and Housing: 1970 PHC(2)-1 United States.

[a] All measures pertain to city, suburb, and SMSA boundaries as defined in 1970.

[b] [(1970 Percentage of blacks − 1960 Percentage of blacks)/1960 Percentage of black] × 100.

[c] [(1970 white population − 1960 white population)/1960 white population] × 100.

[d] [(1970 black population − 1960 black population)/1960 black population] × 100.

corresponding metropolitan increases—a statistic that reflects differential intrametropolitan patterns of white and black population change.

Of particular interest for this study are the changes in suburban racial composition that occurred among the 24 SMSAs during the 1960s. 1970 levels of the measure "Percentage of suburban blacks" are extremely low, particularly outside the South. Moreover, only 10 of the 24 SMSAs have registered increases in that percentage over the 1960–1970 period—increases that were substantially below corresponding increases in the black share of the city population. These data reflect the fact that, although both black and white population growth is occurring in the suburbs, the white growth in many suburbs is still overtaking that of blacks. In the South, this racial disparity in growth patterns is likely to continue and will perhaps widen.

The increase in the percentage of suburban blacks shown for Cleveland is due to the extremely large growth rate of the black suburban population (452.8% as opposed to 23.4% for whites during the period). A similar explanation accounts for the Los Angeles–Long Beach increase in percentage of suburb black. The Houston suburbs display a contrasting pattern. Here, the 1960 black suburban percentage of 12.9 was reduced by 4% during the decade. This change is due almost entirely to the large growth in Houston's white population during the period (63.3% as opposed to 7.7% for blacks) and is characteristic of other Southern suburbs. It should be kept in mind that the data in Table 4.1 represent aggregate changes in racial composition that result from both net migration and natural increase. Although racial differences in migration patterns account for the bulk of the changes assessed (Long, 1975) and are focused upon later, some portion of the aggregate changes must be attributed to the different fertility and mortality patterns that exist between the races (Taeuber, 1972; U.S. Bureau of the Census, 1971).

RACIAL DIFFERENCES IN THE CITY–SUBURB DESTINATION OF MOVERS

In this section, I examine racial differences in the city–suburb destination choices or *destination propensity rates* of residential movers and in-migrants to metropolitan areas. The focus on movers' destination propensities rather than on mobility incidence rates or stream mobility rates is intentional. It is felt that changes in racially discriminatory housing practices are most likely to affect redistribution through this aspect of the movement process, and I provide, first of all, some elaboration of this point.

The Destination Propensity Rate as an Indicator of Racially Constrained Movement [5]

Changes in a suburb's racial composition can be brought about through four types of movement streams, the intrametropolitan city-to-suburb stream, the intrametropolitan suburb-to-city stream, the in-migration stream to the suburbs from outside the metropolitan area, and the out-migration stream of suburban residents to points outside the metropolitan area. The magnitudes of the first three of these streams are dependent on the city–suburb destination propensity rates associated with various black and white mover populations.

The first two of these streams can be viewed as residential mobility streams which, taken together, represent a subset of all residential moves that occur within the metropolitan area during an interval. Previous research on residential movement has shown that different factors are related to a *resident's* decision to make a move than are associated with a *mover's* choice of destination (Butler et al., 1969; Speare et al., 1975). The resident's decision to move is generally associated with a battery of demographic and housing characteristics that are closely linked to the life cycle (Rossi, 1955; Simmons, 1968; Speare, 1970), an association that helps to explain the consistency of mobility incidence for subpopulations both over time and across geographic areas. In contrast, the destination choices of residential movers have been shown to fluctuate markedly from one metropolitan area to another, and across population subgroups (Frey, 1977; 1978). This area- and subgroup-specific variation in destination choice patterns can be attributed to the interaction of subgroup-defined mover preferences for a destination, the availability of preferred destinations in the area, and constraints (financial or other) that prevent the mover from relocating in an existing preferred destination. The constraints imposed by racially discriminatory housing practices will differentially affect the city–suburb destination propensities of black and white residential movers and, in this manner, exert an impact on the racial compositions of the city-to-suburb and suburb-to-city residential movement streams.

For analytical purposes, it becomes a fairly straightforward matter to relate movers' destination propensity rates to stream mobility rates. The

[5] This discussion draws from a fuller treatment of the relationship between mobility rate components and city–suburb redistribution that appears in Frey (1978).

city-to-suburb stream mobility rate can be defined as the product of two components:

$$
\frac{\text{city movers to a suburb destination}}{\text{city residents at the beginning of an interval}} = \frac{\text{city movers to any destination in the SMSA}}{\text{city residents at the beginning of an interval}} \times \frac{\text{city movers to a suburb destination}}{\text{city movers to any destination in the SMSA}} \quad (1)
$$

The first component (on the right side of the equation) is a conventional mobility incidence rate that indicates the proportion of city residents that move anywhere within the metropolitan area during a migration interval. The second component indicates the proportion of city-origin residential movers that relocate in the suburbs during the interval and represents the suburban destination propensity rate of city residential movers. In like manner, the suburb-to-city stream mobility rate can be defined as:

$$
\frac{\text{suburb movers to a city destination}}{\text{suburb residents at the beginning of an interval}} = \frac{\text{suburb movers to any destination in the SMSA}}{\text{suburb residents at the beginning of an interval}} \times \frac{\text{suburb movers to a city destination}}{\text{suburb movers to any destination in the SMSA}} \quad (2)
$$

In this equation, the last factor represents the city destination propensity rate for suburb residential movers.

To illustrate the influence of destination propensity rates on the residential mobility streams of blacks and whites, I have graphed in Figure 4.1 1965–1970 city-to-suburb stream rates and 1965–1970 suburb-to-city stream rates by education level for blacks and whites aged 25 and over in the Cleveland SMSA. In addition, I present corresponding graphs for the mobility incidence and destination propensity components of each stream rate.[6] It is apparent from this figure that most of the racial differences in

[6] These rates were computed from data for 1970 from the *Mobility for Metropolitan Areas* subject report (1973) based on individuals' actual city and suburb residences in 1970 and their reported places of residence in 1965. The denominator for the city-to-suburb (or suburb-to-city) rate includes all individuals who reported a 1965 city (or suburb) residence in the same SMSA. The rates, therefore, do not take into account individuals who have died or out-migrated from the SMSA since 1965. The individuals in a residual category, who moved but did not report a 1965 place of residence or who were abroad in 1965 (the former making up most of the category), were allocated to 1965 residences according to the distributions for individuals in each race–education subgroup who moved and did report a 1965 place of residence.

the stream rates can be attributed to racial differences in the destination propensity components of these rates.

The third movement stream discussed earlier, the in-migration stream to the suburbs from outside the metropolitan area, can also be viewed as a product of two components. Previous studies have shown that long-distance migration between metropolitan or labor market areas is motivated largely by economic or employment considerations (Lansing and Mueller, 1967) and that metropolitan-wide labor market characteristics tend to be strong determinants of the volume of in-migration that an SMSA experiences (Greenwood and Sweetland, 1972). Migration is therefore directed to the labor market or metropolitan area per se. The choice of an intrametropolitan city or suburb location can be viewed as a secondary consideration for the SMSA in-migrant. As with intrametro-politan movement, it is the latter choice that is affected by racially discriminatory housing practices and the one through which the barriers to black suburban in-migration are most apt to operate. In order to isolate this latter effect, the in-migration stream to the suburbs can be decomposed as:

$$
\begin{array}{c}
\text{in-migrants to the} \\
\text{suburbs from outside} \\
\text{the SMSA}
\end{array}
=
\begin{array}{c}
\text{in-migrants from} \\
\text{outside the SMSA}
\end{array}
\times
\frac{
\begin{array}{c}
\text{in-migrants from} \\
\text{outside the SMSA,} \\
\text{locating in a suburb} \\
\text{destination}
\end{array}
}{
\begin{array}{c}
\text{in-migrants from} \\
\text{outside the SMSA}
\end{array}
}
\qquad (3)
$$

so that the last factor in the equation represents the suburb destination propensity rate for SMSA in-migrants. Racial disparities for this rate should be similar to those of the suburb destination propensity rate for city residential movers.

The fourth movement stream discussed earlier, like the third, primarily represents migration between labor markets. Since racially discriminatory practices relate to the housing market choices within the metropolitan area, they are not likely to affect racial differences in migration from the suburbs to other labor market areas. I therefore do not evaluate the impact of this stream on suburban racial composition.

To summarize, I have isolated the three mover populations whose intrametropolitan destination choices will affect the size and composition of suburban population change—city residential movers, suburb residential movers, and in-migrants to the metropolitan area. In the analyses that follow, I shall examine the city–suburb destination propensity rates for blacks and whites in each of the mover populations. I shall examine changes in these rates between the late 1950s and late 1960s and look

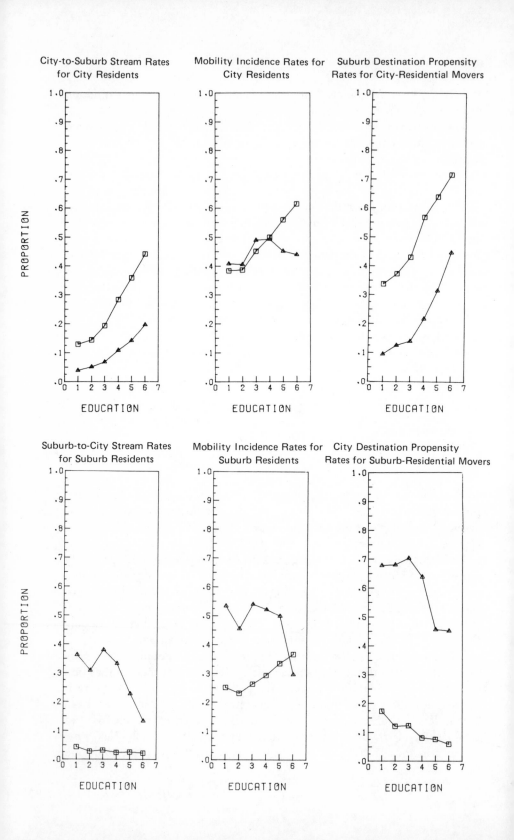

also at the experiences of individual metropolitan areas. These analyses should provide insights into how much progress has been made in eliminating the constraints to black suburban movement, as well as insights into how much more needs to be accomplished.

Mean Patterns: 1955–1960 and 1965–1970

The data in Table 4.2 allow us to examine overall disparities in the city–suburb destination choices of whites and blacks and to identify changes in these disparities over the course of a decade. Presented here are mean destination propensity rates for city residential movers, suburb residential movers, and SMSA in-migrants by race and education for two migration intervals, 1955–1960 and 1965–1970. The mean values were computed over the 24 SMSAs in the study, and the rates pertain to individuals aged 25 and over at the latter date in each migration interval.

Perhaps the most striking findings in the table are the overall disparities that exist between whites and blacks at each level of education and for each period. In every comparison, white suburban propensity rates are substantially higher than black suburban propensity rates for both city residential movers and SMSA in-migrants. Similarly, black city propensity rates are higher than white city propensity rates among suburb residential movers. Given these overall differences at both migration intervals, it is apparent that constraints on black destination selectivity continue to exist at all socioeconomic levels.

Although the gross racial disparities in all comparisons tend to dominate, some encouraging changes can be detected between the late 1950s and late 1960s. For example, 1955–1960 racial differences in the suburb propensities of city movers increase with levels of education. The pattern is caused by progressive increases in the white suburb propensities with additional years of school, coupled with only slight increments in the respective black propensities. By 1965–1970, this gap tends to narrow for the higher educational levels. White city movers with 4 or more years of college in the 1965–1970 period are about 3.4 times as likely to relocate in the suburbs than are their black counterparts. In the earlier

Figure 4.1 1965–1970 Stream Rates, Mobility Incidence Rates for Residents, and Destination Propensity Rates for Movers by Race and Education Level, Cleveland SMSA.

Source: U.S. Bureau of the Census. 1973 Census of Population: 1970 PC(2)-2C.

Education Levels: 1 = Grade School, 0–7 years; 2 = Grade School, 8 years; 3 = High School, 1–3 years; 4 = High School, 4 years; 5 = College, 1–3 years; 6 = College, 4+ years.

Key: ▲—▲—▲ Blacks, 1965–1970; ◻—◻—◻ Whites, 1965–1970.

TABLE 4.2

Mean 1955–1960 and 1965–1970 Destination Propensity Rates by Race and Education for City-Residential Movers, Suburb-Residential Movers, and SMSA In-migrants Aged 25 and Over, Selected SMSAs

	1955–1960 rates						1965–1970 rates					
	Grade school		High school		College		Grade school		High school		College	
Race [a]	0–7	8	1–3	4	1–3	4+	0–7	8	1–3	4	1–3	4+
Suburb destination propensity rates for city-residential movers												
White	.212	.250	.304	.352	.358	.368	.268	.320	.364	.440	.450	.450
Black	.043	.045	.045	.047	.057	.069	.053	.050	.060	.065	.106	.133
City destination propensity rates for suburb-residential movers												
White	.142	.138	.139	.132	.151	.154	.152	.140	.133	.120	.144	.155
Black	.261	.284	.313	.312	.289	.340	.450	.429	.457	.482	.508	.466
Suburb destination propensity rates for SMSA in-migrants												
White	.529	.549	.575	.615	.598	.586	.601	.653	.677	.720	.703	.663
Black	.223	.206	.201	.216	.194	.204	.175	.193	.183	.230	.236	.239

Sources: U.S. Bureau of the Census, 1963. Census of Population: 1960 PC(2)–2C.
U.S. Bureau of the Census, 1973. Census of Population: 1970 (PC(2)–2C.
[a] 1955–1960 rates pertain to whites and non-whites; 1965–1970 rates pertain to non-blacks and blacks.

period, the white suburb propensity rate was 5.3 times the black rate. Both white and black city-to-suburb propensity rates increased over the 10 years; however, the mean data suggest a substantial rise in this rate for highly educated black movers.[7]

Changes in the patterns of racial disparities by education are less clear-cut for the other destination propensity rates, although two general observations might be made. First, black suburban movers have shown a considerable increase in their propensity to relocate in the central city—an increase that is not observed for whites. We might speculate from these data that newly suburbanizing blacks in the 1960s are experiencing a "return movement" to the central city. A second observation pertains to changes in the suburb destination propensity rates of SMSA in-migrants. Here, the overall racial disparity has tended to increase over the course of the decade, in large part due to the greater tendency of white in-migrants to locate in the suburbs. Although highly educated black in-migrants have also increased their propensity for a suburban location, the cross-decade increase among whites is much more substantial and exists at each education level.

Patterns for Individual Metropolitan Areas

The mean destination propensity rates in Table 4.2 tend to mask differences that exist among individual metropolitan areas in the study. In order to underscore these differences, I examine here the destination propensity rates for five individual SMSAs. These include: Detroit, a northern SMSA whose black population is highly concentrated in the central city; Cleveland, the SMSA in our study that experienced the greatest recent increase in its suburban black population; Baltimore, a "border" SMSA; Houston, a prototypic Southern SMSA that experienced large increases in its white population; and Los Angeles–Long Beach, a Western SMSA that, like Cleveland, displayed recent increases in its suburban black population. Graphs of the black and white destination propensity rates for each of these SMSAs in both the late 1950s and late 1960s appear in Figure 4.2.

[7] Although education level represents a crude indicator for status and, in particular, for income, its use in this study is dictated by its availability in both the 1960 and 1970 census mobility reports. In performing income-specific mobility comparisons for the 1965–1970 period in the Philadelphia SMSA, which are analogous to our education-specific comparisons in Table 4.2, Cottingham (1975) obtains similar results. She notes, however, that even income represents a crude control measure due to the greater wealth accumulations of whites at each income level.

A Suburb destination propensity rates for city-residential movers

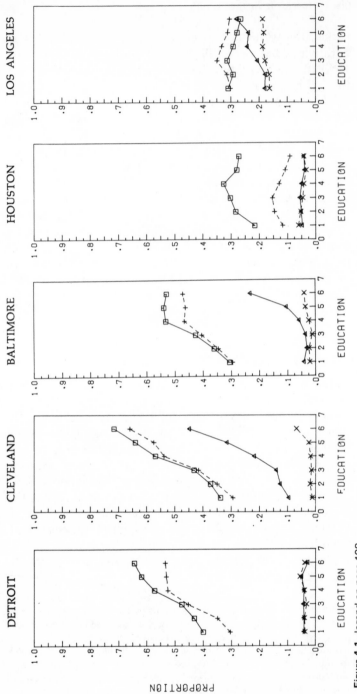

Figure 4.1—legend on page 198.

B City destination propensity rates for suburb-residential movers

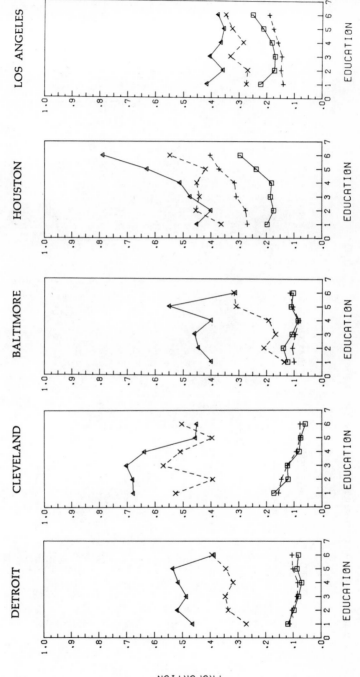

C Suburb destination propensity rates for SMSA in-migrants

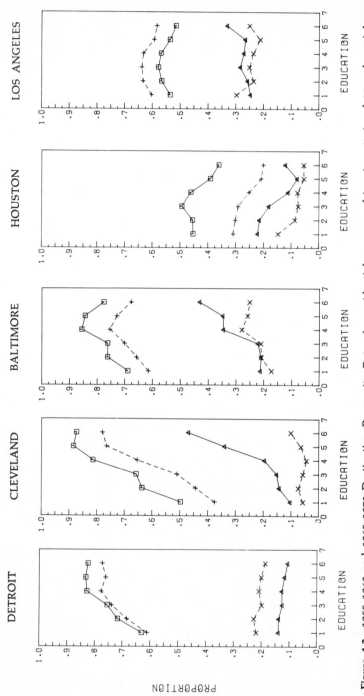

Figure 4.2 1955–1960 and 1965–1970 Destination Propensity Rates for residential movers and in-migrants (aged 25 and over) by race and education level, Detroit, Cleveland, Baltimore, Houston, and Los Angeles-Long Beach SMSAs. Educational levels: 1 = Grade school, 0–7 years; 2 = Grade school, 8 years; 3 = High school, 1–3 years; 4 = High school, 4 years; 5 = College, 1–3 years; 6 = College, 4+ years.

The Detroit pattern of destination propensity rates exemplifies a situation wherein the current movement of blacks and whites serves to reinforce even further an existing, highly segregated city–suburb residential distribution. An examination of suburban propensity rates for Detroit city movers (in Row A of Figure 4.2) reveals increases over time for both the overall level and the status-relatedness of the black–white gap in suburbanward relocation. These increases are due to decade-wide rises in white suburban propensity at all status levels, contrasted with the low, almost constant suburban propensity of blacks. Moreover, white city movers in both periods experienced greater levels of suburban relocation with increased levels of education. This association between status and suburban relocation is not even hinted at for black city movers during either migration interval.

The widening of the racial disparity in Detroit is even more evident when the suburban propensity rates for SMSA in-migrants are examined (in Row C of Figure 4.2). Here, the suburban propensity of whites increases at all status levels between the late 1950s and the late 1960s, whereas the corresponding rates for blacks decrease over the same interval. Furthermore, higher status black in-migrants are less likely to locate in the suburbs than are lower status blacks. Turning to the city propensities of suburban residential movers (in Row B of Figure 4.2), we find that blacks are experiencing a greater rate of central city return in the latter period, whereas white suburban propensities remain low and unchanged. Once again, the racial disparities become wider over the 10-year period.

The Cleveland pattern stands in contrast to Detroit. Here, the suburban propensity rates for city residential movers in the earlier period bear a strong resemblance to the Detroit pattern. The suburban propensity rates of whites tend to be "elastic" to level of education, whereas black suburban propensities are much lower in magnitude and are relatively constant across education level. The late 1960s, however, brought about substantial increases in the suburban propensities for black movers. Although white suburban propensity rates also increased slightly over the period, the large black increases served to close the racial disparity in suburban relocation overall and to narrow the gap substantially at higher status levels. An analogous cross-decade change in the racial gap developed for Cleveland SMSA in-migrants as well, again drastically altering the Detroit-like racial gap that existed in the late 1950s.

It is, of course, true that large racial disparities in destination propensity rates exist among all Cleveland mover populations, even in the most recent period. Yet the decade-wide changes in black destination

propensities that have accompanied Cleveland's recent black suburbanization are encouraging. Increases in black suburban relocation are apparent for all status levels among black central city movers and among
black SMSA in-migrants. And, like suburbanizing whites, suburbanizing blacks are highly selective in status.

To some extent, changes in the suburban propensity rates of Baltimore's black movers resemble the changes in Cleveland. In both SMSAs,
black city movers and black in-migrants with college educations showed
significant increases over the 10-year period in their propensities to
locate in the suburbs. However, unlike Cleveland, overall increases in
suburban relocation are slight among Baltimore's blacks. The suburban
propensity rates of Baltimore's white movers and in-migrants display a
reversed U-shaped relationship with status. White movers who are high
school graduates, rather than the grade-school or college educated, are
most apt to relocate in the suburbs during both migration intervals. This
is consistent with previous research on Southern city–suburb redistribution (Biggar and Biasiolli, 1977; Kirschenbaum, 1972; Schnore, 1972).

In Houston, as in other Southern SMSAs, racial differences in destination propensities have been affected largely by changes in white propensity rates. It can be seen in Figure 4.2 that suburban propensity rates
of white movers and white SMSA in-migrants have increased dramatically over the decade. Similarly, suburban white movers were more
reluctant to choose a city destination in the late 1960s than in the late
1950s. All these changes contributed to a widening of the gap between
the races. (Some caution should be exercised in interpreting these changes
too literally, since 12% of the 1970 Houston metropolitan population
was not included under the 1960 definition.) In comparison, changes in
the black city or suburb destination propensity rates over the course of
the decade were generally smaller or nonexistent.

Of the five SMSAs examined, the racial destination propensity patterns are most unique in Los Angeles–Long Beach. During the recent
period, race differences in suburban propensity of city movers were ex-
ceedingly small. Indeed, black city movers with college educations are
actually more likely to relocate in the suburbs than are whites. Racial
differences are more consistent with other metropolitan areas for the
suburban propensities of SMSA in-migrants and the city propensities of
suburban movers. Because Los Angeles–Long Beach SMSA houses a
large non-black, non-white population (that makes up 26% of its 1970
nonwhite population), comparisons between the 1955–1960 white–
nonwhite propensity rates and the 1965–1970 black–nonblack propensity
rates are not direct. However, the data in Figure 4.2 strongly suggest
that some degree of racial convergence has occurred over the decade.

It is difficult to account for the individual metropolitan variations in black and white destination propensity rate patterns presented here, although explanations have been offered. It has been suggested that the lack of black suburbanization in Detroit can be attributed to the spatial location of the black community, which lies well within the boundaries of the city, and to the widespread availability of intracity housing for blacks—a consequence of sustained white out-migration (Rose, 1976; Schnore et al., 1976). The "high" levels of black suburbanization that are observed in Cleveland and Los Angeles–Long Beach have been interpreted by some to represent a spillover of central city ghettos into contiguous suburban communities (Connally, 1973; Rabinovitz, 1975; Rose, 1976). To attribute the term "black suburbanization" to changes in Houston's suburban racial composition may be highly inaccurate. The long-standing existence of black enclaves in both the cities and the suburbs of Southern metropolitan areas is inconsistent with the Northern model of outward expansion to the suburbs. Indeed, many Southern SMSAs have only recently experienced peaks in white suburbanization. Finally, Baltimore, by virtue of its age and Southern border location, may be experiencing a combination of black redistribution patterns that have been attributed to both Northern and Southern metropolitan areas.

What is apparent from the analysis just presented is that the strong network of constraints that had prevented black movers from entering the suburbs through the late 1950s has continued into the late 1960s for virtually all of the metropolitan areas in this study. This has been convincingly demonstrated in our analysis of black and white destination propensity rates for city residential movers, suburb residential movers, and metropolitan in-migrants. Although a few SMSAs, such as Cleveland and Los Angeles–Long Beach, have shown some tendencies toward reducing these constraints, the progress made even in these metropolitan areas must be viewed as negligible if a color-blind redistribution of movers is the final goal.

MOVEMENT STREAM CONTRIBUTIONS TO SUBURBAN RACIAL CHANGE

The preceding discussion of racial differences in mover destination propensity rates has underscored the degree to which existing barriers constrain the suburban relocation of black movers and in-migrants to levels far below those that are experienced by whites. What remains to be determined is how these black–white differences in destination propensities get translated into aggregate changes in the racial compositions of metropolitan suburbs. In the following analysis, I calculate movement stream contributions to suburban racial changes in the 24 SMSAs, using migration data for the 1965–1970 interval. This is possible because the census data in the *Mobility for Metropolitan Areas* report (1973) indicates the 1965 city, suburb, or outside SMSA place of residence for 1970 city and suburb residents. Hence, we are able to "return" 1965–1970 movers in each stream to their 1965 origins in order to evaluate the aggregate impact of each stream on the 1970 suburban racial composition.[8] The results of this analysis appear in Table 4.3.

We list in Column 1 the black percentage of the suburban population that would have existed in 1970 if no intrametropolitan movement or SMSA in-migration streams had taken place over the 1965–1970 interval. Column 8 shows the net change in that percentage that can be attributed to all of these streams. In Cleveland, for example, the 1970 suburban black percentage would have been 2.0 if no 1965–1970 intrametropolitan movement or in-migration had taken place. The net effect of these streams, however, has been to raise that percentage by +.9 to 2.9%—the actual racial composition of Cleveland's suburban population aged 25 and over. Finally, the intervening Columns, 2–7, indicate the changes that various 1965–1970 race-specific streams exert on the black suburban percentage in Column 1. Of course, both the black streams leading into the suburbs and the white stream leading out of the suburbs serve to increase the black suburban percentage. Contrariwise, both white streams leading into the suburbs and the black stream leading out contribute to a decrease in the percentage suburban blacks.

According to the figures in Column 8, it is first of all apparent that the combined impact of all movement streams serves to bring about only small changes in suburban racial compositions over the 1965–1970 interval. These small changes demonstrate the reinforcing influences that racial differences in suburban destination choice exert on the existing, highly segregated residential distribution. A second point to note from the figures is that the most significant changes in the black suburban percentage are negative changes exhibited in Southern SMSAs.

---

[8] In this analysis, the actual 1970 suburban racial composition is being compared with a number of hypothetical 1970 suburban racial compositions that assume that various 1965–1970 race-specific movement streams did not occur. Therefore, the mortality component of population change does not enter into these comparisons because individuals who have died over the interval would not be included in the 1970 suburban population. Since the population examined includes individuals aged 25 and over in 1970, the fertility component does not affect these comparisons either.

Indeed, the combined impact of these streams serves to effect a positive change in the percentage of the suburb black in only three SMSAs— Cleveland, St. Louis, and Los Angeles—and in each case the black suburban percentage is incremented by less than 1.0. Houston, on the other hand, experiences a reduction of 3.4 in its black suburban percentage—from 11.3 to 7.9.[9]

In evaluating the stream contributions to the suburban racial composition, it is instructive to examine the net contributions of both races for each of the three geographic streams. It is apparent from such an examination that only the city-to-suburb stream (Columns 2 and 3) exerts a substantial net increase in the black suburban percentage, and these increases are only observed for the three SMSAs that registered overall increases in the percentage of suburb black. Largest net decreases in the black suburban percentage are generally brought about through the suburb-to-city stream (Columns 4 and 5) or the in-migration stream to the suburbs (Columns 6 and 7). In Houston, each of the three streams contributed to a negative change in the suburban black composition by one or more percentage points.

Taken together, these findings indicate that recent increases in black suburbanization are almost exclusively a result of black city-to-suburb movement and lend further support to the "ghetto spillover" explanation of this phenomenon. The total impact of all three streams tends to effect only small overall changes in suburban racial compositions. This corroborates what was implied by our earlier examination of destination propensity rates—that the continuing constraints on black residential choices serve to further reinforce existing segregation patterns.

ELIMINATING BLACK–WHITE DIFFERENCES IN RESIDENTIAL CHOICE: THE IMPACT ON SUBURBAN RACIAL CHANGE

In the preceding sections I have established that constraints that had prevented black movers from locating in suburban destinations to the same degree as whites in the 1950s continued to operate in the late 1960s and, furthermore, that the aggregate redistribution of movers

---

[9] The change figures in Column 8 of Table 4.3 are not directly comparable to those in the last column of Table 4.1 because the Table 4.3 changes pertain to the 1965–1970 interval rather than the 1960–1970 interval, pertain only to the surviving population aged 25 and over in 1970 (i.e., natural increase is not taken into account), and do not take into account the impact of the out-migration stream from the suburbs to points outside the SMSA.

TABLE 4.3

Changes in the Percentage of Blacks of the 1970 Suburb Population Aged 25 and Over That Can Be Attributed to 1965–1970 Black and White Streams: City-to-Suburb Mobility, Suburb-to-City Mobility, and SMSA In-migration to the Suburbs, Selected SMSAs

	Percentage of the suburbs black, 1970, under assumption of no 1965–1970 mobility or in-migration a	Change in 1970 percentage of the suburbs black that can be attributed to:						
		1965–1970 city-to-suburb mobility stream		1965–1970 suburb-to-city mobility stream		1965–1970 SMSA in-migration stream to suburbs		All 1965–1970 in-migration mobility and streams
		Black	White	Black	White	Black	White	
SMSAs	(1)	(2)	(3)	(4)	(5)	(6)	(7)	(8)
North								
Detroit	3.8	.4	− .4	− .8	.1	.3	− .3	− .7
Gary–Hammond–East Chicago	.7	.2	− .1	− .3	0	.1	− .1	− .1
Chicago	3.7	.4	− .4	− .8	.1	.3	− .4	− .7
Philadelphia	6.0	.3	− .4	− .2	.1	.5	− .6	− .2
Cleveland	2.0	1.8	− .2	− .7	.1	.4	− .2	+ .9
St. Louis	5.7	1.1	− .4	− .3	.1	.5	− .6	+ .2
Columbus	2.4	.5	− .4	−1.1	.2	.3	− .4	− .8
Cincinnati	3.1	.5	− .3	− .6	.1	.2	− .1	− .4
Youngstown–Warren	2.5	.2	− .2	− .5	.1	.1	− .2	− .6
Buffalo	1.3	.1	− .1	− .1	0	.1	− .1	0
Pittsburgh	3.2	.2	− .1	− .2	0	.1	− .2	− .2
Syracuse	.4	.1	0	− .1	0	.1	0	− .1

South

New Orleans	12.1	1.2	−1.9	−.3	.3	.5	−1.7	−2.0
Birmingham	21.3	.8	−1.7	−1.5	.6	.5	−2.1	−3.2
Baltimore	6.3	.8	−.7	−1.0	.2	.6	−.8	−.9
Atlanta	7.2	1.3	−.9	−1.7	.2	.5	−1.7	−2.0
Houston	11.3	1.0	−2.0	−1.7	.7	.7	−2.4	−3.4
Dallas	7.5	.2	−.9	−2.1	.6	.3	−1.7	−3.1
Louisville	3.4	.5	−.5	−.5	.1	.3	−.5	−.6
Fort Worth	2.0	.1	−.3	−.8	.1	.2	−.6	−1.1
Tampa–St. Petersburg	4.8	.2	−.5	−.6	.2	.6	−1.6	−1.7
Oklahoma City	2.3	.3	−.3	−1.0	.2	.3	−.5	−.9

West

Los Angeles–Long Beach	4.3	1.6	−.4	−.6	.4	.6	−.5	+.6
San Francisco–Oakland	4.9	.6	−.4	−.5	.2	.8	−.8	−.3

Source: U.S. Bureau of the Census, 1973. Census of Population: 1970 PC(2)–2C.

[a] Percentage of blacks of the 1970 suburb population aged 25 and over that would have resulted under the assumptions that 1965–1970 city-to-suburb, suburb-to-city mobility, and SMSA in-migration to the suburbs had not taken place.

resulting from these constraints reinforced the existing city–suburb residential segregation of the races. In this section I shall empirically evaluate the short-run redistributional change that would be brought about by an immediate elimination of racial differences in the city–suburb destination choices of movers and metropolitan in-migrants. This will be accomplished by computing hypothetical suburban racial compositions that would result from alternative sets of destination propensity rates for black and white movers. Suburban racial compositions consistent with an open suburbs reallocation of movers will be compared with expected suburban racial compositions (such as were produced by Hermalin and Farley). This should provide insights into the pace with which complete integration can be achieved.

Actual and hypothetical black suburban percentages for the 24 SMSAs are presented in the first three columns of Table 4.4. Appearing in Column 1 are the actual 1970 values for the percentage of suburban blacks that are consistent with the data reviewed in Table 4.3. These racial compositions assume that actual black and white destination propensity rates occurred during the 1965–1970 interval and serve as a basis for comparison with the hypothetical racial compositions. In Column 2, I have computed hypothetical 1970 suburban racial compositions based on the assumption that all of the elements of the 1965–1970 redistribution process occurred as they had in actuality, with the exceptions of city movers', suburb movers', and SMSA in-migrants' destination propensity rates. However, it is also assumed that blacks and whites in each of the three mover populations took on their respective 1955–1960 destination propensity rates values rather than the 1965–1970 rates. (The attributed 1955–1960 rates were standardized by education status within each racial group.) The values in Column 2 were calculated in order to provide a comparison between redistributional consequences of the actual 1965–1970 destination propensity rates (in Column 1) and those that would have resulted from the destination propensity rates experienced by blacks and whites 10 years earlier.

Finally, in Column 3, hypothetical values for suburban racial compositions resulting from an open suburbs model of mover reallocation are presented. As in the previous simulation, all aspects of the actual 1965–1970 redistribution process are preserved, with the exception of the destination propensity rates for the three mover populations. The assumed destination propensity rates in this simulation completely eliminate racial disparities. This applies to the suburb destination propensity rates of city movers and SMSA in-migrants and to the city destination propensity rates of suburb movers. Although racial disparities in propensity rates are eliminated, educational disparities are preserved. (Education-specific destination propensity rates for the total population of movers are attributed to both black and white movers at each education level.) This elimination of racial disparities, coupled with a retention of educational status disparities, produces a city–suburb redistribution pattern that is predicated only on status-selective destination choice.[10]

We turn first to the comparison of redistribution patterns in Columns 1 and 2 in order to ascertain whether or not the 1955–1960 destination choice patterns of black and white movers—had they occurred in the 1965–1970 period—would have substantially altered the redistribution processes that actually took place in the latter period. The black suburban percentage changes by more than 1.0 for only four SMSAs when the different propensity rates are assumed. The changes in two of these SMSAs might be expected from our earlier results: The 1955–1960 rates would have lowered Cleveland's 1970 percentage of suburban blacks from 2.9 to 1.5 and raised Houston's black suburban percentage from 7.9 to 9.6. Both of these changes are consistent with the data shown in Figure 4.2. In two other Southern SMSAs, Birmingham and Dallas, the 1955–1960 destination propensities would have produced increases in the black suburban percentage. However, the main finding from these com-

[10] The hypothetical redistributions performed here make use of an analytic migration framework that was developed to examine stream components of city–suburb redistribution (see Frey, 1978). The framework consists of demographic accounting equations that can be used to calculate the sizes and compositions of a metropolitan area's city and suburb populations at the end of a migration interval given values for their respective sizes and compositions at the beginning of the interval and a set of migration parameters associated with the following movement streams: intrametropolitan city-to-suburb and suburb-to-city movement, in-migration streams to the suburbs and city from outside the SMSA, and out-migration streams from the suburbs and city to places outside the SMSA (the parameters for the first three streams are defined in Eqs. [1], [2], [3]). With the actual values for all of these parameters, it is possible to reconstruct the actual end-of-interval city and suburb populations. However, by substituting hypothetical values into one or more parameters, the analyst is able to compute end-of-interval population sizes and compositions that would be consistent with these assumed values.

In order to calculate the hypothetical values in Columns 2 and 3 in Table 4.4, actual values were assumed for all parameters except the destination propensity rates (in Eqs. [1], [2], and [3]). The hypothetical figures in Column 2 are arrived at by substituting 1955–1960 destination propensity rates for movers in each race–education-specific category. The figures in Column 3 assume equal destination propensity rates for black and white movers in each education category. These education-specific rates are the weighted averages of black and white (non-black) rates in each education class. Specific details pertaining to both simulations are available from the author on request.

TABLE 4.4

Alternative Values for Percentage of Blacks of the 1970 Suburb Population Aged 25 and Over Resulting from Actual and Hypothetical Destination Propensity Rates of 1965–1970 Movers and In-migrants and from the "Expected" Distribution of Suburban Blacks, Selected SMSAs

| | Values of 1970 percentage of the suburbs black assuming: | | | | Ratios to expected value | |
| | Actual 1965–1970 race and education-specific destination propensity rates | 1955–60 race and education-specific destination propensity rates | No race differences in 1965–1970 destination propensity rates [a] | "Expected" distribution of suburban blacks [b] | (1)/(4) | (3)/(4) |
SMSAs	(1)	(2)	(3)	(4)	(5)	(6)
North						
Detroit	3.1	3.6	7.6	15.3	.20	.50
Gary–Hammond–East Chicago	.6	.8	5.3	14.7	.04	.36
Chicago	3.0	3.2	6.4	13.7	.22	.47
Philadelphia	5.8	5.7	7.7	14.5	.40	.53
Cleveland	2.9	1.5	5.8	13.0	.22	.45
St. Louis	5.9	5.2	7.5	13.0	.45	.58
Columbus	1.6	1.7	4.9	10.0	.16	.49
Cincinnati	2.7	2.7	4.8	9.9	.27	.49
Youngstown–Warren	1.9	2.3	3.8	7.9	.24	.48
Buffalo	1.3	1.3	2.8	6.2	.21	.45
Pittsburgh	3.0	3.0	3.8	6.2	.48	.61
Syracuse	.3	.5	1.4	2.7	.11	.52

South					
New Orleans	10.1	10.9	15.2	25.3	.40	.60
Birmingham	18.1	19.8	20.9	25.9	.70	.81
Baltimore	5.4	5.5	9.6	19.2	.28	.50
Atlanta	5.2	5.8	10.1	18.7	.28	.54
Houston	7.9	9.6	12.2	17.2	.46	.71
Dallas	4.4	5.8	8.2	13.1	.34	.63
Louisville	2.8	3.3	5.5	10.6	.27	.52
Fort Worth	.9	1.4	4.1	8.9	.10	.46
Tampa–St. Petersburg	3.1	3.7	4.9	7.6	.41	.65
Oklahoma City	1.4	1.8	3.5	6.8	.21	.52
West					
Los Angeles–Long Beach	4.9	4.6	6.1	9.2	.53	.66
San Francisco–Oakland	4.6	4.7	6.0	8.6	.54	.70

Sources: U.S. Bureau of the Census, 1963. Census of Population PC(2)–2C.

U.S. Bureau of the Census, 1973. Census of Population PC(2)–2C.

[a] Assumes that blacks and non-blacks of each education class possess the same destination propensity rate—a weighted average of the actual 1965–1970 black and non-black destination propensity rates for that class.

[b] Assumes that the proportion of blacks residing in the suburbs at each education class equals the proportion of blacks residing in the SMSA at each education class in 1970.

parisons is the general consistency in racial redistribution that results from the propensity rates of each period.

The more interesting comparison of redistribution outcomes is made between the actual suburban racial compositions (in Column 1) and those that would have resulted from the elimination of racial differences in city–suburb destination propensities during the 1965–1970 interval (in Column 3). This comparison reveals that the latter, open suburb model of mover reallocation would have effected substantial increases in black suburban percentages. For most Northern suburbs, the percentage of blacks would have more than doubled under the hypothetical redistribution. The Western suburbs in Los Angeles–Long Beach and San Francisco–Oakland would have experienced somewhat more moderate gains due to the fact that minorities were less concentrated in their central cities at the beginning of the interval. The magnitude of racial change that would have resulted in Southern suburbs varies widely across SMSAs, but in most cases significant increases in the percentage of blacks would have occurred.

The results in Column 3 clearly indicate that a reallocation of movers based on status selective (but not racial selective) city-suburb destination choices would result in meaningful short-term increases in black suburbanization, particularly in Northern metropolitan areas. Having established this, I can now return to the question I raised at the outset of the study: Will changes in residential integration brought about by successful open suburbs programs be consistent with the large potential integration levels that other scholars have shown to exist?

In order to make such an assessment, we compute values for an expected percentage of suburban blacks that are consistent with the Hermalin and Farley (1973) expected or potential values of black suburban representation.[11] These might be viewed as the optimum levels of integration that can be achieved given the current economic status levels of a metropolitan area's blacks and whites, and these appear in Column

---

[11] Our measures differ slightly from those produced by Hermalin and Farley (1973). Their "expected" measure assumes that blacks at each status level are represented in the suburbs to the same degree as are whites. Our "expected" measure assumes that blacks at each level are represented in the suburbs to the same degree as the total population. The discrepancy between the two tends to be slight in predominantly white metropolitan areas (later in their analysis [p. 607], Hermalin and Farley employ the same measure I do). As I noted earlier, my definition of metropolitan area, measure of status, and focus on individuals differ from those used to compute the Hermalin and Farley measure. These differences arise from data constraints.

4. To aid in the comparison across SMSAs, I compute two ratios: the ratio of the actual black suburban percentage to the expected black percentage (in Column 5) and the ratio of the black suburban percentage that would result from the open suburbs allocation of movers to the expected black percentage (in Column 6). The ratios in Column 5 tell us the degree to which the suburban racial composition brought about by the 1965–1970 redistribution process is consistent with an optimum level of metropolitan-wide integration. The ratios in Column 6 give us the same information about the racial composition that would have been effected by an open suburbs model of redistribution.

An examination of the actual-to-expected ratios shows that the actual 1970 suburban racial composition falls well below optimum level for most SMSAs and that this disparity is particularly large for metropolitan areas in the North. The ratios in only 3 of 12 Northern SMSAs are greater than .30, and in Gary–Hammond–East Chicago it sinks to .04. The ratios for the two Western metropolitan areas approach 50% of that expected in a completely integrated residential distribution, and in Southern SMSAs, where the percentage of suburban blacks has been high historically, there is wide variation (from .70 in Birmingham to .10 in Fort Worth).

The ratio values resulting from the open suburbs allocation of movers (in Column 6) generally show sharp increases over those associated with the actual 1965–1970 redistribution process. Yet, for the most part, these values are considerably less than 1.00. This seems to indicate that the residential distribution of the races resulting from an open suburbs allocation of movers falls short of the mark of achieving expected metropolitan-wide integration levels, at least over a 5-year period. This is particularly the case for Northern SMSAs. In Gary–Hammond–East Chicago the open suburbs allocation of movers would have increased the black suburban percentage from its actual value of .6 to a value of 5.3. Yet, a redistribution process that would produce a metropolitan-wide integration of the races should yield a black suburban percentage of 14.7. In many Southern and Western SMSAs an open allocation of movers would yield levels of integration that are much closer to those expected than is the case for metropolitan areas in the North. These SMSAs were usually much more integrated—at least in the statistical sense—at the beginning of the migration interval.

The other side of the redistribution process not reported in this table is the concentration of blacks left residing in the central cities. Although a racially equitable redistribution of movers would increase the black percentage of Detroit's suburbs from 3.1 to 7.6, the percentage of blacks residing in the city would only be reduced from 37.6 to 30.6. The expected value for Detroit's black city percentage in an integrated metropolitan area would be 17.6.

To summarize, my comparison of redistribution patterns associated with different sets of destination propensity rates allows us to conclude that changes that occurred in the city–suburb propensities of black and white movers between the late 1950s and late 1960s have not had a marked effect on increasing black representation in the suburbs, that a redistribution process that eliminates all racial differences but preserves all status differences in movers' suburban selectivities would result in substantial short-term rises in the levels of black suburbanization—at least in comparison with existing levels, and that, in comparison with integration levels that are expected to exist in metropolitan areas, the short-term integration gains brought about by opening up the suburbs fall far short of the mark. Although patterns vary to some degree for individual SMSAs, each of these findings is particularly applicable to the migration and redistribution processes of the Northern metropolitan areas in our study.

SUMMARY AND IMPLICATIONS

This study was undertaken to enable urban scholars and policymakers to estimate how much metropolitan-wide residential integration could be accomplished in the short run if successful open suburbs programs were to be implemented. Although recent studies have indicated that the economic potential now exists to bring about a high degree of residential integration, the aggregate migration and redistribution processes that are constantly at work in large metropolitan areas tend to dictate the pace with which this potential can be realized. Through the analysis of migration and residential mobility data from 24 large SMSAs, I have examined the pace of recent residential integration as it has been mediated by these demographic processes in the past. I have also looked at the prospects for future changes in this pace that would accompany a substantial "opening" of the suburbs to blacks. In each part of the study, I focused exclusively on one dimension of racial integration—the suburbanization of metropolitan blacks.

In both the late 1960s and late 1970s, according to our findings, there existed wide disparities in the suburban destination propensities of black and white movers. During each period, white city movers and in-migrants to the metropolitan area were far more likely to relocate in the suburbs than were blacks. Black suburban movers were much more likely than whites to relocate in the central city, a tendency that seems to have increased over the decade. A few metropolitan areas, such as Cleveland and Los Angeles-Long Beach, experienced significant increases in black suburban-ward relocation in the late 1960s. Yet, even in these SMSAs, the overall racial disparity in suburban destination selectivity remained large for the most recent period.

In further analyses designed to assess the aggregate impact of these movement patterns on suburban racial change, I found, not surprisingly, that the destination selectivity patterns in each period did not contribute to a great deal of racial change for most metropolitan suburbs. The small percentage of blacks in Northern and Western suburbs remained relatively unchanged as a result of these movement patterns. In Southern SMSAs the redistribution process served to decrease the black suburban percentage. The major conclusions that emerge from our study of recent movement patterns and suburban racial change are that *constraints that had prevented black movers from locating in suburban destinations to the same degree as whites in the late 1950s continued to operate in the late 1960s* and that *the aggregate redistribution of movers and in-migrants resulting from these constraints served to reinforce existing city–suburb racial segregation patterns.*

The final portion of the study was concerned with estimating the short-run increase in black suburbanization that could be brought about by successful efforts at opening up suburbs to blacks. This estimation was undertaken by simulating hypothetical redistributions of movers and in-migrants that assumed a complete elimination of black–white differences in mover suburban selectivity. Our findings from these simulations indicate that meaningful gains in black suburbanization could be effected in a short, 5-year time period if racial differences in suburban destination propensity were eliminated. However, even these levels of black suburbanization do not measure up to the levels that would arise from an expected metropolitan-wide integration that, according to other scholars, is commensurate with the current economic position of blacks. Based on these findings, *I conclude that an immediate and complete elimination of racial discrimination in suburban entry would bring about increases in black suburbanization that are well above existing levels. Yet, these immediate increases would fall far short of achieving metropolitan-wide racial integration.*

Overall, our examination of the metropolitan redistribution process suggests that the righting of past wrongs—through the elimination of racial residential segregation that has evolved over decades of discrimination—will, at best, occur slowly. This slow pace is largely attributable to the demographic fact of life that residential movement occurs among only a subset of the total population in a given interval of time. The massive redistribution of both blacks and whites that would be necessary to achieve city–suburb (not to mention interneighborhood) racial integration would require more than a 5- or 10-year period even if the constraints to black suburban entry were eliminated. Our evidence from the 1950s and 1960s suggests that the elimination or substantial reduction of these constraints is not imminent. Even in those metropolitan areas that experienced recent increases in black suburbanization, there exist large disparities in the suburban destinations of white and black movers at all status levels. Finally, we reemphasize that our measure of racial integration—the percentage of blacks in SMSA suburbs—greatly overstates the degree of integration that is occurring at the neighborhood level. Studies that have looked at the quality of life experienced by recently suburbanized blacks find few parallels with suburban whites (Rabinovitz, 1973; Rose, 1976). Indeed, the "ghetto spillover" characterization of current black suburbanization may be a fair one.

The implications of our study for long-term strategies directed toward achieving greater racial unity, improving the economic position of minorities, and redeveloping declining central cities might best be assessed by urban planners and policymakers. However, the continuing constraints that are being imposed upon the suburban entry of black movers and in-migrants, as documented here, argue strongly for the vigorous enforcement of existing equal housing laws and for sustained efforts directed toward the elimination of informal discriminatory housing practices that are prevalent in both public and private institutions. Indeed, Glazer's position (1974:110) that "[the residential] integration of blacks is occurring" does not coincide with the data I have presented.

Yet, it is also clear from our study that the sole or heavy reliance on metropolitan-wide residential integration as a means to achieving policy objectives in the short run would be ill-advised. The findings suggest that these objectives might be brought about sooner if emphasis is placed on such interim measures as cross-district busing or reverse commuting programs and if more serious consideration is given to policies aimed at improving the existing social, economic, and physical living environments of central-city residents.

REFERENCES

Biggar, Jeanne C., and Francis C. Biasiolli
    1977   "Metropolitan deconcentration: Subareal in-migration and central city to ring mobility patterns among Southern cities." Paper pre-

sented at the annual meetings of the Population Association of America, St. Louis, Missouri, April.

Butler, Edgar W., F. Stuart Chapin, Jr., George C. Hemmens, Edward J. Kaiser, Michael A. Stegman, and Shirley F. Weiss

1969   Moving Behavior and Residential Choice—A National Survey. National Cooperative Highway Research Program Report No. 81. Washington, D.C.: Highway Research Board, National Academy of Sciences.

Clay, Philip L.

1975   "The process of black suburbanization." Unpublished doctoral dissertation, Chapter 4. Department of Urban Studies and Planning, Massachusetts Institute of Technology.

Connally, Harold X.

1973   "Black movement to the suburbs: Suburbs doubling their black populations during the 1960s." *Urban Affairs Quarterly* 9: 91–111.

Cottingham, Phoebe H.

1975   "Black income and metropolitan residential dispersion." *Urban Affairs Quarterly* 10:273–296.

Downs, Anthony

1973   *Opening Up the Suburbs: An Urban Strategy for America*. New Haven, Connecticut: Yale University Press.

Farley, Reynolds

1970   "The changing distribution of Negroes within metropolitan areas: The emergence of black suburbs." *American Journal of Sociology* 75:512–529.

1975   "Residential segregation and its implications for school integration." *Law and Contemporary Problems* 39 (Winter):164–193.

1976   "Components of suburban population growth." In Barry Schwartz (ed.), *The Changing Face of the Suburbs*. Chicago, Illinois: The University of Chicago Press.

Foley, Donald

1973   "Institutional and contextual factors affecting the housing choices of minority residents." In Amos H. Hawley and Vincent P. Rock (eds.), *Segregation in Residential Areas*. Washington, D.C.: National Academy of Sciences.

Frey, William H.

1977   "Central city white flight: Racial and nonracial causes." Paper presented at the annual meetings of the American Sociological Association, Chicago, Illinois, September. (University of Wisconsin–Madison, Institute for Research on Poverty Discussion Paper 420-77).

1978   "Population movement and city–suburb redistribution: An analytic framework." *Demography* 15 (November), forthcoming.

Glazer, Nathan

1974   "On 'opening up' the suburbs." *The Public Interest* 37:89–111.

Greenwood, M. J., and D. Sweetland

1972   "The determinants of migration between standard metropolitan statistical areas." *Demography* 9:665–681.

Grier, Eunice S.

1973   *Characteristics of Black Suburbanites*. Washington, D.C.: Washington Center for Metropolitan Studies.

Harrison, Bennett
  1974   Urban Economic Development: Suburbanization Minority Oppor-
           tunity, and the Condition of the Central City. Washington, D.C.:
           The Urban Institute.
Hermalin, Albert I., and Reynolds Farley
  1973   "The potential for residential integration in cities and suburbs: Im-
           plications for the busing controversy." American Sociological Review
           38:595–610.
Kain, John F., and Joseph J. Persky
  1969   "Alternatives to the guilded ghetto." The Public Interest 14:74–87.
Kirschenbaum, Alan
  1972   "City–suburban destination choices among migrants to metropolitan
           areas." Demography 3:321–335.
Lansing, John B., and Eva Mueller
  1967   The Geographic Mobility of Labor. Ann Arbor, Michigan: Institute
           for Social Research.
Long, Larry H.
  1975   "How the racial composition of cities changes." Land Economics
           51:258–267.
Long, Larry H., and Celia G. Boertlein
  1976   The Geographical Mobility of Americans: An International Com-
           parison. (U.S. Bureau of the Census, Current Population Reports,
           Special Studies, Series P-23, No. 64) Washington, D.C.: U.S. Govern-
           ment Printing Office.
National Advisory Commission on Civil Disorders
  1968   A Report. New York: Bantam Books.
Palen, John J., and Leo F. Schnore
  1965   "Color composition and city–suburban status differences: A replica-
           tion and extension." Land Economics 41:87–91.
Rabinovitz, Francine F.
  1975   "Minorities in suburbs: The Los Angeles experience." Joint Center
           for Urban Studies of Massachusetts Institute of Technology and
           Harvard University, Working Paper No. 31.
Rose, Harold M.
  1976   Black Suburbanization: Access to Improved Quality of Life or Main-
           tenance of the Status Quo? Cambridge, Massachusetts: Ballinger
           Publishing Company.
Rossi, Peter H.
  1955   Why Families Move. New York: Free Press.
Schnore, Leo F.
  1972   Class and Race in Cities and Suburbs. Chicago, Illinois: Markham
           Publishing Company.
Schnore, Leo F., Carolyn D. Andre, and Harry Sharp
  1976   "Black suburbanization, 1930–1970." In Barry Schwartz (ed.), The
           Changing Face of the Suburbs. Chicago, Illinois: The University of
           Chicago Press.
Simmons, James W.
  1968   "Changing residence in the city: A review of intra-urban mobility."
           Geographic Review 58:622–651.

Speare, Alden Jr.
   1970   "Home ownership, life cycle stage, and residential mobility." *Demography* 7:449–458.
Speare, Alden Jr., Sidney Goldstein, and William H. Frey
   1975   *Residential Mobility, Migration and Metropolitan Change.* Cambridge, Massachusetts: Ballinger Publishing Company.
Taeuber, Irene B.
   1972   "The changing distribution of the population of the United States in the twentieth century." In Sara Mills Mazie (ed.), *U.S. Commission on Population Growth and the American Future.* Population Distribution and Policy, Volume V of Commission Research Reports. Washington, D.C.: Government Printing Office.
Taeuber, Karl E.
   1975   "Demographic perspectives on housing and school segregation." *Wayne Law Review* 21:833–850.
Taeuber, Karl E., and Alma F. Taeuber
   1965   *Negroes in Cities.* Chicago, Illinois: Aldine Publishing Company.
U.S. Bureau of the Census
   1963   Census of Population, 1960. Subject Reports, Final Report PC(2)-2C, Mobility for Metropolitan Areas. Washington, D.C.: U.S. Government Printing Office.
   1971   Census of Population Housing: 1970. General Demographic Trends for Metropolitan Areas 1960 to 1970. Final Report PHC(2)-1 United States. Washington, D.C.: U.S. Government Printing Office.
   1973   Census of Population, 1970. Subject Reports, Final Report PC(2)-2C, Mobility for Metropolitan Areas. Washington, D.C.: U.S. Government Printing Office.
Zimmer, Basil G.
   1973   "Residential mobility and housing." *Land Economics* 49:344–350.

5

Selective Black Migration from the South: A Historical View[1]

STANLEY LIEBERSON

Questions about the nature of black migration from the South occur in a wide variety of contexts. Since blacks in the South presently differ from those residing in the North and West and did even more so in the past and because migration has been a massive factor in the growth of the black population living in the non-South, it is reasonable to consider the nature of this migration whenever one wishes to interpret changes in northern race relations. Even if discrimination is a major causal factor, it is still appropriate to consider the characteristics of blacks when dealing with fluctuations over time in the patterns of northern race relations, since discrimination need not fully explain such shifts. Whether it be temporal changes in segregation patterns, crime

[1] The support of the National Science Foundation (Grant GS-33542) is gratefully acknowledged, along with the suggestion by my colleague, Otis Dudley Duncan, that I use CSRs to deal with the substantive problem.

rates, white attitudes towards blacks, social problems, the magnitude of discrimination, housing, or employment, one must seriously consider the impact of southern migration on the characteristics of the black population living in the North. Most social scientists tend to view fluctuations in northern race relations as a function of other factors outside the characteristics of blacks themselves, but it is certainly a reasonable null hypothesis that shifts in the position of blacks in the North were partially resulting from the differences between black migrants to the North and those who were already living there.

Unfortunately, it is not easy to compare southern black out-migrants with those blacks already in the North. For many of the most interesting census items about black migrants in the North, it is impossible to know whether the data reflect their characteristics before they migrated or reflect their experiences in the North afterward (see Lieberson and Wilkinson, 1976). Before 1940 it is even more difficult, since information on migration was not obtained and the reports on birthplace by residence were tabulated with virtually no characteristics other than age and sex. Accordingly, very little is presently known about the nature of black migration from the South earlier in this century and in the latter part of the nineteenth century. For example, although World War I is widely recognized as a period that "signaled the onset of a great population shift that was to transfer the locus of Negro life in the United States from the rural South to the urban North [Spear, 1967:ix]," we have no idea as yet about the characteristics of these migrants, how they compared with blacks already in the North, and how different they were from earlier migrants and those who followed in later years. Limited data comparing migrants (not always just from the South) with earlier residents are available for Chicago between 1935 and 1940 (Freedman, 1950:Chap. 6); for Chicago between 1940 and 1950 (Duncan and Duncan, 1957:59–62); for a number of leading cities for part of the post-World War II period (Taeuber and Taeuber, 1965a,b); and for southern-born migrants to the North between 1955 and 1960 (Lieberson, 1973:558). But there is no systematic and broad study available of the impact of net migration from the South on the characteristics of the black population living in the North and West earlier in this century.

In this chapter, I shall attempt to remedy this serious deficiency by using U.S. Census Survival Ratios (CSRs) to consider the educational characteristics of black adults migrating to the North and West. At least for this characteristic, it should be possible to determine if net migration was selective by education, the magnitude of this selection, and the consequences it had in the North for black educational characteristics. In the course of pursuing this problem, an important methodological issue that deals with the interpretation of net migration rates was uncovered, and this issue will also be discussed.

DATA AND METHODS

The ideal data are not available. The census migration question initiated in 1940 is not entirely satisfactory for our purposes, since it was restricted in the 1940, 1960, and 1970 censuses to movements during the preceding 5 years and covered only 1 year in the 1950 enumeration. The 1949–1950 period is particularly unfortunate, since a depression occurred during that time span and a net movement back to the South was actually recorded for adult blacks in that period even though there was sizable migration to the North during the 1940s (see Lieberson, 1978). Not only is there no direct census question on migration for the period preceding 1940 but also it was not until then that a question was asked on the educational attainment of adults. Prior to that time, there was information only on the education of those still in school (which is, obviously, not of much value for the problem at hand) and on the literacy of respondents.

In order to estimate the magnitude and direction of the net population movements, CSRs are constructed and applied to each decade for which suitable educational data are available for both the initial and the terminal period. These ratios were determined separately for blacks living in the United States of specific age, sex, and educational (simply literate or illiterate in the period preceding 1940) categories. Since educational level appears to be related to mortality (see, for example, Kitagawa and Hauser, 1973) and because the central topic of the study is education, it was crucial that the CSRs be constructed separately for each educational category among blacks of a given age and sex. They are based on the ratio of the black population of a given age, sex, and education in the United States divided by the corresponding number in the previous census for the population 10 years younger. If there were no black migration into or out of the United States during the decade, if all persons were counted and their age and education correctly enumerated, if their educational situation did not change over the span, if no migrants within the nation died before they were enumerated again in the next census, and if there were no regional differences in mortality, then CSRs would permit an exact and complete determination of the net movements between South and non-South for blacks of different educational levels during each decade. The CSR between Time 1 and Time 2 under these circumstances would give the exact number of survivors expected at Time 2 when applied to the appropriate population living in a given region at Time 1. Any discrepancies between the actual and expected number in the region at Time 2 would be attributed to net migration.

Obviously, there is no census anywhere that meets all of these conditions; the question, however, is whether the deviations from the ideal are serious enough to undermine use of CSRs. Because there was relatively little in the way of new black in-migration to the United States since well before the end of slavery and because black emigration from the nation has not been significant in number, the assumption of a closed population is not too unrealistic. Likewise, regional differences in mortality are probably insignificant between persons of the same educational level. In earlier years, it mattered relatively little, since the overwhelming majority of blacks lived in the South and, hence, the CSR obtained for the nation was certain to be a very close approximation of the mortality experienced by blacks in the South. This becomes less of a case in more recent decades because the group is more evenly split between South and non-South. The undercount of blacks in recent censuses is well-known, and it is concentrated in certain ages (Parsons, 1972). However, it is less of a problem than might appear at first glance. Insofar as the undercount for a given cohort remains consistent between decades and for a given region and educational level, the misestimation is minimal for that category (even if the composition and total number of all migrants is in error). The reason for this is that mortality is estimated in terms of a ratio of two numbers (see Hamilton, 1959:40–42). Another difficulty stems from a true educational upgrading within the adult cohorts over time as well as a misreporting of education (presumably with errors tending to be in a more favorable direction). This means that the CSRs for the more educated (literates in earlier decades) will tend to overestimate survival because there are new persons added to the category in succeeding decades within the same cohort, and, in contrast, the ratios for the less educated categories overestimate mortality because some persons disappear not through death but rather because they report a different educational level in a later census. In order to minimize this problem, the CSRs were computed only for those at least 15–24 when dealing with the literate–illiterate distinction and 25–34 for the post-World War II period. Hence, the distortions due to true educational upgrading should at least be relatively minimal.

Census questions on literacy are not exactly ideal, although they were reasonably consistent throughout the period under study. Two questions were asked in each census: one on the ability to read and the other on the ability to write, with *illiteracy* defined as the inability to write regardless of the ability to read. Since no particular test was used, there is certainly room for errors by respondents (presumably leading to an overestimation of literacy) and errors by enumerators (quite possibly in a direction unfavorable to blacks). These errors are not likely to be trivial, since there is a gray area in the case of literacy for those persons unable to read and write fluently but who are able to do considerably more than merely read and write their own names (U.S. Bureau of the Census, 1933:1219–1220). These reservations notwithstanding, the literacy data are probably reasonably accurate on the whole for measuring educational differences among blacks. Slightly more than 80% of those aged 10 and over were illiterate in 1870, with the figure dropping but still substantial for blacks throughout the period in which literacy was enumerated in the census. Nearly 60% were illiterate in 1890, with the percentage in successive decades dropping to 44.5% in 1900, 30.4% in 1910, 22.9% in 1920 and 16.3% in 1930 (Folger and Nam, 1967:114). Since illiteracy in the South was even higher than these national figures, it is a good indicator of selective migration throughout the period.

Probably the most serious difficulty with the method stems not from the fact that the quality and nature of black enumeration was consistently "off" in each census but that it fluctuated between decades. Coale and Rives (1973) estimate that there were particularly severe undercounts of the black population in the 1890 and 1920 censuses, with generally smaller undercounts in more recent decades (see also Farley, 1970:23–26). To be sure, the crucial issue is the consistency of the undercount in succeeding decades for a cohort with a given level of educational attainment. Although data are not available with such educational detail, a brief review of the undercounts estimated by specific age for black cohorts over time leaves little doubt that the magnitude of the undercount fluctuates by age, independent of the specific census year effect (see Coale and Rives, 1973:21). Some of the CSRs clearly indicate the operation of serious errors; for example, women 45–64 years of age can expect a CSR well below unity in the next 10 years. Yet the number of black women 55–74 years of age in 1970 with 4 or more years of college was actually slightly greater than the number 10 years earlier who were 45–64 and had the same educational attainment (45,134 versus 44,921). To be sure, this can reflect a variety of forces, not the least of which may have been a distortion in the educational attainment claimed by respondents. Notwithstanding the fact that a given age-, sex-, and education-specific CSR may be in serious error, the overall patterns of migration inferred this way are far superior to conclusions obtained through speculation about what occurred in earlier decades. Indeed, in an excellent review of the effect of census errors on net migration measurements, Hamilton (1966) has shown that the CSRs are often superior to other standard methods (for a general review of migration measurements, see Hamilton, 1965; Shryock et al., 1971). As C. Horace Hamilton put it in terms of his own study of education and migration based on survival rates, "We shall simply assume that the application of the method in this case takes us closer to the truth regarding educational selectivity than we would be without using it at all [1959:33]."

THE IMPACT OF MIGRATION ON BLACKS IN THE NORTH

The educational level of adult blacks living in the North and West rose throughout the period under study (1890–1970), a pattern that is hardly surprising given the educational push generally found in the nation. Illiteracy declined from 39.4% among blacks living outside of the South in 1890 to 6.1% in 1930 (see the "actual" figures in Table 5.1). Likewise, in the post-World War II period there is a persistent drop in the proportion of adult blacks with no more than an elementary school education and a concomitant rise in those who attended high school or college (see the "actual" percentage distributions in the bottom half of Table 5.1). The issue, however, is whether black migration to and from the South affected these figures and, if so, in what direction. Would black illiteracy levels have dropped more or less rapidly if, instead of the sizable flow experienced in many of these decades, there had been no migration out of the South or back into it?

Using the CSRs generated for each decade, one can determine what the educational level of adult blacks would have been in the North if there had been no in- or out-migration during the decade and if blacks of a given age, sex, and educational level living there had the mortality experienced by all blacks in the United States with the same characteristics.[2] These are the "expected" figures given in Table 5.1. Nothing can be done for 1940 because the detailed educational characteristics needed to construct 1930–1940 CSRs are not available for 1930, when a literacy question was still in use. The reader should note that the educational level expected for a given decade in the absence of migration is higher than the actual figures for the preceding decade. For example, 13.9% of adults are expected to be illiterate in 1910, whereas 24.7% were actually

---

[2] For convenience I shall use "North" to include also the West and, hence, to refer to the entire non-South.

TABLE 5.1

Educational Attainment among Blacks in the North and West, 1880–1970

Percentage illiterate	1890 [a,b]	1900 [b]	1910 [b]	1920 [b]	1930 [b]
Actual	39.4	24.7	13.6	8.9	6.1
Expected	34.3	19.5	13.9	9.4	5.8
Actual minus expected	5.1	5.2	− .3	− .5	.3

	Percentage distribution					
	1950 [c]		1960 [a,c]		1970 [c]	
Years completed	Actual	Expected	Actual	Expected	Actual	Expected
Elementary						
0–4	21.8	19.1	16.8	14.9	9.3	8.5
5–8	46.5	47.6	39.3	38.0	30.4	30.6
High school						
1–3	15.9	16.6	20.0	21.2	27.6	28.8
4	10.2	10.5	15.7	17.7	22.4	21.8
College						
1–3	3.5	3.6	5.0	4.8	6.4	6.4
4+	2.2	2.5	3.2	3.4	3.9	3.8
Index of net difference	−3.0		−3.7		− .4	

Note: "Expected" figures are based on age- and sex-specific CSRs applied to population living in the North and West 10 years earlier.

[a] Includes all nonwhites.

[b] Ages 25 and over in year indicated.

[c] Ages 35–74 in year indicated.

illiterate in 1900. These differences are due to three factors. First, the more recent period includes a new cohort of adults and, hence, reflects the higher education experienced by that cohort. For example, the 1910 expected figure incorporates those 15–24 living in the North in 1900 and the survivorship rates appropriate to them. Second, since the older adults obviously have greater mortality than the younger adults and because the former are also less educated, an upgrading in the educational level of surviving adults a decade later is to be expected. Finally, there is differential mortality by education within a given age group; that means, in most cases, that more of the highly educated blacks are expected to survive than those of the same age and sex but with less schooling.

A comparison between the actual and the expected figures within a given decade takes all of these factors into account and, hence, the discrepancy between the two numbers is due to the effect of net migration. Although there was net migration of blacks from the South throughout this period, bear in mind that we are dealing with the effects of migration to the South as well as migration from that region. At least for recent decades, the data show that there was a sizable gross flow to the South even though the net movement was substantially in the opposite direction (see Lieberson, 1978). (For the sake of convenience, one talks about the characteristics of migrants from the South, but, in point of fact, net migration is really being measured.) At the tail end of the century, it is clear that the movement of blacks from the post-bellum South tended to lower the educational level of blacks in the North; in both 1890 and 1900, illiteracy in the North and West was about 5 percentage points greater than what would have been expected under the conditions in which there was no in- or out-migration during the preceding decade. The gaps between the actual and the expected figures are, however, not massive and clearly did not prevent an enormous drop in adult illiteracy among northern blacks between 1890 and 1900, from 39.4 to 24.7%. Incidentally, there had been a slight increase between 1880 and 1890 in the actual proportion illiterate in the North, from 37.9 to 39.4%—unfortunately, the data necessary for computing a proper survivorship rate for that decade are not available.

This tendency for net migration to moderately retard the decline of illiteracy among adult blacks living in the North disappeared in the early part of the twentieth century. Net migration was essentially without consequence in the first decade of the new century, with the observed percentage illiterate actually slightly smaller than the figure expected if there were no migration, 13.6 versus 13.9%, respectively. The decade encompassing World War I as well as the following one are very important because the first major migration wave occurred during the war and this, in turn, was succeeded by an even larger flow in the 1920s. As was the case for the 1900–1910 span, net migration was of no importance in altering the decline of illiteracy among black adults living in the North and West from that which CSRs would have generated without any spatial movement. The actual frequency of illiteracy is again slightly lower in 1920 than what would have been the case in the absence of migration. The difference is in the opposite direction for 1930 but is also slight (.3%).

Adult black educational attainment continued its rise during the post-World War II period. The percentage of adults with less than 5 years of schooling declined from 21.8 to 9.3 between 1950 and 1970, and there was a drop of 16 percentage points among those with only 5–8 years of elementary schooling, 46.5 versus 30.4% (see Table 5.1). A comparison between the actual and the expected educational distributions indicates, however, that the educational attainment of blacks in the North increased slightly less rapidly in the post-World War II period because of migration. (The effect being measured in this paper is, of course, an immediate and direct one that is based on the properties of the adult migrants themselves. No attempt is made to deal with the long-term consequences in terms of changes in the age distribution or indirect consequences, such as educational patterns among their children.) The Index of Net Difference (ND), unlike the median, permits a comparison between the entire actual and expected educational distributions rather than merely their fiftieth percentiles. The index is -3.0 and -3.7 in 1950 and 1960, respectively, and is even smaller in 1970, $-.4$. This indicates that, if each adult black living in the North and West in a given year were to be paired with those expected under the conditions of no migration, pairings in which the actual is less educated occurs slightly more often than pairings in which the expected is less educated—the absolute difference in percentages ranging from .4 to 3.7 points (for more details, see Lieberson, 1975).

To summarize, migration earlier in this century had essentially no net effect on the level of black educational accomplishment in the North and West. On the other hand, at the tail end of the nineteenth century and for several decades in the post-World War II period, net migration prevented adult black educational levels from increasing as rapidly as would have otherwise been the case in the North and West. But the impact of net migration in these periods was relatively slight; moreover, it did not prevent a substantial upgrading of black education in the non-South. The terms *direct* and *immediate* must be used in discussing the impact of net migration because the indirect consequences could be another matter. Aside from the demographic possibilities mentioned earlier, such as changes due to the offspring of migrants and their age composition, the growth in the sheer number of blacks in the North could have altered white responses, and, in turn, this may have led to more segregated schools and other institutional changes that had a later bearing on the education of blacks in the North. This is a separate issue that cannot be resolved with the information analyzed here. Indeed, the data in Table 5.1 make it clear that the changing "quality" of black net migration from the South was not responsible for any deterioration in the position of blacks in the North. The reader must recognize that these results deal with only one characteristic of blacks, and, although education is important, there is no assurance that the same pattern holds for other attributes. Moreover, there is always the possibility that important differences exist *within* an educational category between blacks migrating into and out of the North. Nevertheless, it is reasonable to conclude on the basis of the preceding evidence that the net direct effect of migration on the characteristics of adult blacks living in the North was not substantial. Hence, although it is always tempting to attribute changes in the nature of race relations to shifts in the characteristics of members of one or the other group, in this case there is no support for such an interpretation.

NET MIGRATION RATES OVER TIME

Inspection of the actual age-, sex-, and education-specific migration rates is of great value in learning about the sources of migration from the South and the shifts that occurred when blacks moved to the North in increasing numbers around World War I. Although differences between many of the individual rates are not easily understood (and, indeed, may reflect inaccuracies due to the possibly shaky nature of the data on which CSRs are computed and, hence, through which these migration rates are derived), the broad patterns found in Table 5.2 indicate which segments of the Southern black population were especially receptive to the call from the North that occurred after the war in Europe led to a boom but cut off existing sources of unskilled labor.

The raw data generated in the application of survival ratios can be converted into a wide variety of different net migration rates for the South or North. A very simple one is used here:

$$M_{x+t} = \frac{P_{x+t}^t - sP_x^0}{sP_x^0},$$

where x is an age group, t is the number of years between censuses, M_{x+t} is the rate of net migration for the South (out if negative, in if positive), P_x^0 is the black population living in the South of a given age and sex at the time of initial census, P_{x+t}^t is the black population living in the South of the same sex at the time of the second census that was t years later, and s is the CSR for all blacks in the United States of the age, sex, and education specified. There are a variety of different assumptions that could be made about the timing of in- or out-migration during a given span that, in turn, affect the measure used (see Hamilton, 1965), but I believe that the measure used here is adequate for the crude data from which they are derived.

No simple generalization is possible for the first few decades shown in Table 5.2; literate blacks in some ages had higher out-migration rates than the illiterates, whereas the opposite gap occurs at other ages. Indeed, there were cases in which literate blacks appeared, if anything, to be migrating to the South even though illiterates of the same age and

Selective Black Migration from the South

TABLE 5.2

Net Migration Rates from the South, Blacks Grouped by Age, Sex, and Literacy, 1880–1930

Decade and initial age	Net migration rate			
	Male		Female	
	Illiterate	Literate	Illiterate	Literate
1880–1890				
15–20	−.05289	−.03618	−.01605	−.06085
21+	−.02543	.05599	−.01218	−.06101
1890–1900				
15–24	−.01770	−.06530	−.01139	−.07191
25–34	−.01019	−.02228	−.00781	−.02023
35–44	.00941	.03483	−.00504	.02866
45–54	.00317	.01012	−.00566	.05037
55+	.00225	.02669	.00061	.16043
1900–1910				
15–24	−.01355	−.06520	−.01019	−.05679
25–34	−.00465	−.01169	−.00655	−.00591
35–44	.01082	.04272	−.00295	.01838
45–54	.00619	.01779	−.00336	.03499
55+	−.00219	.02426	−.00531	.08007
1910–1920				
15–24	−.03410	−.16668	−.02225	−.12395
25–34	−.02702	−.10043	−.01655	−.06579
35–44	−.01023	−.01738	−.01415	−.05237
45–54	−.00651	−.02741	−.01512	−.06039
55+	−.00657	−.02423	−.00796	−.06072
1920–1930				
15–24	−.04615	−.21719	−.03955	−.18641
25–34	−.03699	−.11343	−.02807	−.09672
35–44	−.01525	−.02376	−.02477	−.06579
45–54	−.01149	−.03655	−.02510	−.06510
55+	−.02014	−.04190	−.01865	−.05742

sex had a net out-migration to the North. Black men 21 years of age and older in 1880, for example, experienced net in-migration to the South during the 1880s, although literate black women in both age categories had higher rates of net out-migration from the South than did illiterate women. In the 1890s, literates in the younger ages were more likely to leave the South than were the illiterates, but the opposite gap held for older blacks. Indeed, out-migration in the first decade of this century was also greater among the older illiterate blacks than among the better educated.

Interpretation of these results is not entirely clear; there are certain technical issues that could have altered the rates. In particular, if there were many blacks who in those days first became literate after reaching adulthood, this would throw off the survivorship rates for both literates and illiterates (by overstating the life chances of the former and underestimating those of the latter). This, in turn, would distort the out-migration rates if illiterate blacks who left the South were particularly likely to learn after residing in the North. Another technical issue pertains to the compositional influence on the interpretation of out-migration rates, but discussion of that is being postponed. These technical cautions notwithstanding, it is quite possible that there was indeed a net movement back to the South around the turn of the century among educated blacks in the older ages. For this was a period in which opportunities for them may have been far greater in the South than elsewhere in the nation. It was a time in which all sorts of opportunities existed for black teachers in the South, where even minimally educated blacks were in short supply. These jobs paid very poorly and the standards were low, but one must contrast them with the opportunities available elsewhere for blacks.

Migration during the decade spanning World War I, as well as in the next 10 years, was sharply different for the two educational groups. On the one hand, net out-migration among illiterates increased only modestly from the rates observed in the previous decade. Rates for women in the 1910s range from −.008 to −.022, in each case somewhat higher than they had been for the same age category a decade earlier. A similar result is found for men. In contrast, the out-migration rates for literate men and women during the World War I period are massively higher than what they had been 10 years earlier—indeed, they are far higher than the rates for the same age and sex among illiterates. Particularly striking is the net out-migration rate of −.167 observed for literate men 15–24, which means that roughly one out of every six black men living in the South in 1910 was living in the North or West 10 years later. (The gross flow to the North is actually higher than this because these are net figures, and, hence, any movement from North to South required an additional compensating move in the opposite direction.) The out-migration rates among literates are also spectacularly high for other young adult ages, −.100 for men 25–34 and −.124 among the youngest cohort of black women (see Table 5.2). From 5 to 6% of literate black women at other ages also left the South during this period (see Table 5.2), and, again, the reader is reminded that these are minimum outflows, since the net migration rates are counterbalanced by whatever movement there was in the opposite direction.

The post-World War I decade witnessed even heavier migration from South to North, and, again, this involved only a modest increase in the net flow of illiterate blacks, although in all ages they exceeded the 1910–1920 rates. The spectacular increases occur among the young adult literates. Roughly 2 out of every 10 black men 15–24 living in 1920 in the South had moved to the North by 1930, and the rate was nearly as high for women, —.186. (Again, these are net figures, and, hence, the gross flow was even greater.) Out-migration is higher in all other ages as well during this span. It is clear, then, that the first great wave of black movement from South to North was extremely selective among adults, drawing heavily not merely from the younger ages but particularly from the better-educated component within each age and sex category. The great pull on southern blacks exerted by the conditions in World War I and its aftermath, as well as the South's unwitting push owing to the dismal outlook for blacks, was particularly powerful among the better-educated young adults of the South. It was these people who had the highest probability of leaving.

I have not supplied the net migration rates for the 1940–1970 period (even though they can be made available) for two related reasons. First, the patterns are very complicated, as well they might be when one deals with a large number of different educational categories at the same time and when the meaning of a given level varies by age because each cohort has more schooling than the preceding cohorts. The second factor is, I believe, not always fully appreciated in research based on net migration figures. Namely, as the proportion of the population living in the various subareas changes (in this case, the proportion of adult blacks living in the South declines radically while it rises elsewhere), the net migration rates will change even if the propensity towards out-migration among a given subset of blacks living in the South remains unaltered over time and the propensity of blacks in the non-South to move to that region likewise remains unaltered. Comparisons between net migration rates, whether it be over time or between educational levels at the same time, will be deeply affected by differences in the numbers of blacks living in each subarea of the nation. This causes little difficulty when analyzing the early decades because the population resides overwhelmingly in the South, but it makes it impossible to infer much about the net migration patterns in the recent decades because a sizable proportion of blacks live in the North. There is, of course, no difficulty in using the methods described earlier to determine the number and the direction of migration between the regions by age, sex, and education; the problem is in interpreting the rates of migration. Rather than sidetrack the substantive concerns any further, the methodological problems in interpreting net migration rates will be discussed in greater detail at the end of this chapter.

CONTRADICTORY INFLUENCES

Even in decades when the minimally educated in each age group were less likely to migrate, for example, the World War I period, the proportion illiterate living in the South was so much greater than in the North and West that the attainment levels in the North would have been lowered anyway. The concentration of out-migration in the younger adult ages was a key factor in minimizing the difference between the actual educational level of adult blacks in the North and that which would have occurred without migration. Although the migrants were more often illiterate than blacks of the same age already living in the North, this was counterbalanced by the fact that migration was most frequent among younger blacks who were still better educated than the average of all adult blacks living in the North.

Table 5.3 should help make these points clearer. The reader will observe that illiteracy for a given age and sex is in most cases somewhat more frequent in the North and West than what would be expected in the absence of any migration. Among young adult men, for example, the actual and expected percentage illiterate in 1920 was 4.2 and 3.1, respectively. Yet the reader will recall that the overall percentage illiterate in 1920 for all black adults in the North was slightly lower than what would have been generated without any migration. The answer lies in the fact that so much of the net migration was concentrated in the younger ages. There were about 280,000 more blacks 25 years of age and older living in the North and West in 1920 than would have occurred without migration. If one compares the actual and expected numbers for different ages shown in Table 5.3, this growth is clearly concentrated in the younger ages. There were nearly 100,000 more men and about 80,000 more women in the 25–34 year bracket because of migration during the preceding decade. Hence, although the proportion illiterate in these ages was somewhat more than would have otherwise occurred, the net effect was to lower overall illiteracy, the reason for this being that these young adult blacks were still far less illiterate than the older blacks who were already living in the North and West.

The differences each year between the actual attainment figures and the educational levels expected in the absence of migration can be broken into two components: that due to the difference in age and sex

TABLE 5.3

Actual and Expected Composition and Percentage of Blacks Illiterate in the North and West, Grouped by Age and Sex, 1920

	Male				Female			
	Actual		Expected		Actual		Expected	
Age	Number	Percentage illiterate	Number	Percentage illiterate	Number	Percentage illiterate	Number	Percentage illiterate
25–34	174,854	4.2	81,056	3.1	167,223	3.2	86,800	2.5
35–44	155,514	6.0	110,621	5.0	130,554	5.8	100,738	4.9
45–54	100,537	10.3	93,749	9.4	72,029	12.5	59,918	11.4
55–64	37,767	17.6	34,125	17.6	31,932	24.9	26,806	23.9
65+	23,762	33.5	21,866	33.4	23,821	43.8	21,230	45.1

composition between the actual adult black population residing in the North and what would have occurred without migration; and the component reflecting educational differences between the actual and expected populations within each age- and sex-specific category. Turning first to the illiteracy rates listed in Table 5.4 and using the Kitagawa components method of standardization (Kitagawa, 1955), one can see that in each year the gap found is always less than what would be generated solely on the basis of the age- and sex-specific illiteracy gaps between the actual and the expected population of northern residents. In other words, illiteracy would have been higher each period and would have been altered more by migration if the age and sex composition of the new migrants had been the same as it was for blacks already living in the North. In 1900, for example, the difference between the actual and the expected percentage illiterate was 5.2; it would have been 6.6% if only differences in age- and sex-specific rates had been considered (by averaging the standard composition between the actual and the expected distributions). Similarly, the differences would have been nearly 1% in 1910 and 1920 rather than —.3 and —.5% in those years. The composition effect is negative in all instances in Table 5.4, thus indicating the pull towards lower illiteracy that occurred because the migrants were concentrated in the ages with less illiteracy.

The result for the post-World War II period (shown in the bottom panel of Table 5.4) is more complicated because numerous educational categories are considered, but basically the same pattern exists. Differences in age and sex composition between the adult black population found in the North in each decade and the distribution expected in the absence of migration are in the direction of generating relatively more highly educated blacks in the North. Witness the negative values in the lower educational categories and the positive values elsewhere. The rate effects are much larger than the compositional effects in most instances, meaning that the gaps between actual and expected are largely due to the differences in illiteracy rates within a given age- and sex-specific category. The overall pattern is rather complex, but it shows that the rates within a given category tend to pull down the northern educational levels, whereas the opposite pull is exerted because of the concentration of migration in the younger adult age groups.

SUMMARY

The question considered in this study is a simple but important one: Was the position of blacks in the North and West undermined by the

TABLE 5.4

Components of the Differences Between Actual and Expected Black Education in the North and West, 1900–1970

Percentage illiterate	Year			
	1900	1910	1920	1930
Actual minus expected	5.2	−.3	−.5	.3
Rate effect	6.6	.9	.8	1.1
Composition effect	−1.4	−1.2	−1.3	−.8

Years completed	1950			1960			1970		
	Actual minus expected	Rate effect	Composition effect	Actual minus expected	Rate effect	Composition effect	Actual minus expected	Rate effect	Composition effect
Elementary									
0–4	.02609	.03654	−.01045	.01879	.02090	−.00210	.00847	.00880	−.00033
5–8	−.01164	−.01061	−.00103	.01381	.01485	−.00104	−.00270	−.00165	−.00106
High School									
1–3	−.00659	−.01287	.00628	−.01118	−.01246	.00128	−.01194	−.01222	.00028
4	−.00319	−.00692	.00373	−.02048	−.02183	.00135	.00610	.00527	.00083
College									
1–3	−.00176	−.00284	.00108	.00108	.00077	.00031	−.00066	−.00083	.00017
4+	−.00292	−.00330	.00038	−.00202	−.00223	.00020	.00074	.00063	.00011

135

massive out-migration from the South through the years as well as by
the numerically important flow in the opposite direction? In particular,
did this great migration stream bring blacks to the North and West
whose potential did not compare with those already there as well as
generate greater white hostility and resistance to blacks generally?
(Note that the changes in black–white relations caused simply by the
growing number of blacks in the North is a separate question that is not
addressed here.) The educational characteristics of adult blacks provides
an indicator that was probably not greatly altered after migration to the
North, and, hence, unlike employment or occupation, is largely a fixed
attribute. Assuming that the CSRs accurately portray the life chances of
various segments of the northern black population, analysis of the
educational composition of adult blacks in the North and West with
what would have occurred if there had been no migration into or out of
the South indicates that net migration had only a moderate impact on
the educational distribution of blacks in the North. In most instances it
lowered this distribution, but not severely. Hence, based on the data
available here, it is extremely unlikely that any deterioration in the position of blacks in the North could be attributed to the changing quality of
the black migration stream. Although gains in the educational level of
black adults in the North was slowed down slightly in many decades
because of migration, the upward thrust was still considerable in each
period because of mortality among the older and less educated blacks,
coupled with the addition of new and more educated cohorts reaching
adulthood. In short, the new migrants had a minimal impact.

NET MIGRATION RATES

An unanticipated result of this study is recognition of certain limitations in the interpretation of net migration rates that are not commonly
noted in the literature. This was particularly the case when the complicated pattern of net migration rates for each specific educational category
was considered for 1950 and later decades. The author began to recognize that these rates were reflecting not merely differences in the propensity for persons of a given age, sex, and educational level to leave
and enter the North and West but were also reflecting the simple number
of blacks residing in each subarea. In other words, if the propensity
towards out-migration remains unaltered among blacks who live in the
South and have a given set of characteristics and if, likewise, the propensity among blacks outside of the South to move to the South is

fixed over time, the observed net migration rate will change as the relative numbers of blacks in the subareas change. Accordingly, one's inferences about the nature and the causes of changes in net migration rates over time as well as differences between educational catgories at the same time can easily be affected by differences in the numbers of blacks living in each subarea of the nation.

The hypothetical case shown in Table 5.5 should make these points clear. It is assumed that 20% of blacks of a given age, sex, and educational class initially living in the South leave during the decade (for simplicity's sake, mortality after migration is ignored). It is also assumed that 10% of non-South residents go to the South during the same period. Note that migration into the South is here constructed in terms of the population exposed to the risk of migrating, that is, the population initially living in the non-South. This is radically different from the conventional in-migration rate based on the population leaving an area divided by the population living in the area of destination. The ramifications of using this alternative way of thinking about in-migration to an area are enormous, as we shall see. In Shryock's (1964:33–34) terminology, this is a "partial out-movement rate." Going further, the four hypothetical situations shown in Table 5.5 all assume that there are 100 expected survivors among those initially living in the South, but there are progressively larger numbers of blacks living in the North and West: First 10 survivors are expected, then 50, then 100, and, finally, 200.

Observe how the net migration rate from the South (bottom line of Table 5.5) varies even though the gross migration rates remain unchanged. First, when there are only 10 expected survivors in the North, gross and net migration rates from the South are virtually identical, —.20 and —.19, respectively, because the number of blacks living in the North is so small that it has little effect on the net migration rate. As a general rule, in situations where the population is very large in one area and relatively small in another, the net migration rate will tend to be fairly similar to the gross rate found in the area with most of the population. (Observe, however, that the in-migration rate is conceived of in terms of the population not living in the area of destination rather than as a proportion of the population living in the area of destination.) We see in Table 5.5 that increases solely in the relative number of northern blacks affects the net migration rate and, of course, makes it less representative of the gross rate in the South. Thus, the net migration rate is zero when there are twice as many blacks in the North as there are in the South. In effect, the net migration rate between Area A and Area B

TABLE 5.5
Influence of Population Composition on the Net Migration Rate Obtained When the Gross Migration Rates Are Constant

Residents of the South (20% out-migration)

Expected survivors	100			
Remaining in the South	80			
Going to North and West	20			
Gross out-migration rate	$\dfrac{80-100}{100} = -.20$			

Residents of the North (10% out-migration)

Expected survivors	10	50	100	200
Remaining in the North	9	45	90	180
Going to South	1	5	10	20
Gross out-migration rate	$\dfrac{9-10}{10} = -.10$	$\dfrac{45-50}{50} = -.10$	$\dfrac{90-100}{100} = -.10$	$\dfrac{180-200}{200} = -.10$
Net migration rate from South	$\dfrac{80-100+1}{100} = -.19$	$\dfrac{80-100+5}{100} = -.10$	$\dfrac{80-100+10}{100} = -.10$	$\dfrac{80-100+20}{100} = 0$

is nothing more than the gross migration rates between the two areas weighted by the relative number of survivors expected in the areas.

Since net migration is determined by the number of persons initially living in each area, coupled with their gross migration rates, an interpretation of net migration rates that ignores the effect of the number living in each area will lead to what might be called the "compositional fallacy." Early in this century, when almost all blacks were living in the South, net migration rates were useful tools for describing the movement between the regions, since they were almost certain to reflect events within the South itself. Indeed, unless either an extraordinarily large proportion of blacks living in the North moved back to the South or blacks in the North had exceptionally better chances of survival, the net migration rate was very similar to the gross out-migration rate from the South because the compositional situation was very much like the first case discussed from Table 5.5, where the population was concentrated in one region. But later in this century, as the relative number of blacks living in the North and West increased considerably, the net migration rate has a different meaning and it is no longer a simple task to interpret because the net rate reflects the gross rates for each region weighted by the numbers residing there. Interpretation is particularly difficult when looking at net out-migration rates over time or for different educational categories because the relative number in each region or category changes. In 1940, for example, 48% of black men 45–54 with 4 or more years of college lived in the North and West, whereas 16% of those with no schooling lived in these regions. The net migration rate for the highly educated will be roughly an average of the southern and non-southern gross migration streams, but the net migration rate for the less educated will largely be a function of the gross migration rate among the southerners.

To be sure, the net migration rate does indicate the direction and relative magnitude of the net movement between areas. But it is also clear that the interpretation of such rates is ambiguous when the relative numbers change over time or if subgroups differ in their initial spatial distribution. Indeed, I suspect that some apparent social changes are partially artifacts generated by this compositional fallacy. As Table 5.5 suggests, the net migration rate may not only change over time but may also even change signs as the relative numbers in each region shift, *even if the gross rates remain unchanged.* For example, the current net movement of blacks from North to South or of urban dwellers to non-metropolitan areas may reflect in part the shifts that would occur if the gross rates remain more or less constant but the composition shifts. This is not to say that the observed changes are simply compositional fallacies, but clearly their magnitude and the point at which they are "discovered" are both deeply affected by the compositional shifts (for a fuller exposition, see Lieberson, unpublished manuscript).

REFERENCES

Coale, Ansley J., and Norfleet W. Rives, Jr.
  1973   "A statistical reconstruction of the black population of the United States, 1880–1970: Estimates of true numbers by age and sex, birth rates, and total fertility." *Population Index* 39:3–36.
Duncan, Otis Dudley, and Beverly Duncan
  1957   *The Negro Population of Chicago.* Chicago, Illinois: University of Chicago Press.
Farley, Reynolds
  1970   *Growth of the Black Population.* Chicago, Illinois: Markham Publishing Company.
Folger, John K., and Charles B. Nam
  1967   *Education of the American Population.* Washington, D.C.: U.S. Government Printing Office.
Freedman, Ronald
  1950   *Recent Migration to Chicago.* Chicago, Illinois: University of Chicago Press.
Hamilton, C. Horace
  1959   "Educational selectivity of net migration from the South." *Social Forces* 38:33–42.
  1965   "Practical and mathematical considerations in the formulation and selection of migration rates." *Demography* 2:429–443.
  1966   "Effect of census errors on the measurement of net migration." *Demography* 3:393–415.
Kitagawa, Evelyn M.
  1955   "Components of a difference between two rates." *Journal of the American Statistical Association* 50:1168–1194.
Kitagawa, Evelyn M., and Philip M. Hauser
  1973   *Differential Mortality in the United States: A Study in Socioeconomic Epidemiology.* Cambridge, Massachusetts: Harvard University Press.
Lieberson, Stanley
  1973   "Generational differences among Blacks in the North." *American Journal of Sociology* 79:550–565.
  1975   "Rank–sum comparisons between groups." In David R. Heise (ed.), *Sociological Methodology: 1976.* San Francisco, California: Jossey-Bass.
  1978   "A reconsideration of the income differences found between migrants and northern-born blacks." *American Journal of Sociology* 83:940–966.
Lieberson, Stanley, and Christy A. Wilkinson
  1976   "A comparison between northern and southern blacks residing in the North." *Demography* 13:199–224.

Parsons, Carole W. (ed.)
  1972   *America's Uncounted People.* Washington, D.C.: U.S. Government
          Printing Office.
Shryock, Henry S.
  1964   *Population Mobility within the United States.* Chicago, Illinois:
          Community and Family Study Center.
Shryock, Henry S., and Jacob S. Siegel and Associates
  1971   *The Methods and Materials of Demography.* Washington, D.C.:
          U.S. Government Printing Office.
Spear, Allan H.
  1967   *Black Chicago: The Making of a Negro Ghetto, 1890–1920.* Chicago,
          Illinois: University of Chicago Press.
Taeuber, Karl E., and Alma F. Taeuber
  1965a   *Negroes in Cities.* Chicago, Illinois: Aldine Publishing Company.
  1965b   "The changing character of Negro migration." *American Journal of
          Sociology* 70:429–441.
U.S. Bureau of the Census
  1933   Census of Population, 1930, Volume II, General Report, Statistics by
          Subjects. Washington, D.C.: U.S. Government Printing Office.

6

Patterns of Marital Instability among Mexican Americans, Blacks, and Anglos[1]

W. PARKER FRISBIE
FRANK D. BEAN
ISAAC W. EBERSTEIN

The study of marital instability has long attracted the interest of social scientists (Bumpass and Sweet, 1972; Burgess and Cottrell, 1939; Carter and Glick, 1966; Duberman, 1974; Farley and Hermalin, 1971; Udry, 1966b), in part because marital disruption has been found to have both negative and positive consequences for both persons and collectivities. For example, where levels of family disorganization are high within a group, chances for economic advancement of the group as a whole seem to be diminished (Moynihan, 1965; Uhlenberg, 1972a:119–128). It has also been reported that marital instability has adverse consequences for social and economic well-being (Herzog and Sudia, 1968:

[1] The authors gratefully acknowledge the support for this research provided by the National Institute of Child Health and Human Development, Grant No. RO1 HD09908.

144   W. Parker Frisbie, Frank D. Bean, and Isaac W. Eberstein

117–182; Uhlenberg, 1972a)[2] and that it negatively affects the emotional quality of the lives of individuals (Campbell, 1975:37–43). Obstacles to the socioeconomic achievement of children also seem to be associated with marital dissolution (Duncan and Duncan, 1969:273–385; Uhlenberg, 1972a,b), perhaps because the disruption of marriage places family members in precarious economic positions and/or because it causes discontinuities in socialization processes.[3] Such conclusions about the deleterious effects of marital instability take on added significance when one considers that rates of family disruption in the United States have increased to the point where they are among the highest in the world (Duberman, 1974; Goode, 1970; Yaukey, 1973).

On the other hand, marital dissolution may often be a positive adaptation in the face of unpleasant alternatives (Billingsley, 1968). For example, Goode (1970:85) adduces evidence that children whose parents do "*not* divorce, but who [have] remained together in disharmony, are more likely to have subsequent histories of personal difficulties than children of divorced parents...." Similar findings are forthcoming from Nye (1957) and Udry (1966b). The latter asserts that "adolescents from broken homes showed *less* psychosomatic illness, *less* delinquent behavior, and *better* adjustment to parents than the adolescents from intact but unhappy homes" (Udry, 1966b:517). Furthermore, Burchinal (1964:44–51) reports no negative effect of divorce on adjustment of adolescents when controls for socioeconomic status are applied (see also Udry, 1966b:Chap. 18).

Whatever the consequences of marital disruption, they may be differentially distributed among various social groups, depending upon the distribution among the groups both of marital patterns and of factors known to affect their occurrence. Determinants of marital patterns may also vary by racial or ethnic group. The present research formulates and tests hypotheses about marital instability among Mexican Americans, blacks, and Anglos, giving particular attention to differences among the groups in relationships between marital instability and certain independent variables. This represents, to our knowledge, one of the few large-scale efforts to study comparatively patterns of marital instability among more than two social groups, as well as the only study to undertake such an inquiry within a framework allowing for the explicit statistical control of the factors examined.

[2] But this is by no means true in every case (cf. Nye, 1968:434–440).

[3] There are, of course, numerous other demographic reasons for interest in this subject, not the least of which is the fact that fertility varies inversely with marital instability (e.g., see Kiser and Frank, 1967:427–449).

FACTORS INFLUENCING MARITAL INSTABILITY

Several factors are known to affect marital instability. One of the most important is age at first marriage (Bumpass and Sweet, 1972; Burgess and Cottrell, 1939; Glick, 1957; Glick and Norton, 1971; Nye and Berardo, 1973). The relationship is invariably inverse and has usually been explained in terms of higher education being associated with later age at marriage (Udry, 1966a,b). This means that higher levels of occupation and income will also tend to be associated with later age at marriage (Blau and Duncan, 1967; Featherman, 1971). Couples with greater social and financial resources at their disposal have generally been thought to be less likely to dissolve their marriages (Goode, 1964). The age of marriage relationship may be due to other factors as well, such as "(1) the impact on young marriages of the struggle for independence from the family of orientation, (2) the effect of subsequent changes in young adult role perceptions . . . [Bumpass and Sweet, 1972: 755]," and (3) the possibility that individuals who marry at younger ages may be less emotionally mature (Blood, 1962). Whatever the case, controls for age at first marriage greatly weaken the relationship between education and marital instability (Cutright, 1971) and virtually eliminate the "Glick effect" [4] (cf. Bauman, 1967; Bumpass and Sweet, 1972:757; Glick, 1957:154). If nothing else, this raises the possibility that racial–ethnic group differences in marital instability may in part reflect differences in age at marriage.

Apart from their association with age at marriage, education, occupational status, and income are also important variables in considering racial–ethnic differences in marital dissolution. Educational level (Duberman, 1974; Glick, 1957; Glick and Norton, 1971; Hicks and Platt, 1970; Monahan, 1962; Udry, 1966a, 1967) and occupational status (Hicks and Platt, 1970; Kephart, 1966; Monahan, 1955, 1962; Udry, 1966a) are both inversely related to marital instability, and the interpretation of their consequences for marital solidarity is usually made in terms of their effects on income (Blau and Duncan, 1967), which is inversely related to marital dissolution (Udry, 1966a, 1967). When controls for income are introduced, neither education nor occupation is found to have a strong relationship with marital instability (Cutright, 1971).

The divergent positions of Anglos, blacks, and Mexican Americans

---

[4] The "Glick effect" is the finding that "dropouts" from high school or college are characterized by higher degrees of marital instability than those who complete these schooling threshholds. This implies that the factors that "affect . . . persistence in education also affect . . . persistence in marriage [Glick, 1957:154]."

with respect to these variables have implications for intergroup patterns of marital instability. In median years of school completed, "Mexican Americans in 1960 fell far short of the performance not only of Anglos but also of nonwhites in general [Grebler et al., 1970:143]." In 1970, this situation is unchanged, as is shown by the percentage over age 25 who have completed 4 or more years of high school: Anglos, 58.6%; blacks, 34.7%; and Mexican Americans, 26.3% (Uhlenberg, 1972b:50). In 1970, the black–Mexican-American differential in the percentage below the low-income level was .4 points (29.8 and 29.4%, respectively). Both figures are much larger than the corresponding 11.3% for Anglos (Uhlenberg, 1972b:50). Thus, on the basis of educational performance if not income levels, Mexican Americans might be expected to be characterized by levels of marital instability higher than those of both blacks and Anglos and not lower, as has been previously found (Eberstein and Frisbie, 1976; Frisbie et al., 1977).

Another factor, racism, is often mentioned in concert with low socioeconomic standing to explain higher levels of black marital instability (Frazier, 1939; Moynihan, 1965). "The existence of large numbers of broken Negro families is fully explained by contemporaneous poverty and discrimination [Ryan, 1971:70]." In the case of Mexican Americans, however, discrimination has been argued to be less virulent than that directed against blacks (cf. Fogel, 1965; Howard, 1970:1–9; Murguía, 1975:47–54; Pinkney, 1969), so that in the Southwest the probability of converting educational attainment to occupational and income gains may be greater for Mexican Americans than for blacks (cf. Frisbie and Neidert, 1977). Nevertheless, it is questionable that discrimination against Mexican Americans has been so much less severe that the differential in marital instability between the two minority groups can be attributed to this factor alone. Certainly, other factors operate as well, as is indicated by the finding that marital instability is less prevalent among Mexican Americans than among Anglos (Eberstein and Frisbie, 1976; Frisbie et al., 1977).

ALTERNATIVE HYPOTHESES

Two basic themes in the literature suggest explanations of differential levels of racial–ethnic group marital instability. One derives from certain characterizations of black and Mexican American family life. For example, blacks in the United States have often been depicted as having a form of family organization that, although originating in the effects of slavery and of historical socioeconomic deprivation, is seen as self-perpetuating (Moynihan, 1965). In this view, the structure of black families is seen as fragmented, and the position of the male vis-à-vis the female is thought to be weak relative to the normative expectations of society (Blood and Wolfe, 1960:34–35; Frazier, 1939; Moynihan, 1965). In sharp contradistinction, Mexican Americans have often been seen as possessing a solidaristic family structure characterized by traditionalistic, patriarchal, and familistic emphases, with the position of the male being strong (Madsen, 1964; Murillo, 1971; Rubel, 1966). For convenience of discussion, we term these ideas, which are at least partially stereotypes, "family structural perspectives." On the basis of presumed variations in strength of family solidarity, they imply that marital instability will be greatest among blacks, followed in descending order by Anglos and Mexican Americans.

These perspectives have been sharply questioned (Casavantes, 1971; Feagin, 1968; Grebler et al., 1970; Hill, 1972; Rainwater and Yancey, 1972; Ryan, 1965), largely on the grounds that the patterns observed are either class-specific or are generally attributable to variations in socioeconomic status. In this alternative view, cultural or ethnic factors are not seen as important underlying bases of black and Mexican American family systems. Rather, if black family ties are weak and Mexican American family ties are strong, it is because of current socioeconomic conditions. In short, levels of marital instability, whether relatively high or low, are a result of socioeconomic factors. Hence, controls for socioeconomic variables should wash out or, more realistically, reduce instability differences to negligible magnitudes. This perspective, then, which might be termed a "socioeconomic perspective," would predict no significant differences in family instability among the three groups after the introduction of appropriate controls.

A third possibility may also be derived by considering that the forces suggested by the family structural perspective may affect the influence of age at marriage and education. For example, if certain factors, including "familism" (Bean et al., 1977; Farris and Glenn, 1976) and Catholicism (Alvírez, 1973), support intact families among Mexican Americans, then it is anticipated that the effects of age at marriage and socioeconomic status on marital instability will be of lesser magnitude among Mexican Americans than among Anglos and (especially) blacks. To illustrate, if Mexican American families caught in untenable economic positions are more able than are Anglo or black families to call upon and receive support from kin, the impact of socioeconomic variables on family stability may be mitigated. Some increase in the viability of marriages is also to be expected where economic conditions are favorable. Thus, whereas marriages of Mexican Americans with lower levels of socioeconomic status may tend to be less stable than those of more affluent Mexican Americans, they are expected to be more stable than the marriages of poor Anglos or blacks. A similar argument may be advanced for relationships involving age at marriage. In short, this view would predict an interaction effect on marital instability between racial–ethnic group membership and age at marriage and socioeconomic status.

DATA

The data utilized in this research were obtained from the 1970 1/100 (5%) Public Use Samples for the five southwestern states—Arizona, California, Colorado, New Mexico, and Texas. The entire Mexican American, black, and Anglo populations of ever-married women aged 25–64 listed in the Public Use Samples were included. Blacks were identified as "Negroes" of non-Spanish surname and non-Spanish origin, Mexican Americans as whites who self-identified as of Mexican origin (cf. Hernandez et al., 1973), and Anglos as whites of non-Spanish surname and non-Spanish (including non-Mexican) origin. The sample sizes are 6601, 5580, and 59,469 for the Mexican, black, and Anglo groups, respectively.

Analysis is limited to the Southwest for two reasons. The vast majority of Mexican Americans reside in the southwestern states (Bradshaw and Bean, 1973; Grebler et al., 1970; U.S. Bureau of the Census, 1973:1), and there are sufficient differences in the socioeconomic milieu of the Southwest to distinguish it from the rest of the country (Browning et al., 1973). More important, divorce rates are higher in western sections (including the Southwest) than in other areas of the nation (cf. Kephart, 1966; Landis, 1955; U.S. Department of HEW, 1973:32; Weed, 1974). Thus, "a comparison of the relative frequency of marital instability with a national sample of other racial or ethnic groups would artificially inflate instability levels of Mexican Americans relative to the others [Eberstein and Frisbie, 1976:612]."

Marital instability is operationalized using information on the number of times married combined with indicators of current marital status. This resulted in the seven marital status categories utilized in 1970: (1) spouse present, married once; (2) spouse present, married more than once, first marriage ended due to death of spouse; (3) spouse present, married more than once, first marriage ended for reasons other than death of spouse; (4) widowed; (5) divorced; (6) separated, including deserted; and (7) spouse absent for other reasons. Marital instability is measured by summing the proportions of persons in categories three, five, and six. We recognize that, even after separating the remarried widowed from the remarried divorced, some unknown degree of measurement error remains because a small number of persons will have married more than twice, and some fraction of these will have had their first marriage dissolved by the death of their spouse and later marriage(s) terminated by divorce or separation. However, the number of persons marrying three or more times comprises so small a proportion of the ever-married population that any distortion should be minimal (Eberstein and Frisbie, 1976:612). The separated category "includes persons deserted or living apart because of marital discord, as well as legally separated persons [U.S. Bureau of the Census, 1972:147]," and the married with spouse absent for other reasons category refers to:

> Married persons whose spouse was not enumerated as a member of the same household, *excluding separated*. [It also] includes those whose spouse was employed and living away from home, whose spouse was absent in the Armed Forces, or was an inmate of an institution, all married persons living in group-quarters, and all other married persons whose place of residence was not the same as that of their spouse [U.S. Bureau of the Census, 1972:147; emphasis added].

This latter group does not necessarily include marriages characterized by marital discord. Hence, we do not combine it with the divorced and separated because to do so might well lead to an erroneously high estimate of marital instability.

It should be noted that census data on prevalence of marital instability are less than ideal as an indicator of the incidence of marital disruption. Sweet (Chapter 10 of this volume) puts the matter concisely: "Prevalence measures confound differences in marital disruption, remarriage rates, age at marriage distribution, and age structure differences in a single measure." Although acknowledging the cogency of this comment, we note that most of the difficulties mentioned do not apply to the present analysis. First, the 1970 enumeration allows, for the first time, a distinction to be made between remarried widows and remarried divorcees based on responses to the question of whether or not the first marriage was broken by divorce or by death of spouse. Second, both age at first marriage and current age are specifically taken into account. Of course, inaccuracy of reporting is a problem in the census as in all surveys that depend on the memory and veracity of respondents, and it would be useful to have full marital histories in order to trace changes over time. Despite these difficulties, the benefits to be derived from the information available in the census would seem to far outweigh the disadvantages. In fact, census records represent *the only large-scale data set* that permits the identification and comparative analysis of marital instability among Mexican Americans.

Selection of independent variables was guided by the considerations noted above, the availability of data, and concern for the temporal sequence of the variables. Thus, educational level will be employed as the primary indicator of socioeconomic position, since, unlike income and occupation, education can for the most part be considered prior to marriage (cf. Davis and Bumpass, 1976). The sample is limited to women because of sex differences in remarriage and mortality (Glick, 1957) that result in marital instability being more prevalent among women than among men. The age group 25–64 is used so as to preclude illogical combinations of categories of current age and age at first marriage. The analysis is based on age at first marriage, education, and ethnicity-specific standardized (via direct standardization, see Shryock *et al.*, 1976) marital instability rates. Age at first marriage is dichotomized into the categories 14–19 and 20+, and education is partitioned into the categories 0–8, 9–11, and 12+ years of education completed.[5]

Variable	Category	β *
Age at first marriage	14–17	11.74
	18–19	4.25
	20–21	.56
	22–24	− 5.40
	25+	− 8.89
Education	0–7	− 3.31
	8	.63
	9–11	2.75
	12	− .72
	13+	.89
Current age	25–34	− 5.02
	35–44	.94
	45–54	3.46
	55–64	1.16

[5] Initially, all three independent variables (as well as ethnicity) were included in the analysis and were categorized in a more detailed fashion. However, after inspection of the main effects of these variables, it was decided that collapsing the detailed categories and including direct standardization for age would result in no loss of information and would sharpen the presentation. The main effects of each category of these variables on the odds of marital instability, on which this decision was based, are presented in standard form. If β * ≥ 1.65, the significance of the effect of that category is less than or equal to .05, using a one-tailed test.

METHOD

A major concern in choosing a technique for analysis is that dichotomous dependent variables (such as marital instability) create problems for which standard multiple regression analysis is not well suited. Central to conventional regression techniques are the assumptions of homoscedasticity (equal variances of Y for each value of X) and a normal distribution of Y in each population analyzed. With a dichotomous dependent variable, the latter assumption is violated. A dummy variable regression with these data may generate predicted proportions of marital instability outside the logical range of possibilities (e.g., less than 0 and over 1), as well as provide biased estimates of effect parameters. For these reasons, the analysis applies a log-linear technique specifically designed for the analysis of qualitative data (cf. Goodman, 1970, 1972).

The analytic technique has a more general application than will be utilized here. It may be used for analysis of sets of variables when one is seen as dependent, as in the present research, as well as for sets of variables in which none are conceptually dependent (Fienberg, 1977). The analysis focuses on fitting models to the data that presuppose different possible relationships among all variables in the table. In the present case, marital instability is analyzed as a dependent variable, since it is impossible to conceive of marital dissolution "causing" differences in racial–ethnic group membership, age at first marriage, or, for the most part, educational attainment.

The analysis begins with the input of cell frequencies from a crosstabulation of all the variables of interest. Next, a series of hypotheses are specified, which are fitted to the observed data, until a best-fitting (measured by a maximum likelihood χ^2 statistic) and parsimonious model is discerned (cf. Davis, 1974). The sequence is somewhat comparable to "backward elimination" in stepwise regression analysis where, from a saturated model, specific interaction terms are hypothesized to have no effect and a R^2 difference is used as a test of these hypotheses (Kerlinger and Pedhazur, 1973:389–390).

The specific form of the dependent variable in this type of analysis is an "odds-ratio" of one category of the dependent variable (i.e., marital instability) relative to another (i.e., marital stability), examined at every level of the other variables in a cross-classification (cf. Davis, 1974; Goodman, 1972:30–31). Main and interaction effects for the independent variables may be calculated so as to yield estimates of parameters analogous to conventional regression coefficients, although the model is stated in multiplicative rather than in additive form. These parameter estimates

(γ) may be converted to additive form through a natural logarithmic transformation (ln $\gamma = \beta$). The statistical significance of the effect of each category of the independent variables on the odds of falling in certain categories of the dependent variable may then be ascertained through the conversion of each β to standard form ($\beta^* = \beta/SE\beta$) and the use of a table of areas under the normal curve (Goodman, 1972:Fn. 17).

FINDINGS

The data used in this analysis are shown in Table 6.1 along with both the percentage of women in each row with a history of marital dissolu-

TABLE 6.1

Percentage Distribution of Ever-Married Women Aged 25–64 by Marital Status, Education, Age at First Marriage, and Ethnicity: 1970 [a]

Ethnicity	Education	Age at first marriage	Marital status Unstable (N)	Stable (N)	Unstable (%)	Odds of instability
Mexican American	0–7	14–19	334	1,173	22.16	.28
		20+	241	1,355	15.10	.18
	8–11	14–19	262	759	25.66	.35
		20+	185	744	19.91	.25
	12+	14–19	119	373	24.19	.32
		20+	179	877	16.95	.20
Anglo	0–7	14–19	376	979	27.75	.38
		20+	206	812	20.24	.25
	8–11	14–19	3,144	5,873	34.87	.54
		20+	1,241	4,528	21.51	.27
	12+	14–19	4,606	10,741	30.01	.43
		20+	4,705	22,258	17.45	.21
Black	0–7	14–19	170	278	37.95	.61
		20+	131	275	32.27	.48
	8–11	14–19	544	641	45.91	.85
		20+	338	570	37.22	.59
	12+	14–19	480	577	45.41	.83
		20+	481	1,095	30.52	.44

Source: U.S. Bureau of the Census. 1970 1/100 5% Public Use Samples: Southwest.

[a] Cell frequencies for Mexican Americans and blacks are standardized to the Anglo age distribution within categories of education and age at first marriage.

tion and the odds of marital disruption. A cursory inspection indicates, first, that women who married for the first time after age 19 are, without exception, characterized by a lower relative frequency of marital instability than those who married between the ages of 14 and 19. Second, the Glick effect is observable in that, in general, women with 8–11 years of schooling have a greater relative frequency of marital disruption than comparable women with other, higher levels of education. Among both Mexican American and black women who married for the first time between the ages of 14–19, however, marital instability among those not completing high school but finishing the eighth grade is about the same as for those who completed 12 or more years of school. A somewhat different situation is indicated for Anglos who first married *after* age 19 in that those who completed between the eighth and the eleventh grades evidence about the same level of marital instability as do those women who have not completed any grade beyond the seventh.

A third observation from Table 6.1 is that, among those with later age at marriage, Mexican American women with at least a high school education show the same odds of marital instability as do comparable Anglo women. Also, Mexican American women marrying after age 20 and with 8–11 years of education have a level of marital instability about 1.6 percentage points less than comparable Anglos. However, in every other instance Mexican American women show a level of marital instability at least 5 percentage points less than Anglos. Black women consistently exhibit a relative frequency of marital instability that is at least 10 percentage points *higher* than that among Anglos.

Thus, rough inspection of the data suggests support for the first hypothesis but rejection of the second. However, even with a table composed of only 18 rows, it becomes difficult to go beyond such general impressions. Although the main effects of these variables on marital instability seem to appear in the data, the estimation of their relative magnitude, together with that of possible interaction effects, requires further analysis.

The log-linear models fitted to the data in Table 6.1 are presented in Table 6.2, along with the effects on marital instability that they include. As is illustrated in the table, model H_6 is the most parsimonious model that minimally fits the data (the errors in prediction from this model are significant at about the 2% level). Model H_3, however, which includes an education by age at first marriage interaction and is, thus, less parsimonious than H_6, fits the data better, as is indicated by the probability level associated with the errors in prediction. In order to choose between these models, several points were considered. First, the decrement of errors of prediction associated with inclusion of the age at

TABLE 6.2

Some Hypothetical Models Pertaining to the Odds of Marital Instability Fitted to the Data in Table 6.1

Fitted marginals[a]		df	x^2	p	γ parameters in model
H_0	{ABCD}	0	0.00	—	$\gamma\gamma A\gamma B\gamma C\gamma AB\gamma AC\gamma BC\gamma ABC$
H_1	{ABC}{ABD}{ACD}{BCD}	4	8.88	.064	$\gamma\gamma A\gamma B\gamma C\gamma AB\gamma AC\gamma BC$
H_2	{ABC}{ACD}{BCD}	6	17.48	.008	$\gamma\gamma A\gamma B\gamma C\gamma AC\gamma BC$
H_3	{ABC}{ABD}{ACD}	8	13.92	.084	$\gamma\gamma A\gamma B\gamma C\gamma AB\gamma AC$
H_4	{ABC}{ABD}{BCD}	6	22.35	.001	$\gamma\gamma A\gamma B\gamma C\gamma AB\gamma BC$
H_5	{ABD}{ACD}{BCD}	6	40.76	.000	—
H_6	{ABC}{ACD}{BD}	10	21.04	.021	$\gamma\gamma A\gamma B\gamma C\gamma AC$
H_7	{ABC}{BCD}{AD}	8	44.11	.000	$\gamma\gamma A\gamma B\gamma C\gamma BC$
H_8	{ABC}{ABD}{CD}	10	30.84	.001	$\gamma\gamma A\gamma B\gamma C\gamma AB$
H_9	{ABC}{AD}{BD}{CD}	12	51.60	.000	$\gamma\gamma A\gamma B\gamma C$
H_{10}	{ABC}{AD}{BD}	14	594.63	.000	$\gamma\gamma A\gamma B$
H_{11}	{ABC}{AD}{CD}	14	195.02	.000	$\gamma\gamma A\gamma C$
H_{12}	{ABC}{BD}{CD}	13	1,340.48	.000	$\gamma\gamma B\gamma C$
H_{13}	{ABC}{AD}	16	778.64	.000	$\gamma\gamma A$
H_{14}	{ABC}{BD}	15	1,897.84	.000	$\gamma\gamma B$
H_{15}	{ABC}{CD}	15	1,704.23	.000	$\gamma\gamma C$
H_{16}	{ABC}{D}	17	2,313.78	.000	γ
H_{17}	None	35	148,074.95	.000	—

[a] A = Age at first marriage, B = Education, C = Ethnicity, and D = Marital status.

first marriage by education interaction is only marginally significant ($\chi^2\gamma_{AB} = 7.12$; $df = 2$; $.02 < p < .05$). Second, an examination of the pattern of deviations associated with this interaction (not shown) indicates that in no instance is any single deviation large enough to be considered significant at the 5% level (two-tailed test). Given the large sample size, the overall significance of this parameter is obviously marginal at best. Third, a comparison of the magnitude and direction of the parameters included in both models (not shown) indicates only trivial differences between them. Fourth, the interaction of age at first marriage and education is not directly relevant to any of the three alternative hypotheses of interest. For these reasons, only the parameters of model H_6 will be discussed here. These parameters are shown in Table 6.3 (in multiplicative, additive, and standardized form) and will be examined in relation to the three alternative hypotheses noted earlier.[6]

---

[6] Because the age at first marriage by ethnicity interaction (γ^{AC}) is included in both models H_3 and H_6 and since the exclusion of all interactions by ethnicity results in significant errors of prediction [(H_8); (H_9)], the difference between models H_3 and $H_{6'}$ occasioned by the inclusion or exclusion of the age at marriage by education interaction (γ^{AB}), is not relevant to a test of the three alternative hypotheses.

Also, these models are summarized in Table 6.4 in a manner usually seen in analysis of variance presentations. This table is calculated from the information in Table 6.2 and is included only to relate more closely the log-linear results to the kind of statistics associated with other, more widely recognized techniques.

Our first hypothesis was derived on the basis of what we have called the "family structural" view of Mexican American and black families. We have interpreted this perspective to mean that such variables as education and age at first marriage are related to marital instability in the same way (the relationship takes the same form) within all three groups but that differences in marital instability among them are due to the properties of family structure of each group (such as the allegedly fragmented family structure among blacks and a presumed familistic structure among Mexican Americans). We have also interpreted this view to imply that no interaction effects between age at first marriage and ethnicity or between education and ethnicity will be necessary to fit the data in Table 6.1. All of the differences in the odds of marital instability between these groups are seen as due only to the main effects of racial–ethnic group membership. Although the ranking predicted by this hypothesis is found in the data, tests of H_8 and H_9 (Table 6.2)

TABLE 6.3

Effects of Independent Variables on the Odds of Marital Instability, Estimated by Model H_6 in Table 6.2

Variable [a]	β	γ	β * [b]
D	−.998	.368	−60.779
A	.260	1.297	15.814
B–1	−.102	.904	− 4.010
B–2	.164	1.177	7.554
B–3	−.062	.939	− 2.751
C–1	−.374	.687	−14.902
C–2	−.136	.872	− 6.909
C–3	.510	1.667	20.806
A (C–1)	−.056	.945	− 2.237
A (C–2)	.084	1.088	4.313
A (C–3)	−.028	.972	− 1.167

[a] A = Age at first marriage (1 = 14–19; 2 = 20+), B = Education (1 = 0–8; 2 = 9–11; 3 =12+), C = Ethnicity (1 = Mexican American; 2 = Anglo; 3 = black), and D = Marital instability.

[b] If β * $\geqslant$ 2.33, $p \leqslant .01$ for main effects (one-tailed test); if β * $\geqslant$ 1.95, $p \leqslant .05$ for interactions (two-tailed test).

TABLE 6.4

Analysis of the Variation in the Odds of Marital Instability in the Data in Table 6.1[a]

	Source[b]	df	x^2	p
1.	Total variation due to main effects of A, B, C, and interaction effects among these variables	17	$x^2(H_{16}) = 2313.78$	$p < .001$
1a.	Due to variation unexplained by main effects (H_9)	12	$x^2(H_9) = 51.60$	$p < .001$
1b.	Due to variation explained by main effects	5	$x^2(H_{16}) - x^2(H_9) = 2262.18$	$p < .001$
	Partition of (1a)			
2a.	Due to variation unexplained by γ^{AC} (H_6)	10	$x^2(H_6) = 21.04$	$p = .021$
2b.	Due to variation explained by γ^{AC}	2	$x^2(H_9) - x^2(H_6) = 30.56$	$p < .001$
	Partition of (2a)			
3a.	Due to variation unexplained by γ^{AB} (H_3)	8	$x^2(H_3) = 13.92$	$p = .084$
3b.	Due to variation explained by γ^{AB}	2	$x^2(H_6) - x^2(H_3) = 7.12$	$.02 < p < .05$
	Partition of (3a)			
4a.	Due to variation unexplained by γ^{BC} (H_1)	4	$x^2(H_1) = 8.88$	$p = .064$
4b.	Due to variation explained by γ^{BC}	4	$x^2(H_3) - x^2(H_1) = 5.04$	$.05 < p < .10$

[a] Based on Table 6.2.
[b] A = Age at first marriage, B = Education, and C = Ethnicity.

indicate that the main effects and/or interactions not involving ethnicity are not sufficient to fit the data.

Our second hypothesis was drawn from a critique of the conventional view of minority families. This hypothesis predicted that, if socioeconomic factors are indeed responsible for the different degrees of marital instability among blacks, Mexican Americans, and Anglos, then controls for these variables would eliminate observed differences in marital instability. That this hypothesis must be rejected in the present case is evident from the fact that ethnic differences in marital instability remain when education is controlled. Of course, the inclusion of socioeconomic data for husbands (particularly for first husbands) might change this conclusion. However, this information is available neither in the present data nor in any other data set that provides a large enough subsample of Mexican Americans to make the analysis of these three groups possible.[7] Hence, on the basis of the data and results available here, this perspective cannot be said to be supported.

The third hypothesis predicted that minority status per se would have some effect on marital instability in that education and age at first marriage would interact with ethnicity in their effects on marital instability. The effect of age at first marriage on marital instability does, in fact, vary by ethnicity, with this relationship being significantly stronger among Anglos than among either blacks or Mexican Americans. That is, early marriage increases the odds of marital disruption more among Anglos than it does among either minority group. This interaction is necessary to fit the data since, as a comparison of models H_3 and H_8 shows, omitting the interaction term is associated with a large increase in errors of prediction ($\chi^2 \gamma_{AC} = 16.92$; $df = 2$; $p < .001$).

The parameters in Table 6.3 offer the greatest support for the third hypothesis. The presence of the age at first marriage by ethnicity interaction is inconsistent with the first hypothesis, and the significantly different main effects for the three ethnic groups contradict the second hypothesis. However, the fact that an education by ethnicity interaction seems unnecessary to fit the data indicates only partial support for the third hypothesis. The observed interaction of age at first marriage and ethnicity distinguished Anglos from the other two groups, and the main effect of ethnicity indicates that the odds of marital dissolution are reduced among Mexican Americans and increased among blacks. Contrary to the predictions of the third hypothesis, however, age at marriage differentials in marital instability are not higher among blacks than among Mexican Americans (or Anglos). This finding has implications that are explored in the following discussion.

DISCUSSION AND CONCLUSION

The family structural view of blacks and Mexican Americans has been drawn upon in formulating both the first and the third hypotheses. Both rest on the assumption that historical economic deprivation, in combination with other important factors that may have impinged uniquely on the given minority groups, has led to patterns of adaptation

---

[7] The same is true regarding data on duration of marriage. For example, in the case of a previously divorced but currently married woman, there is no information on when the divorce occurred and, therefore, no way of determining how long either the first or the second marriage endured.

that have had important consequences for minority family structures, weakening them in the case of blacks and strengthening them in the case of Mexican Americans. However, whereas in the first hypothesis this is seen as a sufficient reason for predicting different levels of marital instability among the groups, the importance these conditions have for modifying the effects of other variables (such as age at marriage) is emphasized in the third hypothesis. Thus, early age at marriage was predicted to have the least debilitating effect among Mexican Americans. In fact, this pattern emerged for Mexican Americans but not for blacks, with both groups showing less of a tendency than Anglos for early age at marriage to be associated with greater odds of marital instability (and, conversely, more of a tendency for later age at marriage to be associated with greater odds for marital stability).

The logic of the third hypothesis suggested that age at first marriage might not have as strong an impact on marital instability among Mexican Americans as among Anglos and (especially) blacks because of Mexican American familism (and, perhaps, Catholicism). The fact that blacks also exhibit less of a negative relationship[8] than might be expected between age at first marriage and marital instability suggests that some other explanation is needed. Though clearly post hoc, one possible explanation lies in the lesser access of the minority groups to socioeconomic opportunities. This may mean that later age at marriage is differentially selective across the majority–minority groups of persons likely to defer marriage for the sake of socioeconomic attainment. With less access to economic opportunity, minority persons may have little reason to defer marriage. Conversely, marriage deferral may enable greater socioeconomic resources to be brought to Anglo marriages. The result would be that later age at first marriage leads to a greater reduction in the odds of marital instability among Anglos than among the minority groups.

As noted earlier, the education–marital-instability relationship does not vary significantly by ethnicity. This is somewhat surprising given the modified family structural interpretation of ethnic group differences in marital instability indicated by the age at marriage and ethnicity interaction, as well as by other evidence suggesting that Mexican Americans who go on to higher levels of education may be more acculturated (Carter, 1970) and thus less inclined to adhere to traditional forms of family structure. The lack of a significant difference in the relationship between education and marital instability among these racial–ethnic

---

[8] This is evidenced by a *positive* coefficient (given the fact that marital *instability* was coded as category one).

groups, however, suggests that elaboration of the modified family structural perspective (the third alternative hypothesis) is necessary before its explanatory power can be thoroughly evaluated. Unfortunately, the data necessary for such an analysis are simply not available, especially for Mexican Americans. For example, the role of education in perpetuating or breaking down traditional views of the family among Mexican Americans, together with the role of other factors (such as Catholicism, physical and social proximity to Mexico, and a continuing influx of immigrants), cannot be addressed via census data. Before Anglo–Mexican American and black–Mexican American differences in marital instability are fully understood, the paucity of comprehensive and valid comparative information must be remedied.

In conclusion, the present research has focused upon three hypotheses implicit in the literature dealing with racial–ethnic group differences in marital instability. The analysis suggests that neither ethnicity-specific nor socioeconomic factors alone are adequate explanations of these differentials but that these two sets of variables interact in the determination of racial–ethnic differences in family solidarity. However, only partial support is evident for this conclusion, in that the relationship between age at first marriage and marital instability varies significantly by race–ethnicity, although the relationship between education and marital instability does not. Additional investigation is necessary to ascertain more clearly the relative validity of these three perspectives on racial–ethnic differences in family dissolution.

REFERENCES

Alvírez, David
    1973   "The effects of formal church affiliation and religiosity on the fertility patterns of Mexican-American Catholics." *Demography* 10 (February):19–36.
Bauman, Karl E.
    1967   "The relationship between age at first marriage, school drop-out, and marital instability: An analysis of the Glick effect." *Journal of Marriage and the Family* 29:672–680.
Bean, Frank D., Russell L. Curtis, Jr., and John P. Marcum
    1977   "Familism and marital satisfaction among Mexican Americans: The effects of family size, wife's labor force participation, and conjugal power." *Journal of Marriage and the Family* 39:759–767.
Billingsley, Andrew
    1968   *Black Families in White America.* Englewood Cliffs, New Jersey: Prentice-Hall.

Blau, Peter M., and Otis Dudley Duncan
1967   *The American Occupational Structure.* New York: John Wiley and Sons.

Blood, Robert O. Jr.
1962   *Marriage.* Glencoe, Illinois: The Free Press.

Blood, Robert O. Jr., and Donald M. Wolfe
1960   *Husbands and Wives.* Glencoe, Illinois: The Free Press.

Bradshaw, Benjamin S., and Frank D. Bean
1973   "Trends in the fertility of Mexican-Americans, 1950–1970." *Social Science Quarterly* 53:688–696.

Browning, Harley L., Sally C. Lopreato, and Dudley L. Poston, Jr.
1973   "Income and veteran status: Variations among Mexican Americans, Blacks and Anglos." *American Sociological Review* 38:74–85.

Bumpass, Larry L., and James A. Sweet
1972   "Differentials in marital stability: 1970." *American Sociological Review* 37:754–766.

Burchinal, Lee G.
1964   "Characteristics of adolescents from unbroken, broken and reconstituted families." *Journal of Marriage and the Family* 26:44–51.

Burgess, E. W., and Leonard S. Cottrell, Jr.
1939   *Predicting Success or Failure in Marriage.* New York: Prentice Hall.

Campbell, Angus
1975   "The American way of mating: Marriage si, children only maybe." *Psychology Today* 8:37–43.

Carter, Hugh, and Paul C. Glick
1966   "Trends and current patterns of marital status among nonwhite persons." *Demography* 3:276–288.

Carter, Thomas P.
1970   *Mexican Americans in School.* Princeton, New Jersey: College Entrance Examination Board.

Casavantes, Edward
1971   "Pride and prejudice: A Mexican American dilemma." Pp. 46–51 in N. W. Wagner and M. J. Haug (eds.), *Chicanos.* Saint Louis, Missouri: Mosby.

Cutright, Phillips
1971   "Income and family events: Marital stability." *Journal of Marriage and the Family* 33:291–306.

Davis, James A.
1974   "Hierarchical models for significance tests in multivariate contingency tables: An exigesis of Goodman's recent papers." Pp. 189–231 in Herbert L. Costner (ed.), *Sociological Methodology.* San Francisco, California: Jossey-Bass.

Davis, Nancy J., and Larry L. Bumpass
1976   "The continuation of education after marriage among women in the United States: 1970." *Demography* 13:161–174.

Duberman, Lucille
1974   *Marriage and Its Alternatives.* New York: Praeger.

Duncan, Beverly, and Otis Dudley Duncan
1969   "Family stability and occupational success." *Social Problems* 16: 273–285.

Eberstein, Isaac W., and W. Parker Frisbie
    1976   "Differences in marital instability among Mexican Americans, Blacks and Anglos: 1960 and 1970." *Social Problems* 23:609–621.
Farley, Reynolds, and Albert I. Hermalin
    1971   "Family stability: A comparison of trends between Blacks and Whites." *American Sociological Review* 36(1):1–17.
Farris, B. E., and Norval Glenn
    1976   "Fatalism and familism among Anglos and Mexican Americans in San Antonio." *Sociology and Social Research* 60:393–402.
Feagin, Joe R.
    1968   "Kinship ties of Negro urbanites." *Social Science Quarterly* 48:660–665.
Featherman, David L.
    1971   "The socioeconomic achievement of white religio–ethnic subgroups: Social and psychological explanations." *American Sociological Review* 36:207–232.
Fienberg, Stephen E.
    1977   *The Analysis of Cross-Classified Categorical Data.* Cambridge, Massachusetts: M.I.T. Press.
Fogel, Walter
    1965   *Education and Income of Mexican Americans in the Southwest.* Mexican American Study Project, Advance Report No. 1. Los Angeles, California: University of California, Graduate School of Business Administration.
Frazier, E. Franklin
    1939   *The Negro Family in the United States.* Chicago, Illinois: University of Chicago Press.
Frisbie, W. Parker, and Lisa J. Neidert
    1977   "Inequality and the relative size of minority populations: A comparative analysis." *American Journal of Sociology* 82:1007–1030.
Frisbie, W. Parker, Isaac W. Eberstein, and Frank D. Bean
    1977   "Marital instability among Mexican Americans: Is the trend converging with that of Blacks?" Paper presented at the annual meeting of the American Sociological Association, September 5–9, Chicago.
Glick, Paul C.
    1957   *American Families.* New York: John Wiley and Sons.
Glick, Paul C., and A. J. Norton
    1971   "Frequency, duration and probability of marriage and divorce." *Journal of Marriage and the Family* 33:307–317.
Goode, William J.
    1964   *The Family.* Englewood Cliffs, New Jersey: Prentice-Hall.
    1970   *World Revolution and Family Patterns.* 2nd Edition. New York: The Free Press.
Goodman, Leo A.
    1970   "The multivariate analysis of qualitative data: Interactions among multiple classifications." *Journal of the American Statistical Association* 65:226–256.
    1972   "A modified multiple regression approach to the analysis of dichotomous variables." *American Sociological Review* 37:28–46.

Grebler, Leo, Joan W. Moore, and Ralph C. Guzman
  1970   The Mexican-American People. New York: The Free Press.
Hernández, Jose, Leo Estrada, and David Alvírez
  1973   "Census data and the problem of conceptually defining the Mexican
          American population." Social Science Quarterly 53(4):671–687.
Herzog, Elizabeth, and Cecilia E. Sudia
  1968   "Fatherless homes: A review of research." Children 15:177–182.
Hicks, Mary W., and Marilyn Platt
  1970   "Marital happiness and stability: A review of the research in the
          sixties." Journal of Marriage and the Family 32:553–574.
Hill, Robert B.
  1972   "The strengths of Black families." Pp. 262–290 in D. G. Bromley and
          C. F. Longino, Jr. (eds.), White Racism and Black Americans. Cam-
          bridge, Massachusetts: Schenkman.
Howard, John R.
  1970   "Introduction: Ethnic stratification systems." Pp. 1–9 in John R.
          Howard (ed.), Awakening Minorities. Chicago, Illinois: Aldine Pub-
          lishing Company.
Kephart, William M.
  1966   The Family, Society and the Individual. 2nd Edition. Boston, Massa-
          chusetts: Houghton Mifflin.
Kerlinger, Fred N., and Elazar J. Pedhazur
  1973   Multiple Regression in Behavioral Research. New York: Holt, Rine-
          hart and Winston.
Kiser, Clyde, and Myrna Frank
  1967   "Factors associated with the low fertility of nonwhite women of
          college attainment." Milbank Memorial Fund Quarterly 45:427–449.
Landis, Paul H.
  1955   Making the Most of Marriage. New York: Appleton, Century-Crofts.
Madsen, William
  1964   Mexican Americans of South Texas. New York: Holt, Rinehart and
          Winston.
Monahan, Thomas P.
  1955   "Divorce by occupational level." Marriage and Family Living 17:
          322–324.
  1962   "When married couples part: Statistical trends and relationships in
          divorce." American Sociological Review 27:625–633.
Moynihan, Daniel P.
  1965   The Negro Family: The Case for National Action. Washington,
          D.C.: U.S. Department of Labor. Reprinted in Lee Rainwater and
          W. L. Yancey (eds.) (1967), The Moynihan Report and the Politics
          of Controversy. Cambridge, Massachusetts: The M.I.T. Press.
Murguía, Edward
  1975   Assimilation, Colonialism, and the Mexican American People. Aus-
          tin, Texas: Mexican American Studies Center, University of Texas
          Press.
Murillo, Nathan
  1971   "The Mexican American family." Pp. 97–108 in N. W. Wagner and
          M. J. Haug (eds.), Chicanos. St. Louis, Missouri: Mosby.
Nye, F. Ivan
  1957   "Child adjustment in broken and in unhappy unbroken homes." Pp.

434–440 in M. B. Sussman (ed.), *Sourcebook in Marriage and the Family.* 3rd edition (1968). Boston, Massachusetts: Houghton Mifflin.

Nye, F. Ivan, and Felix M. Berardo
 1973　*The Family: Its Structure and Interaction.* New York: Macmillan.
Pinkney, Alphonso
 1969　*Black Americans.* Englewood Cliffs, New Jersey: Prentice-Hall.
Rainwater, Lee, and W. L. Yancey
 1967　*The Moynihan Report and the Politics of Controversy.* Cambridge, Massachusetts: The M.I.T. Press.
Rubel, Arthur J.
 1966　*Across the Tracks.* Austin, Texas: University of Texas Press.
Ryan, William R.
 1965　"Savage discovery: The Moynihan report." Pp. 457–466 in Lee Rainwater and W. L. Yancey (eds.), *The Moynihan Report and the Politics of Controversy* (1967). Cambridge, Massachusetts: The M.I.T. Press. Reprinted from *The Nation* (November 22).
Ryan, William R.
 1971　*Blaming the Victim.* New York: Random House.
Shryock, Henry S., and Jacob S. Siegel and Associates
 1976　*The Methods and Materials of Demography.* Condensed edition by E. G. Stockwell. New York: Academic Press.
Udry, J. Richard
 1966a　"Marital instability by race, sex, education, and occupation using 1960 census data." *American Journal of Sociology* 72:203–209.
 1966b　*The Social Context of Marriage.* Philadelphia, Pennsylvania: Lippincott.
 1967　"Marital instability by race and income based on 1960 census data." *American Journal of Sociology* 72:673–674.
Uhlenberg, Peter
 1972a　"Demographic correlates of group achievement: Contrasting patterns of Mexican-Americans and Japanese-Americans." *Demography* 9: 119–128.
 1972b　"Marital instability among Mexican Americans: Following the pattern of blacks?" *Social Problems* 20:49–56.
U.S. Bureau of the Census
 1972　"Public use samples of basic records from the 1970 census: Description and technical documentation." Washington, D.C.: U.S. Government Printing Office.
 1973　Census of population: 1970. Persons of Spanish Origin. Final Report PC (2)-1C. Washington, D.C.: U.S. Government Printing Office.
U.S. Department of Health, Education, and Welfare
 1973　Vital and Health Statistics. Series 21, No. 33. Divorces: Analysis of Changes, U.S. States, 1969. Rockville, Maryland: National Center for Health Statistics.
Weed, James A.
 1974　"Age at marriage as a factor in state divorce rate differentials." *Demography* 11:361–375.
Yaukey, David
 1973　*Marriage Reduction and Fertility.* Lexington, Massachusetts: Lexington Books.

7

Racial-Ethnic Differences
in Labor Force Participation:
An Ethnic Stratification Perspective

TERESA A. SULLIVAN

Documenting racial and ethnic differences in labor force participation rates (LFPRs) is easy. Interpreting them is not. Part of the hermeneutic difficulty lies in the measures we use; part of it lies in the enterprise of minority demography. The LFPR is an ambigious indicator. Its rise or fall does not correspond in any straightforward way to the success or failure of the group. Yet, because work-related income and occupational identities are conferred only on those in the labor force, labor force participation is linked to the stratification system, including the stratification of racial and ethnic groups. Nevertheless, stratification has been a muted theme in the literature of minority demography. Minority demography has remained more descriptive than theoretical and more devoted to documenting the size and extent of differences among minorities than to explaining them.

In this chapter it is argued that minority demography requires a firmer conceptual basis for defining "minority groups." I propose an ethnic

The Demography of Racial and Ethnic Groups.

stratification perspective that defines *minority groups* by access to resources and that stresses the interaction of the minority population with
a dominant population (and other minority populations). From this
perspective it appears that demographers should study the *type* of labor
force participation and should not just study the participation rate. Type
of labor force participation implies a strategy of resource control that in
turn may imply other demographic consequences.

RACIAL–ETHNIC DIFFERENCES
IN LABOR FORCE PARTICIPATION RATES

The LFPR (also called the economic activity rate or the refined activity
rate) is the most common indicator used by demographers to measure
economic activity. The LFPR is the ratio of persons in the labor force to
all noninstitutionalized persons over the age of 16 during a reference
week. The labor force includes all those who worked at least 1 hour
during the week for pay or profit, unpaid family workers who worked at
least 15 hours, and persons who were actively seeking work. In other
words, the labor force includes the employed and the unemployed. Although the labor force concept has been under attack, the LFPR has the
advantage of being easy to understand, available in time series, and in
wide use around the world. It has also been used as the dependent variable in a number of landmark studies (Bowen and Finegan, 1969;
Durand, 1975).[1]

Unfortunately, the interpretation of the LFPR is not straightforward.
A higher participation rate does not necessarily mean that the group is
financially better off. For example, a group of recent immigrants may
have high participation rates because such a large proportion of them
are in the prime working ages. An older immigrant group, because it has
more retirees, might have lower rates but might be more financially
secure. But a lower participation rate is not necessarily a sign of affluence. A lower rate might mean that a group can afford to let young
people prolong schooling and let old people retire. But it might also
mean that group members have withdrawn from the labor force in
discouragement. Nor is there a rule of thumb for what levels are "high"
or "low." Demographers might agree that a crude birth rate of 40 is
high and that one of 10 is low. There is much less consensus about
LFPRs, especially as applied without controls for age, marital status,
and other factors.

---

[1] I distinguish between studies that use the rate with a group as the unit of
analysis and studies that use labor force participation with the individual as the
unit of analysis. For an example of the latter, see Sweet, 1973.

TABLE 7.1

Labor Force Participation Rates for Ten Racial–Ethnic Groups
by Sex, 1970

Racial–Ethnic groups	Male	Female
Cuban	83.7	51.0
Japanese	79.3	49.4
Filipino	79.0	55.2
Hawaiian	77.9	48.5
Mexican	77.4	36.4
Korean	75.5	41.5
Puerto Rican	75.5	35.3
Chinese	73.2	49.5
Negro	69.8	47.5
American Indian	63.4	31.6
All whites [a]	73.8	38.9

Source: Table 7.3.
[a] Includes Hispanic groups.

Table 7.1 provides 1970 labor force participation rates by sex for a variety of racial–ethnic groups in the United States. American Indians had the lowest rates for both sexes. The male rate was 20 points lower than that of the highest male rate (Cubans). The female rate was 23 points below the highest female rate (Filipinos). This means that one in every five American Indians would have to join the labor force to equal the highest rates. Table 7.1 serves several functions. First, it shows the danger of lumping together "Hispanics" or "Asians," let alone "nonwhites," for labor force studies (see also Lyman, 1974:26 and Roberts and Lee 1974:505). Second, it shows clear differences in participation by sex. Mexican men participate at much higher relative levels than do Mexican women.[2] On the basis of their rates, Chinese and Filipino women rank higher among women than Chinese and Filipino men do among men. However, this table does not permit any further conclusions about Cubans as compared with American Indians or about Puerto Ricans as compared with Mexicans.

Table 7.2 sets the problem in a longer time perspective because Table 7.1 shows the lowest census LFPR ever reported for black males. Blacks account for 90% of nonwhites, and so, despite the shortcomings of the nonwhite classification, Table 7.2 can be taken as a proxy for black–white differences. Table 7.2 shows a long-run decline in nonwhite male LFPR and a more modest secular decline in the LFPR of white men. In

[2] These are persons defined in the census subject reports as "of Mexican origin."

168   Teresa A. Sullivan

TABLE 7.2

Decennial Census Labor Force Participation Rates by Race, 1890-1970

	Total		Male		Female	
	White	Negro and other	White	Negro and other	White	Negro and other
1890	51.0	62.4	84.0	86.6	15.8	37.7
1900	52.4	65.0	84.4	88.5	17.3	41.2
1920	53.2	64.2	84.1	87.5	20.7	40.6
1930	52.1	63.2	81.7	86.1	21.8	40.5
1940	52.1	58.1	79.7	80.0	24.5	37.3
1950	53.1	56.1	79.2	76.6	28.1	37.1
1960	55.2	56.3	78.0	72.1	33.6	41.8
1970 [a]	55.7	54.2	73.8	65.4	38.9	44.4

Source: U.S. President, 1976, Table BB-3.

[a] 1970 data exclude 14- and 15-year-old workers.

1950 the rate for nonwhite males slips below that of white males and stays well below it, with the largest decennial drop occurring between 1960 and 1970 for both groups. In this perspective, the high 1970 rates for Cubans, Japanese, and Filipinos may look "anachronistic" rather than "high."

White female participation rates have increased steadily since 1890, with an acceleration beginning in 1940. By contrast, the rates for nonwhite women dropped throughout the first five decades of this century, converging toward white women's rates but always exceeding them. Between 1950 and 1970, there was an increase in nonwhite women's participation rates. Are nonwhite women "better off" than white women in the labor market? It is an interpretation given by some (Farley, 1977; Freeman, 1976:179, speaking of college graduates). Are nonwhite men "worse off" in the labor market than white men in 1970 as compared to their relative position in 1890? It seems unlikely. Could it be that a lower participation rate is a "good sign" for men, whereas a higher one is a "good sign" for women (Long, 1958)? The decline in nonwhite male participation rates has been defined as a "problem," usually with the connotation that it indicates economic disadvantage (Farley, 1977; Levitan, Johnston, and Taggart, 1975:69ff.). This is certainly one possible interpretation. The problem with the LFPR taken in isolation is that it lends itself to many interpretations.

There are several possible interpretations for the decline in nonwhite participation. The agnostic interpretation points out that a number of variables must be controlled before any further conclusions about eco-

TABLE 7.3

Labor Force Characteristics and Children Ever Born for Ten Racial–Ethnic Groups, United States, 1970

Indicator	Mexican	Cuban	Hawaiian	Korean	Puerto Rican	American Indian	Filipino	Negro	Japanese	Chinese
Male labor force participation rate	77.4	83.7	77.9	75.5	75.5	63.4	79.0	69.8	79.3	73.2
Male LFPR, aged 35–44	92.7	95.4	92.1	91.3	88.2	80.6	94.9	88.1	96.9	95.5
Unemployment rate	6.1	4.3	5.1	3.6	6.2	11.6	4.7	6.3	2.0	3.0
Part-time workers (%)	NA[a]	NA[a]	5.3	5.9	NA[a]	6.4	12.7	12.2	6.5	5.3
Full-time, low income workers	NA[a]	NA[a]	15.8	11.8	NA[a]	10.9	5.5	12.3	4.6	2.6
Mismatched (%)	NA[a]	NA[a]	10.5	11.8	NA[a]	7.3	10.9	6.2	19.0	18.4
Median income in 1969	$4735	$5532	$6485	$6435	$5105	$3509	$5019	$4158	$7574	$5223
Female labor force participation rate	36.4	51.0	48.5	41.5	31.6	35.3	55.2	47.5	49.4	49.5
Female LFPR, aged 35–44	41.4	64.1	59.4	51.7	36.4	43.4	62.3	60.4	52.7	59.1
Unemployment rate	8.9	7.3	5.6	5.4	8.3	10.2	4.7	7.7	3.0	3.7
Median income in 1969	$1892	$2825	$2931	$2741	$2938	$1697	$3515	$2041	$3236	$2686
Self-employed (%)	4.1	4.5	2.9	5.0	2.6	5.1	3.4	3.3	10.1	9.7
Unpaid family work (%)	.4	.3	.3	.4	.2	.5	.2	.2	1.0	1.5
CEB, women aged 35–44	4530	2064	4181	2287	3503	4554	3300	3817	2301	3005

Source: U.S. Bureau of the Census, Census of Population: 1970, Subject Reports: Persons of Spanish Origin, Final Report PC(2)-1C; Japanese, Chinese, and Filipinos in the United States, Final Report PC(2)-1G; Puerto Ricans in the United States, Final Report PC(2)-1E; American Indians, Final Report PC(2)-1F; Negro Population, Final Report PC(2)-1B, and 1970 Public Use Samples.

[a] NA = not available.

nomic position can be drawn. Age, as mentioned above, can affect comparative rates. (Table 7.3 also shows male participation rates for ages 35–44. In that age group, there is much less variation than in the overall male rates.) For women, the number and age of children and the availability of household help can affect participation. Among Hispanic groups, such factors may affect the difference between Cuban and Mexican women's participation rates (U.S. President, 1974:96). The specific issue of declining black male participation has been approached with "neutral" explanatory factors, such as marital status (King and White, 1977) and census undercount (Rives, 1976).

The optimistic interpretation points to the decline in participation by all males, which is not generally taken to be an alarming indicator. Declining male participation rates can be due to such benevolent developments as early retirement, longer schooling, and improved disability benefits (Siskind, 1975; U.S. President, 1973:23). Such falling male participation rates result from affluence, and for nonwhites to participate in these declines as widely as whites would be a sign of equality and economic progress. In a large cross-national study, Durand (1975) cross-classified participation rates by level of development. Despite the problems of drawing long-range conclusions from cross-sectional data, Durand concluded that a falling participation rate is consistent with economic development. If nonwhite males could be thought of as a group that is developing economically, Durand's analysis suggests a very sanguine interpretation of the dropping participation rates. At least some aspects of the optimistic interpretation do fit black males, especially those pertaining to longer schooling and to better disability payments. Unfortunately, we do not know if we could go so far as to say that the decline in nonwhite men's participation *exceeds* that of white men's because their rate of economic improvement is even faster.

The negative interpretation argues that high unemployment leads to discouragement and that discouragement leads to withdrawal from the labor force. A variant of this argument is that men withdraw from the "legitimate" labor force in favor of clandestine or illegal activities. The falling participation rate, then, is defined as a problem, not just in the sense of its being a puzzle for social scientists but also in the sense of its being a social problem.

Table 7.4 shows black participation rates by sex for 1968 to 1975. The largest decreases in male participation rates occurred in years with large unemployment increases. In the case of the 1970–1971 dip, there had been 2 years of higher unemployment. A slightly larger decline in 1974–1975 followed another 2 years of increased unemployment. The

TABLE 7.4

Labor Force Participation Rates, Unemployment Rates, and Adjusted Rates, Negro and Other Races, by Sex, with Black–White Ratio for Leaving Labor Force Due to Economic Reasons [a]

	Black males				Black females		Black-White ratio of those leaving LF for economic reasons
	LFPR	Un-employ-ment rate	Ad-justed rate [b]	LFPR	Un-employ-ment rate	Ad-justed rate [b]	
	(1)	(2)	(3)	(4)	(5)	(6)	(7)
1968	77.6	5.6	4.4	49.3	8.3	4.1	1.2
1969	76.9	5.3	4.1	49.8	7.8	3.9	1.2
1970	76.5	7.3	5.6	49.5	9.3	4.6	1.3
1971	74.9	9.1	6.8	49.2	10.8	5.3	1.3
1972	73.7	8.9	6.6	48.7	11.3	5.5	1.2
1973	73.8	7.6	5.6	49.1	10.5	5.2	1.3
1974	73.3	9.1	6.7	49.1	10.7	5.3	1.4
1975	71.5	13.7	9.8	49.2	14.0	6.9	1.5

Source: Cols. 1, 2, 4, 5: U.S. President, 1976, Tables A-3, A-7, A-13, A-18.

[a] Spanish origin LFPR in 1974 was 61.0, with 8.1% unemployment; 1975 figures were 60.7, with 12.2% unemployment.

[b] Unemployment per 100 adults aged 16 and over.

women's rate was a little different. Although black female unemployment is even larger than that of black males, a small decrease in the black female unemployment rate raises participation more than does a larger decrease in unemployment for males. At an aggregate level, unemployment seems to be an important indicator to consider with LFPRs. Because unemployment is a component of LFPRs, the adjusted rate in Columns 3 and 6 is designed to present unemployment per 100 adults aged 16 and over. This has the effect of lowering black female unemployment because unemployment is not expressed as a percentage of labor force participation. But the adjustment shows that even the dropping LFPRs did not offset rising unemployment.

With unemployment so serious a problem, it is not surprising to find a high ratio of blacks to whites who leave the labor force for economic reasons. The ratio does not quite correspond to the unemployment rate. In 1973, although unemployment improved and LFPRs went up for both males and females, the ratio of labor force leavers continued to climb. These data suggest that the negative interpretation of participation rates cannot be shrugged off.

This discussion of conflicting interpretations underscores the problem of interpreting the LFPR for even one group, black Americans. How do we interpret the difference in rates between blacks and other groups? What is the basis for a comparative demography of economic activity? The following sections set forth a tentative approach for grounding studies of economic activity among minority groups. A rather lengthy theoretical excursion will be necessary before resuming the discussion of economic activity indicators.

ETHNIC STRATIFICATION AND THE DEMOGRAPHY OF MINORITY GROUPS

Robert Merton (1973:457) applies the term "Matthew effect" to the familiar observation that control of resources leads to further control of resources: The rich get richer. In this chapter I develop a stratification perspective on minority group demography that defines and analyzes minority groups in terms of their control of resources and adds a twist from demographic folk wisdom: The rich get richer and the poor get children. We are accustomed to speaking of rich individuals, not so much of rich groups. Here, however, the unit of analysis must be the group. Although there is at least implicit recognition that stratification ranks groups as well as individuals, demographic treatments of stratification usually emphasize the atomized individual and not the group. An ethnic-group stratification perspective helps define minority groups and provides an analytic framework for comparing economic activity among minority groups. Although these ideas are exploratory, they provide a theoretical base for grounding minority demography. Without some such base we may go on mistaking the study of minority individuals for the study of minority groups.

Wherever there is a system of stratification, we may expect it to have demographic consequences. Ethnic stratification deserves special attention for its role in generating and juxtaposing demographic differences. Any stratification system, whether based on class, caste, or ethnic group, distributes life chances. Life chances include mortality and morbidity, for poor people are more exposed to the risks of illness and early death. Life chances include shared patterns of nuptiality and fertility. Life chances are associated with the cultural division of labor, and so demographic indicators of economic activity should also reflect stratification. But the ethnic stratification system also juxtaposes the differences in indicators. In an urbanized society, the ethnic stratification system must distribute differences in life chances among groups that share the same life space. Consequently, demographic differences can be woven into the ideology that justifies the initial stratification. Ethnic stratification may generate demographic differences, but, even more importantly, the demographic differences may affect subsequent inter-group relations. Such differences give the dominant group one more reason for thinking "They are not like us." [3]

An ethnic stratification perspective goes far toward defining a subject matter and an approach for the demography of minority groups. From this perspective, a *minority group* is a highly endogamous population that is culturally distinct, claims a common putative origin, and controls significantly fewer resources and their revenues than the economically dominant group with whom it shares the territory. In contrast, the *dominant group* controls a disproportionately large share of resources and the revenues generated by them. These definitions provide a basis for understanding how the rich get richer. Several further points about these definitions are worth noting.

First, "minority group" is not just another classification reached by cross-tabulating race, birthplace, or some other variable. The definitions let us examine the behavior of statistical majorities whose economic position is more similar to that of statistical minorities in the United States. For example, we might expect the relative demographic characteristics of blacks and whites in South Africa to be like those of American Indians and whites in the United States, although South African blacks are statistically a majority and American Indians are not.

The second point is that the exchange of resources becomes the most important point of contact between the two populations. The more lopsided the resource control, the more important the exchange becomes. Where there are more than two minority groups, the potential exchange relations are, of course, multiplied, and the analyst's problem becomes greater. Much of the following analysis is based upon resource exchange.

Third, the dominant group can be relatively heterogeneous. In the case of the United States, it would not be reasonable to include all whites in the dominant group. The dominant group would be defined principally by revenues and resources; they are likely to be white. The dominant

---

[3] Indeed, ethnic stratification may focus attention on the between-groups variation in demographic indicators, although the within-group variation may be as great or greater. Lower-class members of the dominant group may have fertility as high or higher than that of minority groups. Class-based stratification encourages an emphasis on the different demographic characteristics of classes within groups; the ethnic stratification system encourages the emphasis on the different demographic characteristics of groups. Where the ethnic stratification system assumes greater salience, the demographic differences between groups will be more threatening than those between classes.

group would certainly include the top 1% of the population in terms of wealth. At about the time of the 1970 census, this group accounted for 14% of real estate holdings, about 50% of corporate stocks, 53% of bonds, and 14% of cash (U.S. Bureau of the Census, 1976:Table 694).

Nothing in these definitions precludes individual social mobility, and so a member of a minority group could enter the dominant group. Individual social mobility could also occur within the class structure of the minority group. But the stratification perspective suggests that the more interesting kind of mobility would be that of entire groups changing their relative rank in the stratification system—for example, the kind of mobility that the Chinese may have experienced in the United States since 1940.

The ethnic stratification perspective counteracts two problems in the current literature: the ad hoc selection of minority groups for study and the fragmentary treatment of demographic characteristics. First, the stratification perspective requires a search for general principles of what constitutes a minority population and what the interactions of minority and majority populations might be. By contrast, an ad hoc research policy looks at each new group as it gains sufficient publicity or political clout to intrude itself on the researcher's consciousness. The ad hoc selection of minority groups as subjects is also influenced by the availability of census codes, which reflect political activism and public attention to the group (Shryock et al., 1973,I:252–263). Using census categories can produce useful and interesting results and can lead to extensive comparative studies (Kritz and Gurak, 1976). Nevertheless, it is unsystematic because the identification of groups to be studied is haphazard. Specifically, a small but politically unglamorous group may be overlooked despite its critical position in the ethnic group hierarchy. The emphasis on resource control not only suggests a way to define minority groups but also suggests a way to define those minority groups that are most (theoretically) interesting.

Second, the stratification perspective poses a research agenda: What are the demographic consequences of social position? The answer to this question is currently carved up into specialties. For example, labor force demographers examine participation patterns, occupational inheritance, and mobility. (Do the rich get richer?) Fertility specialists examine differential fertility and the quality versus quantity tradeoff as one moves up the social hierarchy. (Do the poor get more children?) It is rare to find a more holistic treatment.[4]

---

[4] For example, Easterlin (1968) makes the relationship only at a highly aggregated level.

A partial exception to this generalization is found in the literature on differential fertility. Two competing hypotheses have been studied: the minority status and social characteristics theses (Bean and Wood, 1974; Goldscheider and Uhlenberg, 1969; Ritchey, 1975). The two hypotheses differ as to whether class or ethnicity is thought of as the more important basis of stratification. The social characteristics thesis may be seen as a formulation of the "poor get children" hypothesis. To the extent that minority groups are disproportionately poor, they have more children. Presumably, individual social mobility would result in lower fertility. The implicit model of stratification is a top-to-bottom ranking by social class, with minorities included on the same basis as whites. The minority group hypothesis may be seen as an argument that membership in a minority group consciously or unconsciously translates itself into behavioral correlates. For example, political consciousness may lead to higher fertility (Kennedy, 1973) or upwardly mobile groups may be more sensitive to reference norms and may decrease their fertility beyond what would otherwise be expected. (A different hypothesis for this will be suggested later.) The implicit model of stratification here is a ranking of *groups*, or a quasi-caste formulation. A better-developed stratification perspective might make obsolete the tension in these studies between "characteristics" and "minority status." To the extent that ethnic stratification is the cource of both characteristics and status, the discussion becomes somewhat like the controversy about whether light is composed of particles or waves.

The stratification perspective suggests that social position may have demographic consequences besides fertility. Tracing these consequences may lead to a more mature demography of the minority group as a population, something that can be done today only by splicing together bits and pieces from the differential characteristics literature. The study of the group *as a group* could lead to richer and more sophisticated theories of differential fertility as well as of intergroup relations.

The stratification perspective is certainly not the only one from which to view the demography of minority groups. It is useful because it sets an agenda: It suggests what groups should be studied, and it hints at what problems are important. Because all stratification systems are closely linked to the economic system, the study of economic activity should be an important one for demographers. But stratification and its demographic consequences are mutually reinforcing, and with no consequence is this so obvious as with the study of economic activity. This simultaneously makes economic activity an essential study for minority group demographers, but one that is prone to tautological reasoning.

ECONOMIC ACTIVITY AND THE DEMOGRAPHY
OF MINORITY GROUPS

The preceding section argues that minority groups can be ranked from highest to lowest by the extent of the resources they control. This ranking implies differences in economic activity and in other kinds of demographic indicators. Groups with many resources should have different economic activity from groups with fewer resources. The danger of tautological reasoning lies in the fact that resource control is so closely related to economic activity that one risks using the same indicator to define both. Figure 7.1 shows schematically the outline of the argument

Figure 7.1. Ethnic group stratification and economic activity: Mutual influences.

so far. Stratification (resource control) affects economic activity, but economic activity also affects resource control. Using the same variable to measure both—say, occupational attainment or income—is a fruitless exercise. There are two problems, then: defining what is meant by resource control, an independent variable, and providing indicators of economic activity, a dependent variable. As a rough-and-ready measure, male median income is used as the indicator of resource control for 10 culturally distinct, endogamous ethnic groups.[5] The income data are given in Table 7.3. I turn now to the problem of defining resource control.

TYPES OF RESOURCES

Resource control has been operationally defined in terms of median income. Similarly, *type* of resource might be defined by type of income. Labor is the principal resource that every minority group has at its disposal. As a resource, it can be improved through education, experience, training, and migration. Labor is exchanged for wages and salaries, which account for 63–65% of personal income in the United States. Over time, savings can be converted into other types of resources that produce a different type of income. Acquisition of property makes rent

[5] The Spearman rank correlation between male and female median income for the 10 groups is +.60.

possible. Or, the ownership of a firm makes possible profits or fees for service. Miscellaneous monies can be invested for interest. An ethnic group could improve its ranking (i.e., its resource control) by garnering more of the same kind of revenue—say, higher wages—or by converting its wages into different sorts of revenue-producing resources.[6] For example, group savings from wages in the first generation might purchase small stores in the second generation and professional practices in the third generation.

The exchange of these four kinds of income—wages, rents, profits, and interest—can occur entirely within the ethnic group. The ethnic group can serve as the clientele for such small businesses as grocery stores and restaurants that specialize in the foods of the old country. Historically, professional and personal services in the black community were provided by blacks. The ethnic group can serve as a source of investment monies and can pay interest within the group (Light, 1972: 19–44; Lyman, 1974:120). It is quite common for some ethnic groups to serve as employers and landlords for other members of the group. For example, this was the case among the Japanese in California before World War II.

As a rule, however, the relative ranking of ethnic groups will depend on the amount and types of resources exchanged with other groups. Because of economic growth, resource control need not be a zero-sum game. The law of supply and demand is not analogous to the law of the conservation of energy and matter. In theory, the resources of each group may increase without diminishing the resources of the other groups. In practice, however, the "Matthew effect" comes into play. Control of resources can be concentrated, but the lack of resources can only be diffused. Economic ghettoization is an example of how the dominant group's resource control can be increased. Ghettoization is characterized by only one form of income flowing into a group while flows of other income types that are equally large or larger go to other groups. Sharecropping is one example. The sharecropper exchanged labor for wages (or shares) but paid interest on money loaned against the crop, gave some of the profits to the plantation store, and often paid rent to the landlord. Ghettoization usually involves interest, profits, and rent going to the dominant group and wages going to the minority group.

Ghettoization tends to concentrate resources in the dominant group. It is the most extreme case, but it is not the only pattern. Patterns of

---

[6] I have not covered the case of transfer payments because they are paid by the corporate political body. Political power, of course, is one of several nonmonetary resources that deserves consideration. It is beyond the scope of this chapter.

resource control do change, and, as they change, the ethnic stratification system may become more fluid. As the group gets more resources, some of the flows to the dominant group can be stopped or reduced. Employment, rents, investments, and profits can be provided within the group. This is the separatist position. In moving to the other extreme, more equal resource control, income flows may reverse or become reciprocal. The minority group may begin to provide employment, investment funds, and more goods and services to the formerly dominant group.

Income is a guide to stratification. But if incomes are equal, an examination of the reciprocity of flows helps establish the "distance" that a minority remains from the dominant group.[7] On the other hand, if incomes are unequal, the less reciprocal the income flows, the less resource control the minority group has. In particular, if the minority group receives only wages from the dominant group, its probability of unemployment helps determine how much control it has over the resource it does control.

This very sketchy outline of resource exchanges enhances our understanding of how the group rankings come about and how they might change. It also helps one understand both the two-group situation and the multiple-group situation. In addition, three more points should be made.

First, the transfer of savings into proprietorships and other sources of revenue is not solely a result of the group's industry and frugality. Dishonorable goods and services and unfashionable clienteles may be relegated to minority groups to provide and to cater to. The more minority groups there are, the more likely it is that the lowest-ranked group will be served by merchants and lenders of another minority group—the so-called middleman minorities (Bonacich, 1973; Loewen, 1971). Minority groups may provide menial or dishonorable services to the dominant group, either for wages or for profits. For example, domestic service is provided by blacks and Mexican Americans for wages, but the laundry service was provided in many areas by self-employed Chinese. In Europe, moneylending was done by Jews. A so-called middleman minority may pay rent to the dominant group and may receive profits from both the dominant group and other minority groups. To the extent that goods and services are defined as dishonorable (dirty, menial) or clienteles are defined as causing loss of status to the dominant group,

---

[7] Data on reciprocal flows are difficult to find. Some data are available, usually for blacks. O'Connell (1976) documents the small share of receipts by black businesses.

there is an "ecological niche" created that can be a resource, in addition to their wage-labor, for minority group members.

Second, resource control varies by the kind of reseources a group controls and not just by the number of resources it has. The provision of goods and services for profit or interest has an advantage over wages as a resource: The worker is dependent on one employer, but the person who receives profits, interest, or rents has a number of possible clients. Thus, entrepreneurs can protect themselves in a way wage-laborers cannot.

Third, resources can be parlayed into more resources, but lack of control can only be diffused. A group that only earns wages from the dominant group can only send more workers to the dominant group, and the dominant group can refuse to hire them.

Resource exchange can be considered the dynamic aspect of ethnic stratification. How does such a perspective help us to understand the differences in economic activity among minority groups? The data for a full treatment are not available, but some progress can be made over an approach that considers only LFPRs.

A REEXAMINATION OF ECONOMIC ACTIVITY BY MINORITY GROUPS

Economic activity indicators can be viewed as indicators of resources. According to the preceding discussion, we might expect that the groups with the least resource control would have the highest unemployment. This would indicate that their wage employment is a principal source of income but that they have not had as much success as other groups in securing employment. (The reason for this may be a lack of related resources, such as human capital, but that does not contradict the argument.) A group that relies on labor alone should also have a high LFPR. Put differently, it should diffuse its lack of control by sending more workers out into the market. However, unemployment is negatively correlated with LFPRs (Spearman rank-correlation coefficient is —.56 for males, —.43 for females). And so, if the highest unemployment groups are examined, the worst-off of those groups should have the lowest labor force participation and the better-off should have higher labor force participation.[8] For the men, this puts American Indians and

[8] The unemployment rate is a component of the LFPR. The reason that this relationship probably holds is that high unemployment drives some workers from the labor force; as a result, the LFPR is lower.

blacks in the lowest group and Puerto Ricans, Mexicans, and Filipinos in the second-lowest group.

The remaining groups had low unemployment. To the extent that they are wage-earners, their labor force participation should be high. But, in addition, we would expect them to have other sources of income. Another way to put this is to say that they should have higher percentages of self-employed and unpaid family workers among them. These indicators are given in Table 7.3, and Table 7.5 shows enterpreneurship by ethnic group. The first column (in Table 7.5) refers to workers who entered the labor force between 1965 and 1970 and who were *entrepreneurs*—that is, self-employed workers who reported income from their own business, practice, or farm in 1969 or who were unpaid family workers. The second column is made up of workers who were in the labor force in 1965 but who changed their work to become entrepreneurs in 1970. The third group is made up of workers who were entrepreneurs in both 1965 and 1970. The fourth column is made up of

TABLE 7.5

Entrepreneurship among Eight Racial–Ethnic Groups, 1970 [a]

	Current					
	1970 entrant	1970 change	1965 and 1970	Former	Total entrepreneur	All workers (%)
Negro	46	44	89	87	266	4343
	(17.3)	(16.5)	(33.5)	(32.7)	(100.0)	(6.1)
American Indian	1	1	2	1	4	110
						(3.6)
Japanese	4	5	22	1	32	153
	(12.5)	(15.6)	(68.8)		(100.0)	(20.9)
Chinese	2	4	14	2	22	114
		(18.2)	(63.6)		(100.0)	(19.3)
Filipino	1	1	3	3	7	110
						(6.4)
Hawaiian	0	0	0	0	0	19
						(0.0)
Korean	0	0	0	1	1	17
						(5.9)
Other	1	2	0	3	6	52
						(11.5)

Source: 1970 Public Use Samples.
[a] Numbers in thousands, with percentages.

workers who were self-employed in 1965 and in the labor force in some other capacity by 1970. Most of the numbers in this table are too small to be reliable, but, among the largest groups, it is clear that the Chinese and the Japanese were far more likely to be entrepreneurs. Blacks were less likely to be entrepreneurs, and their entrepreneurial status was far more volatile than that of the Japanese or the Chinese. From these data we would expect the Japanese, Chinese, Koreans, and Cubans to rank relatively high in resources.

Confirmation for these classifications can be taken from some other data in Table 7.3. Education may be considered as an "extra" resource that an elite minority group may have, although it may not be able to translate it into high-level jobs. That is, it may be a resource over which control is limited by the employment relationship. This is measured by the indicator called "mismatch," which is the percentage of the ethnic group who work full-time but whose education is significantly higher than that of other workers in their detailed occupational group.[9] We would expect blacks and American Indians to have the lowest mismatch score and the Japanese and Chinese to have the highest. This is indeed the case.

Two other variables in Table 7.3 should be positively correlated with unemployment, for they represent dimensions of the lack of control over employment but do not represent any extra resource, as mismatch does. These variables are the percentage of part-time workers and the percentage of full-time workers whose earnings put them below the poverty level. These indicators are correlated positively with each other and with unemployment. Low income is strongly negatively correlated with labor force participation. This lends a little extra confirmation to the earlier classification. These results lead us to Table 7.6. By operationalizing unemployment, LFPR, and class of workers as indicators of resource control, we come much closer to approximating the ethnic stratification given by income than we do by using LFPR alone.

DISCUSSION

Table 7.6 shows high agreement between the "objective" stratification of ethnic groups ranged by median income and the expected economic activity based on resource control. At one level, this can be dismissed as merely showing that a number of labor force variables are related.

[9] This indicator is explained in some detail in Sullivan (1978).

TABLE 7.6

A Comparison of Stratification by Income, LFPR, and Classification by Resource
Indicators

Independent ranking (male median income, 1969)	LFPR only	Ranking by resource indicators
Japanese	79.3	Highest group: Japanese,
Hawaiian [a]	77.9	Chinese, Korean, Cuban
Korean	75.5	
Cuban	83.7	
Chinese	73.2	Intermediate group: Puerto
Filipino	75.5	Rican, Mexican, Filipino
Puerto Rican	79.0	
Mexican	77.4	
Blacks	69.8	Lowest group: Blacks, American
American Indians	63.4	Indians

[a] Did not fall clearly into the ranking by resource indicators.

Certainly this is true, but the advantage of the stratification perspective
is that it can show how they are related. For example, instead of puzzling
over whether black participation rate declines are promising or threatening indicators, black participation can be put into the context of
other indicators and into the context of other ethnic groups. A number
of nonobvious inferences are available from this perspective. For example,
instead of explaining the entrepreneurship of Asian-American groups
by cultural background or innate qualities, the expected locations of
their "ecological niches" can be predicted. Similarly, one can safely
predict that most black entrepreneurs are still serving the black community and are not selling their goods and services to other groups.
(This is the case: In 1972, over 35% of black proprietorships were found
in service industries, with only 1.7% in manufacturing industries, 9.8%
in construction, and .8% in wholesale.)

Furthermore, this perspective suggests ways to interpret future
changes in participation rates. Declines in Japanese, Cuban, and Korean
participation rates should be neither surprising nor alarming. Reasonably affluent ethnic groups with high levels of entrepreneurship can
probably "afford" lower participation. On the other hand, a further
decline in the participation of black and American Indian males, especially if their unemployment remains high, should be cause for concern.

FURTHER POINTS

Relatively little has been said about the labor force participation of women of ethnic groups. Table 7.7 presents Spearman rank correlations for male and female indicators of labor force participation and unemployment, with the number of children ever born to women 35–44 included. For the most part, there is a strong positive correlation between men's and women's indicators on the same variable. Men's unemployment is negatively related to women's participation and income, and women's unemployment is negatively related to men's participation and income. These rank–order correlations point to a roughly similar ranking of the ethnic groups regardless of sex.

The stratification perspective should imply other demographic consequences besides economic activity. The strong negative correlations of most labor force indicators with children ever born and the strong positive correlation for unemployment with children ever born suggest that "the poor get children." Equally striking is the correlation between men's median income and children ever born to women aged 35–44 (−.69). The limitation of children among upwardly mobile groups can be attributed to the desire for assimilation or to self-consciousness. But it can also reflect the desire to concentrate control of hard-won

TABLE 7.7

Spearman Correlations for Male and Female Labor Force Indicators and Children Ever Born to Women Aged 35–44 of Ten Racial Groups, 1970

	Women's LFPR	LFPR, women aged 35–44	Women's un-employment	Women's median income	CEB to women
Male LFPR	.60 [a]	.43	−.44	.69 [a]	−.53 [a]
LFPR, aged 35–44	.73 [b]	.36	−.76 [b]	.48	−.60 [a]
Unemployment	−.62 [a]	−.27	.89 [b]	−.48	.79 [b]
PT (%)	.31	.36	−.37	.18	NA
Low income FT (%)	.02	.26	−.13	−.07	NA
Mismatch (%)	.41	.14	−.82 [b]	.30	NA
Median income	.37	.17	−.71 [a]	.60 [a]	−.64 [a]
CEB	−.56 [a]	−.42	.67 [a]	−.49	—

Source: Table 7.4.
[a] $p < .05$.
[b] $p < .01$.

resources rather than to disperse them within a sibship. The upwardly mobile groups are those that can create an inheritance. On the other hand, in a group that has only its labor as a resource, there is little incentive for any family to limit the number of potential laborers. This is true even when unemployment is high. Each child may be seen as a lottery ticket with a chance of winning a job. This kind of analysis may seem overly rational, but it deserves discussion in contrast to more subtle hypotheses in which the mechanisms are left unclear.

Finally, these data suggest that different minority groups more or less self-consciously follow different strategies of resource control. To a large extent, these strategies are not voluntary. The ethnic stratification system constrained the choice of possible strategies. The Japanese and

TABLE 7.8

Minority Employment in Firms with One Hundred or More Employees, 1966 and 1969–1974 [a]

Year	Negroes	Spanish	Orientals	American Indians
1966 total	8.2	2.5	.5	.2
WC	2.5	1.2	.7	.1
BC	10.8	3.4	.3	.3
1969 total	9.5	3.2	.6	.3
WC	4.1	1.7	.8	.2
BC	12.6	4.4	.4	.4
1970 total	10.3	3.6	.6	.3
WC	4.8	1.9	.8	.2
BC	13.2	4.9	.3	.4
1971 total	9.5	3.5	.6	.3
WC	4.6	2.0	.8	.2
BC	12.7	4.9	.3	.4
1972 total	10.2	3.8	.7	.3
WC	5.2	2.1	1.0	.2
BC	13.3	5.3	.3	.4
1973 total	10.8	4.1	.8	.4
WC	5.6	2.3	1.1	.3
BC	13.9	5.7	.4	.5
1974 total	11.0	4.3	.8	.4
WC	5.9	2.4	1.1	.3
BC	14.1	5.8	.4	.4

Source: U.S. President, 1976, Table 6–10; Manpower Report of the President, 1973, Table 6–7; Manpower Report of the President, 1974, Table 6–10.
[a] Quantities are percentages of all workers.

the Chinese have tended to become small business owners, at least in the current generation; the coming generation may well concentrate more on professional practices. Blacks have tended to be employees, and current government policy seems to be reemphasizing fair employment after a disappointing attempt to stimulate black capitalism. Affirmative action policies emphasize employment, and the government requires affirmative action reports from firms that report 100 or more workers. These are significant firms, if only because job security is likely to be somewhat greater in those firms. Table 7.8 shows the progress that minority groups have made in being hired by these firms. To the extent that a minority group relies on employment as its strategy of resource control, assuring job security seems to be an important subordinate goal.

CONCLUSIONS

Taken by itself, the LFPR is difficult to interpret for even one minority group, let alone several. Set within a conceptual framework that defines minority groups by access to resources and by the type of income those resources generate, the labor force participation rate becomes part of a set of variables that can describe the ethnic stratification system and changes within it. The unemployment rate, a component of the participation rate, becomes one important indicator, and a measure of entrepreneurship becomes another.

The ethnic stratification perspective helps define minority groups, define what is problematic about them, and identify the ecological niches in which minority groups may flourish. Economic activity varies by position in the stratification hierarchy, as does one measure of fertility. Other demographic consequences can also be expected.

REFERENCES

Bean, Frank D., and Charles H. Wood
    1974   "Ethnic variations in the relationship between income and fertility."
            Demography 11(November):629–640.
Bonacich, Edna
    1973   "A theory of middleman minorities." *American Sociological Review*
            38(October):583–594.
Bowen, William G., and T. Aldrich Finegan
    1969   *The Economics of Labor Force Participation*. Princeton, New Jersey:
            Princeton University Press.

Durand, John
   1975   *The Labor Force in Economic Development.* Princeton, New Jersey:
           Princeton University Press.
Easterlin, Richard A.
   1968   *Population, Labor Force and Long Swings in Economic Growth.*
           New York: National Bureau for Economic Research.
Farley, Reynolds
   1977   "Trends in racial inequalities: Have the gains in the 1960s disap-
           peared in the 1970s?" *American Sociological Review* 42(2)(April):
           189–208.
Freeman, Richard B.
   1976   *The Overeducated American.* New York: Academic Press.
Goldscheider, Calvin, and Peter R. Uhlenberg
   1969   "Minority status and fertility." *American Journal of Sociology* 74
           (January):361–372.
Kennedy, Robert E., Jr.
   1973   "Minority group status and fertility: The Irish." *American Socio-
           logical Review* 38(February):85–96.
King, A. G., and R. White
   1976   "Demographic influences on labor force rates of black males."
           Monthly Labor Review 99(November):42–43.
Kritz, Mary M., and Douglas Gurak
   1976   "Ethnicity and fertility in the United States: An analysis of 1970
           Public Use Sample data." *Review of Public Data Use* 4(May):12–23.
Levitan, Sar A., William B. Johnston, and Robert B. Taggart
   1975   *Still a Dream: The Changing Status of Blacks since 1960.* Cam-
           bridge, Massachusetts: Harvard University Press.
Light, Ivan H.
   1972   *Ethnic Enterprise in America.* Berkeley, California: University of
           California Press.
Loewen, James W.
   1971   *The Mississippi Chinese: Between Black and White.* Cambridge,
           Massachusetts: Harvard University Press.
Long, Clarence
   1958   *The Labor Force under Changing Income and Employment.* Prince-
           ton, New Jersey: Princeton University Press.
Lyman, Stanford M.
   1974   *Chinese Americans.* New York: Random House.
Merton, Robert K.
   1973   *The Sociology of Science.* Norman W. Storer, (ed.). Chicago, Illinois:
           University of Chicago Press.
O'Connell, John H. Jr.
   1976   "Black capitalism." *Review of Black Political Economy* 7(Fall):67–84.
Ritchey, P. Neil
   1975   "The effects of minority group status on fertility: A re-examination
           of concepts." *Population Studies* 29(July):249–257.
Rives, Norfleet
   1976   "Effects of census errors on labor force estimates." *Industrial Rela-
           tions* 15(May):252–256.

Roberts, Robert E., and Eun Sul Lee
   1974   "Minority group status and fertility revisited." *American Journal of Sociology* 80 (September):503–523.
Shryock, Henry S., and Jacob S. Siegel and Associates.
   1973   *The Methods and Materials of Demography.* Washington, D.C.: Government Printing Office.
Siskind, Frederic B.
   1975   "Labor force participation of men, 25–54, by race." *Monthly Labor Review* 98 (July):40–42.
Sullivan, Teresa A.
   1978   *Marginal Workers, Marginal Jobs.* Austin, Texas: University of Texas Press.
Sweet, James A.
   1973   *Women in the Labor Force.* New York: Seminar Press.
U.S. Bureau of the Census
   1976   Statistical Abstract of the United States:1976. 97th ed. Washington, D.C.:Government Printing Office.
U.S. President
   1973   Manpower Report of the President. Washington, D.C.:Government Printing Office.
   1974   Manpower Report of the President. Washington, D.C.:Government Printing Office.
   1976   Employment and Training Report of the President. Washington, D.C.:Government Printing Office.
   1977   Employment and Training Report of the President. Washington, D.C.:Government Printing Office.

8

Differential Fertility and the Minority Group Status Hypothesis: An Assessment and Review[1]

FRANK D. BEAN
JOHN P. MARCUM

According to the most recently available evidence, many racial and ethnic groups in the United States have average family sizes noticeably larger or smaller than those prevailing within the majority white population—differentials that have persisted for some time. Although documentation of these differentials has been extensive, our understanding of the forces underlying racial and ethnic fertility and of how those forces operate remains incomplete. The present chapter addresses the general question of why racial and ethnic group membership is associated with differential fertility by (a) summarizing fertility differences among racial and ethnic groups; (b) analyzing attempts to explain such differences in terms of the so-called "minority group status" hypothesis; and (c) suggesting a possible direction for further investigation.

---

[1] The authors' names are listed alphabetically to reflect their equal contributions to the chapter.

FERTILITY LEVELS AND TRENDS

A brief glance at fertility levels for various American racial and ethnic groups reveals a broad range of reproductive patterns. Table 8.1 presents 1970 United States Census data on children ever born for women 35–44 in the major racial and ethnic groups. Noticeable differences in average family size are apparent, although almost every group reveals average fertility within the 2–4-child range usually considered normative in the United States (Griffith, 1973). Of the groups listed, only Cubans fall below the two-child mean (1932 per 1000 women) and only Mexican Americans (4222) and American Indians (4267) exceed the four-child average. In all three cases, however, the levels are not far beyond the limits of the normative range. This observation is not intended to understate the magnitude of between-group differences (Mexican American fertility, for example, is double that of Cubans) but rather to keep these differences in perspective. Despite variation, most groups average at least two children per woman but fall far short of reproductive capacity.

In comparing fertility differences among racial and ethnic groups, we take as a baseline the fertility of the majority white population, that is, the native-born, urban white population. As Table 8.1 shows, women aged 35–44 in this group in 1970 had 2803 children ever born for every 1000 women. Only two groups—Cubans (1932) and Japanese Americans (2149)—reveal lower average childbearing. All other groups have higher fertility, although in many instances the differences are small: Chinese Americans, Filipinos, and Koreans, for example, have fertility levels only very slightly higher than those of native-born urban whites. Increasingly higher fertility is found among Puerto Ricans (3240), blacks (3489), Hawaiians (3940), Mexican Americans (4222), and American Indians (4267). On the average, the women in the last three groups have about one child more than do majority white women.

Some tentative patterns emerge. First, racial and ethnic groups almost invariably have fertility at or above the level characteristic of assimilated whites. Of the two exceptions, the very lowest—Cubans—represents a rather select group of recent immigrants. Of groups with extended residency in the United States, only Japanese Americans deviate to an extent that is noticeably below the white rate. (Most other Oriental origin groups have fertility near the white rate.) A second pattern is that the highest fertility is exhibited by groups whose members have been in the United States for the longest time—blacks, Mexican Americans, Hawaiians, and American Indians—groups whose members have historically been concentrated in rural areas and have been the objects

TABLE 8.1

Children Ever Born for Women 35–44, by Race and Ethnicity: 1970

Group	Children ever born per 1000 women
Total	2958
White [a]	2891
Native	2913
Urban	2783
Urban native	2803
Rural	3179
Spanish Origin	3443
Mexican	4222
Puerto Rican	3240
Cuban	1932
Other Spanish	3041
Black	3489
American Indian	4267
Japanese	2149
Chinese	2833
Filipino	2981
Hawaiian	3940
Korean	2891
Other	3222

Source: U.S. Bureau of the Census, Census of Population, 1970. Subject Reports, Final Report PC(2)-3A, Women by Number of Children Ever Born. Washington:U.S. Government Printing Office, 1973, Tables 8 and 13.

[a] Includes persons of Spanish origin.

of discrimination (Ryder, 1973). In addition, the table suggests the importance of separating certain origin groups into subgroups. Appreciable differences exist among the Spanish origin subgroups, for example, and similar differences might obtain if American Indians could likewise be divided into tribal groupings.

Historical fertility data are not available for all groups; for those for which records exist, the evidence indicates that current differentials are not of recent origin. Blacks, for example, have almost invariably revealed total fertility rates above those of the white population over the last century and a half, except for a brief period during the Great Depression (Farley, 1972). Moreover, fluctuations in black fertility over this period have closely paralleled those of the white population. Black and white fertility apparently respond similarly to social and economic factors, but black fertility remains at a higher level. Somewhat sketchy evidence (see Bradshaw and Bean, 1972) also indicates that the differential between Mexican Americans and Anglo fertility probably existed as far back as the mid-nineteenth century.

A more comprehensive attempt to catalogue recent fertility trends for American racial and ethnic groups has been undertaken by Rindfuss and Sweet (1977: Chap. 5), who examine own-children data for urban white women and for women of five racial or ethnic groups: blacks, American Indians, Mexican Americans, Chinese Americans, and Japanese Americans. Their overall comparison is reproduced in Figure 8.1. For most groups, fertility shows some fluctuation from the trend typical of whites, but, on balance, there exists a remarkable similarity in the patterns. Groups with higher fertility remained higher over the period 1955 to 1969, although Mexican Americans and American Indians exchanged positions at the top of the range and black fertility converged somewhat to the level of whites. For the two lowest groups a similar change in ranking occurred, with Chinese Americans revealing the lowest total fertility rate in 1969. This latter result is discrepant with that of Table 8.1 (where Japanese Americans were lowest) and suggests that current fertility among recent cohorts for these two Oriental groups

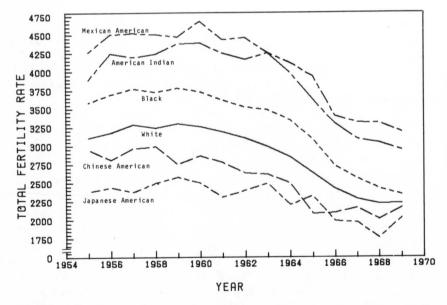

Figure 8.1. Total fertility rates for six racial or ethnic groups: 1955–1969. Source: Rindfuss and Sweet, 1977:90.

may have changed from the pattern typical of cohorts completing reproduction around 1970.

EXPLANATIONS OF DIFFERENTIAL FERTILITY

There have been numerous efforts to interpret the magnitude and persistence of fertility differences among racial and ethnic groups. Two principal explanations have emerged in the literature—the so-called "social characteristics" and "minority group status" hypotheses. The *social characteristics* hypothesis attributes variation in racial–ethnic fertility patterns to differences in socioeconomic composition between racial–ethnic and majority populations. For example, several studies have suggested a convergence of black and white fertility rates as differences in the distribution of socioeconomic variables between the two groups disappear. Lee and Lee (1959:231) assert that "higher Negro fertility can be explained in terms of differences in education and socioeconomic level. Whenever Negroes and whites are equated, no matter how roughly, Negro fertility seldom appears much higher than white and it is often lower." Petersen (1961:226) writes in a similar vein: "Negroes have no cultural trait that affects natality independently of their occupation or education. Race is not a cause of family size but an index of social class." Parallel statements have been made by others, including Thomlinson (1965:178), Farley (1966), Bogue (1969:696), and Presser (1971). In addition, other writers have stressed the importance of black urbanization for the convergence of black and white fertility (Huyck, 1966), a point on which Smith (1960:322), writing about black fertility in the 1950s, was especially emphatic: "Because Negroes are still residents of the most rural region of the country [i.e., the South] and probably because they tend to live in the most rural sectors of that region, their rate of reproduction is slightly higher than that of whites." Similar arguments have stressed the importance of social, economic, and demographic factors in bringing about the observed lower fertility for Jews in the United States (see Freedman *et al.*, 1961:608; and Thomlinson, 1965:179).

In short, the social characteristics hypothesis views fertility differences between majority and racial–ethnic populations as tied to differences in the distribution of socioeconomic factors. It thus contends that fertility, as a major behavioral expression of subgroup norms and values, will vary completely with the degree to which racial–ethnic groups have become socioeconomically assimilated into the majority population.

Holding constant the distribution of socioeconomic characteristics, fertility differentials presumably reduce to zero.

Goldscheider and Uhlenberg (1969:361) attempted a test of the characteristics hypothesis, focusing on four minority groups—Negroes (nonwhites), Jews, Japanese Americans, and Catholics. Relying alternately upon previously published studies not specifically designed to address the issue (e.g., Westoff et al., 1961; Whelpton et al., 1966) and upon incomplete descriptive presentations of aggregate census data that ignore such key socioeconomic variables as income and occupation, they compiled evidence that suggested that a new hypothesis might better explain fertility differences. This alternative interpretation, in addition to considering socioeconomic differences, acknowledged the "independent role of minority group status [Goldscheider and Uhlenberg, 1969: 369]." In brief, their data seemed to indicate that fertility differences do not disappear when the distribution of socioeconomic characteristics is controlled. Instead, when compared with majority whites, Catholics appeared still to have higher fertility, whereas Jews, higher status blacks, urban Japanese Americans, and Japanese Americans outside the West all appeared still to have lower fertility. To account for these residual fertility variations, Goldscheider and Uhlenberg proposed that other aspects of minority life besides those associated with socioeconomic status contribute to minority fertility patterns, a general explanation that has come to be known as the *minority group status* hypothesis.

Goldscheider and Uhlenberg also presented a detailed but speculative formulation of "in what ways, and under what conditions, minority group status operates as an independent factor influencing fertility [1969:361–362]." In their view, higher Catholic fertility constitutes an exception, reflecting the pronatalist norms of Catholicism. Their general explanation is applied to the lower fertility of Jews and certain segments of the Negro and Japanese American populations. To account for this lower fertility, they suggest a social–psychological explanation postulated in terms of the "insecurities associated with minority group status [1969:370]." Their first assumption is that minority couples are *acculturated*, that is, that they embrace the norms and values of the larger society, including those pertaining to socioeconomic attainment. Full realization of these goals, or complete assimilation, however, does not often occur. Hence, some minority couples find themselves becoming assimilated on some dimensions (e.g., education or occupation) but not on others (e.g., primary group attachments or intermarriage). This discrepancy in the degree to which different types of assimilation are experienced places minority couples in marginal positions, thus producing insecurities with respect to the socioeconomic attainment that has occurred. To counteract such feelings and to solidify their socio-economic position, minority couples limit childbearing. Such an effect is presumed to operate most strongly among those minority couples who are sufficiently socioeconomically assimilated to experience this kind of insecurity (i.e., among higher status couples).

The initial effort to investigate minority fertility in light of Gold-scheider and Uhlenberg's ideas was undertaken by Sly (1970). Drawing upon United States census data on children ever born per 1000 women aged 35–44, Sly made preliminary cross-classifications of fertility for white and nonwhite women by region and socioeconomic indicators, then used a three-way analysis of variance design to sort out the effects. This approach led him to reject the characteristics hypothesis as an explanation of between-group fertility variation, as did the results of analyses of variance for data on the entire nation. However, after recomputing his results with data for the South omitted, Sly obtained results that more nearly supported the characteristics explanation.

Another study designed to test the hypothesis, one by Roberts and Lee (1974), demonstrated that results vary according to the definition of minority group employed, as well as according to region. Drawing upon United States census data from the 1960 1% Public Use Sample for women aged 15–49 living in one of the five southwestern states, they repeated their analysis for three varying majority and minority classifications: white–nonwhite, majority–minority (the same as white–nonwhite but with Spanish surname shifted to the nonwhite category), and Spanish surname–other-white–Negro (with other nonwhites excluded entirely). More variation in fertility was apparent between categories when the last two classification schemes were used, and the independent variables (ethnicity, education, income, occupation, and rural–urban residence) explained a greater percentage of variation in either cumulative or current fertility when the majority–minority breakdown was used as opposed to the white–nonwhite one and when the Spanish-surname–other-white–Negro breakdown was used as opposed to either of the other two. Even more important, support for the social characteristics hypothesis was considerably greater in the case of the white–nonwhite breakdown than in the case of the Spanish-surname–other-white–Negro categorization, indicating that conclusions may be altered significantly by the operationalization of majority and minority group status.

Others have argued for a different research approach. Rather than assessing the independent explanatory power of minority group status relative to that of various social, economic, and demographic factors, they have suggested examining relationships between socioeconomic factors and fertility separately *within* minority and majority groups. As Browning (1975:311) noted, the latter approach appears to be in keeping with Goldscheider and Uhlenberg's view that understanding minority fertility requires the recognition that general minority fertility tendencies result from an averaging of various patterns within subgroups of the minority, patterns that reflect individual differences in such factors as identification with the minority group, interaction with other minority persons, and variation in socioeconomic position relative to other members of the minority group. In this same vein, Goldscheider (1971:297) noted:

> The nature of minority group identification assumes that intergroup social contact is fostered, particularly primary group relations. Indeed, the quality of minority group cohesion and integration becomes a key axis of fertility heterogeneity *within* the minority group. In this sense, differentials *within* subgroups must be interpreted. The degree of minority group integration and the accentuated marginal position between acculturation and structural separation will determine the behavior patterns of minority group members, all other things considered, vis-à-vis the majority community.

Other alternatives to the exclusive focus on either between-group or within-group differences are presented by Bean and Wood (1974) and Pohlmann and Walsh (1975). Their approach involves a different conceptualization of the problem. Instead of simply comparing fertility levels between majority and minority groups, they looked at patterns of relationship between fertility and other variables as computed separately for each group. Thus, it was possible to establish between-group variation by comparing the patterns of relationship and to gain some understanding of within-group variation by examining the separate patterns. Bean and Wood applied this approach to the relationship between income and fertility. Taking data from the Public Use Samples of the 1960 and 1970 censuses of the United States for once-married Anglo, Mexican American, and black women aged 40–49 whose age at marriage was under 30 and who lived in one of the five southwestern states, they estimated the effect of actual and relative income on the number of children ever born, adjusting for the wife's education, age at marriage, and rural–urban residence. Markedly different patterns of relationship appeared between income and fertility within the racial–ethnic groups. For example, they observed a positive effect for both actual and relative income on fertility among Anglos, a negative actual income but a positive relative income effect among Mexican Americans, and a negative effect for both income variables among blacks. The evidence for between-group variation was clear-cut, but the nature of the patterns was not given further interpretation in terms of distinguishing the characteristics and minority group status hypotheses.

Pohlmann and Walsh presented a similar analysis but incorporated a larger number of independent variables and focused only on a single minority group, blacks. Using data from the 5% 1/1000 Public Use Sample of the 1970 United States Census on all women aged 15-59 (except those of Spanish descent), children ever born was regressed separately for each 5-year age cohort on age at first marriage, woman's education, woman's income, a dummy variable for chief income recipient, housing adequacy, family income, racial status, a dummy variable for rural farm residence, a dummy variable for renting or not renting one's residence, and a dummy variable for woman's employment status. Separate stepwise regressions were run for the black and white subsamples. Though the evidence clearly revealed fertility differences by race, the within-group analyses did not indicate that radically different sorts of relationships between the independent variables and fertility produced each group's pattern. Rather, the findings suggested that other variables beyond those considered might have operated to produce fertility differences.

Another approach to differential minority fertility has emphasized the importance of the sociocultural and/or political climate in which reproduction occurs. At least two studies (Kennedy, 1973; Ritchey, 1975) have presented evidence that the contextual setting may independently affect fertility. In an effort to explore differential fertility outside the United States, Kennedy (1973) examined fertility in the Republic of Ireland and in Northern Ireland. These two societies provide an unusual setting. Although they possess similar populations (having been unified until as recently as 1921), the positions of majority and minority groups in the two areas are reversed. In the Republic Catholics form a large majority, whereas in Northern Ireland Protestants outnumber Catholics by about two to one. Using aggregate census data going back as far as 1861 but principally for the period 1937–1961, Kennedy examined estimated crude birth rates and child–woman ratios for Catholics and Protestants in both societies. At every time period for which data were available, Catholics had higher fertility than Protestants on either side of the border. Among Protestants, little difference in the mean fertility between the two societies was apparent; however, among Catholics, fertility in Northern Ireland was usually somewhat higher than in the Republic. This can be clearly seen in child–woman ratios for the four groups in 1961: Republic Catholics, 4.25; Northern Irish Catholics, 4.76; Republic Protestants, 2.47; Northern Irish Protestants, 2.45.

Apparently, much of the differential in fertility is attributable to religion. Beyond this, however, Catholic fertility is, on the average, about a half-child greater, in the North than in the Republic. Part of this difference may be due to younger age at marriage among Northern Ireland's Catholics. The rest, Kennedy has suggested, may be evidence of a minority group status effect attributable to the social context: Catholics as a minority group in the North face different societal circumstances than do minority Protestants in the Republic, and these circumstances operate in such a way as to enhance fertility. In particular, the access of Irish Catholics in the North to channels of mobility is more limited, and the relative size of the Catholic minority is greater, both of which factors could encourage higher reproduction.

A contextual approach to the study of the fertility of blacks and whites in the United States has also been undertaken by Ritchey (1975). In addition to examining the effects of individual-level variables, such as race and education, Ritchey attempted to investigate racial inequality in the state of residence as it might affect reproduction. Individual data were drawn from the 1970 1/1000 Public Use Sample (5% questionnaire) to create a sample of all once-married women with husband present and aged 15-44. Racial inequality in each woman's state of residence was determined by an index of 10 factors drawn from various sources and intended to measure socioeconomic inequality between blacks and whites as well as degree of racial segregation and discrimination. Respondents were grouped into three categories based in the index score of their state of residence, and separate analyses were computed for these three subsamples (women in states of high inequality, medium inequality, and low inequality). For each subsample, the number of children ever born was regressed on race and education (the independent variables), age and labor force status (the control variables), and three first-order multiplicative interaction terms: Race × Education, Race × Age, and Labor force status × Age. For all three subsamples, race, as well as the Race × Education interaction, was significantly related to fertility. The effects are such that blacks revealed a higher overall fertility than whites but exhibited a more negative relationship between education and fertility. Most importantly, both of these effects declined in magnitude as racial inequality decreased. Apparently, minority group status not only independently affects fertility but also does so in combination with both socioeconomic status (education) and the social milieu.

Another study (Beaujot et al., 1977) merits attention for its findings about assimilation. Although no measure of socioeconomic status was used, the authors compared reproductive levels among Canadian ethnic groups according to other measures of assimilation: length of generational residence in Canada, language preference, and intermarriage. In general, their sample exhibited only narrow differences in childbearing. (The range was from a current family size of 1.49 for the British to one of 2.08 for the French.) Nevertheless, within-group comparisons revealed an interesting finding: For most groups, particularly when assimilation was measured by intermarriage, less-assimilated segments deviated most strongly in the direction that was typical of their group; that is, such segments showed even higher fertility if they belonged to a high fertility group and even lower fertility if they belonged to a low fertility group. This pattern suggests that distance from other groups in society reinforces the specific reproductive norms of each group. The implication is that minority group status interacts with degree of assimilation in its effects on fertility.

The preceding studies do not exhaust the recent research on racial–ethnic group fertility patterns, but, as of the time this chapter went to press, they included the major research efforts (to our knowledge) that had attempted to test the ideas of Goldscheider and Uhlenberg. Most other research has either been largely descriptive (e.g., Bradshaw and Bean, 1972; Farley, 1972) or not explicitly concerned with interpreting observed racial–ethnic differences in terms of the minority group status hypothesis (Anderson and Smith, 1975; Baumann and Udry, 1973; Cain and Weininger, 1973; Detray, 1973; Gardner, 1972; Gregory *et al.*, 1972; Ryder and Westoff, 1971; Westoff and Ryder, 1977).

AN ASSESSMENT OF PREVIOUS RESEARCH

A major problem in interpreting racial–ethnic group fertility differences in terms of minority group status inheres in the definition of minority group. Various subpopulations have been investigated without explanation of why they qualify as minority groups. The major problem has been the use of data on "nonwhites" to represent Negroes, along with the use of a white–nonwhite dichotomy to represent majority and minority populations (Goldscheider and Uhlenberg, 1969; Sly, 1970). Such a division ignores culture, physiognomy, and other traits that distinguish racial–ethnic groups. For example, the white–nonwhite distinction places Mexican Americans, Cubans, and Puerto Ricans in the white category (e.g., Ritchey, 1975), whereas Negroes, Native Americans, Chinese Americans, Japanese Americans, and other Orientals are agglomerated as nonwhites. This situation may be particularly troublesome in studies that omit the South, since a higher percentage of nonwhites who are not blacks live outside the South, as do most of the Spanish-heritage groups classified as whites. Clearly, any sub-population designated as a minority group should reflect more than a statistical aggregate.

What, then, constitutes a minority group? The work of Roberts and Lee (1974) demonstrated that results may vary depending on the definitions used. Consequently, it is important that the individuals under investigation be members of groups meeting certain qualifications in addition to constituting a statistical aggregate. The following criteria have been variously proposed as minimum conditions establishing eligibility for minority status. A *minority group* has been defined as any racial, ethnic (national origin), or religious population characterized by: (a) small size relative to the total societal population (Blalock, 1967:46; Browning, 1975:299); (b) a "relatively clearly defined subculture and separate pattern of social interaction [Petersen, 1964:237]"; (c) a historical pattern of opposition from and discrimination by the dominant population (Browning, 1975:229; Petersen, 1964:237); and (d) membership determined by ascription through a "socially invented 'rule of descent' [Wagley and Harris, 1959:7]." The most important of these is probably the third. All of the definitions, however, would eliminate analyses of statistical aggregates (such as nonwhites) as well as broad, heterogeneous groups such as Catholics that are, in reality, agglomerations of two or more smaller ethnic groups, some of which may no longer be minority groups, especially according to the third criterion. However, Mexican Americans and blacks continue to qualify as minority groups.

Other problems are methodological. Previous research (e.g., Rindfuss, 1975; Ritchey, 1975; and Sly, 1970) has not always taken (or been able to take) into account the *simultaneous* effects of income, education, and occupation on fertility or the effects of minority group status extraneous of all three socioeconomic variables (Bean and Wood, 1974). Confounding variables, such as wife's education, labor force participation, and age at marriage, have not always been controlled for (Sly, 1970). Sometimes variables have been controlled by delineating the sample, as in Sly's (1970) exclusion of the southern region and Roberts and Lee's (1974) elimination of women who were not working and of women who married after the age of 25. This not only may have the effect of truncating variance in some variables but may also eliminate women with characteristics relevant to the predictions of the minority status hypothesis (e.g., poor women from the South and higher status women who are employed). Although the investigation of contextual effects may prove to be an important approach for understanding the mechanisms that underlie the minority group status effect, more thought should be given to the nature of the contextual aggregate. Large units such as societies (Kennedy, 1973) or states (Ritchey, 1975) may be inappropriate. Ritchey, for example, categorizes individuals based on the overall degree of inequality for their state of residence, a procedure that ignores the fact that the degree of inequality is not uniform throughout each state. To assign all residents of Texas only one value, "high," and all residents of Kentucky only one value, "low," on the index of racial inequality obscures the fact that parts of Kentucky may be higher in inequality than parts of Texas. The states (or any large aggregate) as a unit of analysis may mask as much variation as is revealed.

Another difficulty is that it has not always been entirely clear what results would support the minority group status hypothesis as opposed to the social characteristics hypothesis. For example, the latter hypothesis is presumably supported if fertility differences between racial and ethnic groups disappear after controlling for socioeconomic variables. And, in fact, this has been the approach taken by a number of studies, as noted before. However, adjustment for population differences in the distribution of certain socioeconomic characteristics requires the assumption that the socioeconomic variables are related to fertility in the same way *within* racial and ethnic groups. That is, there must be no statistical interaction between racial and ethnic group membership and socioeconomic factors in their effects on fertility (e.g., Kerlinger and Pedhazur, 1973).

When the possibility of such interaction is considered, however, it is apparent that different patterns of results might be taken as evidence in support of the minority group status hypothesis. On the one hand, racial–ethnic differences in the relationship between social characteristics and fertility might constitute a minority status effect. In fact, when Goldscheider and Uhlenberg speak of high socioeconomic status blacks as having lower fertility than their white counterparts and lower socioeconomic status blacks as having higher fertility than their white counterparts, this is the kind of effect to which they seem to be referring. On the other hand, if it is assumed that there are no differences between blacks and whites in relationships between socioeconomic variables and fertility, adjustments for differences in the distribution of these factors can be made to see if fertility differences remain after taking them into account. If such differences do persist, then this would provide evidence in support of minority–majority fertility differences that could not be attributed to differences in socioeconomic status. However, this would not be a minority group status effect in the sense in which the term seems to be used by Goldschneider and Uhlenberg. Graphs of these alternatives, which we have termed, respectively, an "effect difference" and a "levels difference" (the pattern of similar relationships but different levels of fertility owing to the fact that distributional differences in socioeconomic factors do not account for all of the fertility differences), are depicted in Figure 8.2.

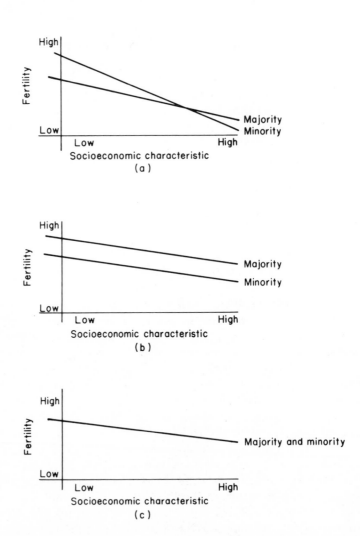

Figure 8.2 Graphs illustrating minority differences in fertility rates in relationship to the majority fertility rate and to socioeconomic variables, as projected by the three leading hypotheses outlined in the text.

It is important to specify which of these patterns constitutes evidence in support of the minority group status hypothesis. In reality, the patterns imply that different social processes bring about differential racial–ethnic fertility. The effect difference implies the kind of process about which Goldschneider and Uhlenberg (1969) spoke–acculturation preceding socioeconomic assimilation, with the result that higher status members of minority groups resort to exaggeratedly low (by majority standards) fertility in order to overcome the insecurities of minority group status and to sustain progress toward the achievement of socioeconomic goals acquired in the process of acculturation. The levels difference, however, implies a process that makes no supposition about acculturation preceding socioeconomic assimilation. If anything, this pattern is more consistent with the possibility that socioeconomic assimilation occurs before acculturation in that fertility differences between racial or ethnic groups remain (at all socioeconomic levels) even after accounting for as much of the difference as possible by differences in socioeconomic status.

The lower portion of Figure 8.2 presents an example of the circumstances necessary to satisfy the characteristics hypothesis. In this case, socioeconomic differences are sufficient to account for fertility differences between racial and/or ethnic groups. It is important to emphasize, however, that this conclusion is warranted only if it is first established that different relationships between socioeconomic characteristics and fertility do *not* exist within the racial and/or ethnic groups being examined. It is also worth reiterating that evidence of minority–majority differences in relationships between socioeconomic characteristics and fertility does not, in itself, provide a sufficient basis for inferring the existence of a minority group status effect. That is, the finding of a statistically significant interaction effect is not necessarily equivalent to support for the minority group status hypothesis. It also must be shown that this results in lower average fertility for minority women of higher socioeconomic status as compared to the average fertility of majority women of similarly high socioeconomic status.

A POSSIBILITY FOR FURTHER RESEARCH

The minority group status hypothesis involves the prediction of a particular pattern of interaction between racial–ethnic group membership and socioeconomic status in their effects on fertility. Specifically, a minority group status effect is most likely to be found among those members of minority groups who have experienced the greatest socioeconomic attainment but who nonetheless have been denied the benefits of complete integration into the majority society (e.g., who still find intermarriage and perhaps other kinds of primary group relationships proscribed owing to continuing discrimination and prejudice). In short, the effect is thought to come about as a result of felt discrepancies in the rate at which various kinds of assimilation occur. With rising socioeconomic attainment (i.e., increasing socioeconomic assimilation), minority "insecurity" is assumed to increase, at least as long as reminders of discrimination and racism linger in the society.

Carrying this line of reasoning further, we would expect minority group status effects to be more evident in some contexts than in others. In particular, under conditions in which the social and economic distance between the members of the minority and the majority group are minimized, the minority group status effect on fertility might be expected to be strongest. In the rest of this discussion, we suggest three factors that may be related to diminished socioeconomic distance between minority and majority groups and, thus, that may condition the effect on fertility of minority group status. These are (a) residence in an urban versus a rural place; (b) residence in an integrated as opposed to a segregated area; and (c) membership in a generational group that is distant from, rather than proximate to, some place of origin. We consider these factors as they might influence the fertility patterns of blacks and, in some cases, Mexican Americans.

Urban versus Rural Residence

Occupational achievement is higher in urban than in rural places (Blau and Duncan, 1967:248–249). Moreover, in all four (census) regions of the country (North Central, North East, South, and West), urban blacks (males, aged 16 and over) have higher median years of schooling completed than do rural farm or rural nonfarm blacks. Also, urban blacks have higher median incomes than do rural blacks (farm or nonfarm) within each region (U.S. Bureau of the Census, 1973). Hence, minority group status effects on fertility might be hypothesized to be stronger in urban than in rural areas. Indirect evidence in support of this hypothesis is found in a study by Slesinger (1974) that reported greater average differences in children ever born calculated by educational level for black men living in larger places than for black men living in smaller places. No test was conducted in that study for a minority status effect, however, since the purpose of the research was not to examine minority–majority fertility differences.

Other factors besides minority group status, however, may make for the possibility of higher-order interaction effects on fertility among racial–ethnic group membership, socioeconomic status, and rural–urban residence factors. For example, rural to urban migration has generally been found to increase socioeconomic differentials in fertility among urban women (Duncan, 1965; Freedman and Slesinger, 1961; Goldberg, 1959). Also, a disproportionate share of urban men with farm backgrounds are black (Blau and Duncan, 1967). Hence, if urban residence, socioeconomic status, and racial–ethnic membership were found to interact in their effects on fertility, this would not in itself constitute support for the minority group status hypothesis. This result must be shown to involve the pattern wherein the fertility of *higher status* black women is lower than the fertility of their white counterparts.

Integrated versus Segregated Residential Area

A minority group status effect may also be more likely in some urban contexts than in others. There are numerous references in the racial–ethnic group literature that affirm the importance of residential segregation for reinforcing the norms of subcultures and for providing the milieu in which intraethnic interaction can occur. These have covered a variety of minority groups, including the Chinese (Fong, 1965), the Russians (Simirenko, 1964), the Italians (Myers, 1950), blacks (Blalock, 1967), and various European immigrant groups (Lieberson, 1963; see also Beshers, 1962, Park, 1952:20 and Timms, 1971). Not only do ethnic neighborhoods reinforce distinctive minority behavior, but a complementary process is also at work—one that might be called "migratory emulation"—whereby individuals desiring assimilation into the majority society may move out of the ethnic neighborhood and into majority residential areas, whereas ethnics more satisfied with their heritage may remain behind. Timms (1971:98) notes "that residential location and relocation may be seen as strategies for minimizing the social distance between the individual and populations which he desires to emulate and for maximizing that from groups he wishes to leave behind."

This is not entirely a unidirectional process, but, overall, the balance of moves to and from an ethnic enclave may reflect efforts to make residence more harmonious with values. Although, as has been noted in other research (Wilensky, 1965:136), the break with the old area may not be complete; thus, the frequency of visits to a former neighborhood would not seem to be as crucial an indicator of assimilationist potentialities as actual residence itself. It might thus be hypothesized that the more socioeconomically assimilated members of minority groups living in integrated residential areas will experience more insecurity than the more socioeconomically assimilated persons living in nonintegrated areas. Hence, one might predict that a minority group status effect on fertility would be more likely in the former case than in the latter. Or, if present in both cases, one would expect it to be stronger under the former circumstances.

In nonurban areas, the mediating influence of residential segregation on minority fertility patterns appears to be less predictable. On the one hand, living in an area that includes appreciable numbers of whites might be hypothesized to heighten the insecurity of higher status minority persons in rural as well as in urban areas. On the other hand, residential location in rural areas may not reflect assimilationist preferences and outcomes as much as it may in urban areas.

Generational Distance versus Generational Proximity

Another variable that may affect the strength of a minority group status effect is generational distance from region of origin. Among blacks, numerous studies have shown appreciable differences in education and income among southern blacks, northren blacks born in the South, and northern blacks born in the North (Lieberson and Wilkinson, 1976; Long and Hansen, 1977; Long and Heltman, 1975). The former two groups exhibit higher socioeconomic achievement than do northern blacks born in the North. This greater assimilation (in the sense of higher socioeconomic achievement relative to other groups of blacks) provides a basis for hypothesizing that minority group status effects on fertility may be more likely among northern blacks born in the South than among the other two groups and more likely among northern blacks born in the North than among southern blacks. We do not hypothesize comparable fertility differences between first and later generation northern blacks born in the North because such differences have not been previously found with respect to other variables (Lieberson and Wilkinson, 1976).

Mexican Americans constitute a group that might be expected to be an exception to the minority group status hypothesis. Not only are Mexican Americans seemingly pronatalist (Bradshaw and Bean, 1972), but they are also predominantly Catholic (Grebler et al., 1970:487), although their religion has been argued not to be a factor in their pronatalism (Alvirez, 1973; Browning, 1975). Whatever the case, recent studies indicate that assimilation processes among Mexican Americans may be affected by the fact that Mexico is such a proximate point of socioeconomic reference for members of this minority group (e.g., Bean and Wood, 1974; Dworkin, 1970; Marcum and Bean, 1976). In particular, Marcum and Bean found among Mexican Americans that the effects on fertility of intergenerational occupational mobility did not take hold until after the second generation, at which point they had a depressing effect on the fertility of both upwardly (especially) and downwardly mobile couples. This suggests that among Mexican Americans the minority group status hypothesis may be more likely to find empirical support among later than among early generation couples.

SUMMARY AND CONCLUSION

In this chapter we have (a) presented an overview of certain aspects of racial–ethnic group fertility differences in the United States; (b) reviewed and evaluated the research efforts aimed at interpreting these differences; and (c) suggested a particular research strategy for further investigations of the "minority group status hypothesis." In this latter regard, we have argued that if minority group status affects reproductive behavior in the way suggested by Goldcheider and Uhlenberg (1969), then minority couples of higher socioeconomic status will exhibit lower fertility than majority couples of similar socioeconomic standing. We have also hypothesized that a minority group status effect on fertility is more likely to emerge under conditions of less socioeconomic distance between majority and minority groups. Whether or not these possibilities actually prove to be the case is an empirical question that invites our further investigation.

REFERENCES

Alvirez, David
    1973   "The effects of formal church affiliation and religiosity on the fertility patterns of Mexican-American Catholics." *Demography* (10 (February):19–36.
Anderson, John, and Jack Smith
    1975   "Planned and unplanned fertility in a metropolitan area: Black and white differences." *Family Plannning Perspectives* 7:281–285.
Bauman, Karl E., and J. Richard Udry
    1973   "The differences in unwanted births between blacks and whites." *Demography* 10(August):315–328.
Bean, Frank D., and Charles H. Wood
    1974   "Ethnic variations in the relationship between income and fertility." *Demography* 11(November):629–640.

Beaujot, Roderic P., Karol J. Krotki, and P. Krishnan
  1977   "The effects of assimilation on ethnic fertility differentials." Paper
            presented at the annual meetings of the Population Association of
            America. St. Louis, Missouri, April.
Beshers, James M.
  1962   *Urban Social Structure*. New York: The Free Press of Glencoe.
Blalock, Hubert M. Jr.
  1967   *Toward a Theory of Minority Group Relations*. New York: Capri-
            corn Books.
Blau, Peter M., and Otis Dudley Duncan
  1967   *The American Occupational Structure*. New York: John Wiley and
            Sons.
Bogue, Donald J.
  1969   *Principles of Demography*. New York: John Wiley and Sons.
Bradshaw, Benjamin S., and Frank D. Bean
  1972   "Some aspects of the fertility of Mexican-Americans." Pp. 140–164
            in Charles F. Westoff and Robert Parke, Jr. (eds.), Demographic and
            Social Aspects of Population Growth, Research Reports, Volume 1,
            Commission on Population Growth and the American Future. Wash-
            ington, D.C.: U.S. Government Printing Office.
Browning, Harley L.
  1975   "The reproductive behavior of minority groups in the U.S.A." In
            William Montagna and William A. Sadler (eds.), *Reproductive Be-
            havior*. New York: Plenum Publishing.
Cain, G., and A. Weininger
  1973   "Economic determinants of fertility: Results from cross-sectional
            aggregate data." *Demography* 10(May):205–233.
Detray, D.
  1973   "Child quality and the demand for children." *Journal of Political
            Economy* 81(no. 2 supplement)580–590.
Duncan, Otis Dudley
  1965   "Gradients of urban influence on the rural population." *Midwest
            Sociologist* 18(Winter):27–30.
Dworkin, A. G.
  1970   "Stereotypes and self-images held by native-born and foreign-born
            Mexican Americans." In John H. Burma (ed.), *Mexican Americans
            in the United States*. New York: Holt, Rinehart and Winston.
Farley, Reynolds
  1966   "Recent changes in Negro fertility." *Demography* 5(February):188–
            203.
  1972   "Fertility and mortality trends among blacks in the United States."
            Pp. 111–138 in Charles F. Westoff and Robert Parke, Jr. (eds.),
            Demographic and Social Aspects of Population Growth, Research
            Reports, Volume 1, U.S. Commission on Population Growth and
            the American Future. Washington, D.C.: U.S. Government Printing
            Office.
Fong, Stanley L. M.
  1965   "Assimilation of Chinese in America: Changes in orientation and
            acculturation." *American Journal of Sociology* 71(November):265–
            273.

Freedman, Ronald, and Doris P. Slesinger
1961   "Fertility differentials for the indigenous nonfarm population of the United States." *Population Studies* 15(2):161–173.
Freedman, Ronald, Pascal K. Whelpton, and John W. Smit
1961   "Socioeconomic factors in religious differences in fertility." *American Sociological Review* 26(August):608–614.
Gardner, B.
1972   "Economic aspects of the fertility of rural–farm and urban women." *Southern Economic Journal* 38:518–924.
Goldberg, David
1959   "The fertility of two-generation urbanites." *Population Studies* 12 (3):214–222.
Goldscheider, Calvin
1971   *Population, Modernization, and Social Structure.* Boston, Massachusetts: Little Brown and Company.
Goldscheider, Calvin, and Peter R. Uhlenberg
1969   "Minority group status and fertility." *American Journal of Sociology* 74(January):361–372.
Grebler, Leo, Joan W. Moore, and Ralph C. Guzman
1970   *The Mexican-American People.* New York: The Free Press.
Gregory, P. R., V. M. Campbell, and B. S. Cheng
1972   "A simultaneous equation model of birth rates in the United States." *The Review of Economics and Statistics* 54:374–380.
Griffith, Janet
1973   "Social pressure on family size intentions." *Family Planning Perspectives* 5:237–242.
Huyck, Earl E.
1966   "White–nonwhite differentials: Overview and implications." *Demography* 3(2):548–565.
Kennedy, Robert E. Jr.
1973   "Minority group status and fertility: The Irish." *American Sociological Review* 38(February):85–96.
Kerlinger, Fred N., and Elazar J. Pedhazur
1973   *Multiple Regression in Behavioral Research.* New York: Holt, Rinehart and Winston.
Lee, Everett S., and Anne S. Lee
1959   "The future fertility of the American Negro." *Social Forces* 37 (March):228–231.
Lieberson, Stanley
1963   *Ethnic Patterns in American Cities.* New York: The Free Press of Glencoe.
Lieberson, Stanley, and Christy A. Wilkinson
1976   "A comparison between northern and southern Blacks residing in the North." *Demography* 13:199–224.
Long, Larry H., and Kristin A. Hansen
1977   "Selectivity of black return migration to the South." *Rural Sociology* 42:317–331.
Long, Larry H., and Lynne R. Heltman
1975   "Migration and income differences between black and white men in the North." *American Journal of Sociology* 80(May):1391–1409.

Marcum, John P., and Frank D. Bean
    1976   "Minority group status as a factor in the relationship between mo-
            bility and fertility: The Mexican American case." *Social Forces* 55
            (September):135–148.
Myers, Jerome K.
    1950   "Assimilation to the ecological and social systems of a community."
            American Sociological Review 15(June):367–372. Reprinted in George
            A. Theodorson (ed.), *Studies in Human Ecology.* New York: Harper
            and Row, 1961:273–279.
Park, Robert Ezra
    1952   *Human Communities.* Glencoe, Illinois: The Free Press.
Petersen, William
    1961   *Population.* London: The Macmillan Company.
    1964   *The Politics of Population.* New York: Doubleday and Company.
Pohlmann, Vernon C., and Robert H. Walsh
    1975   "Black minority racial status and fertility in the United States,
            1970." *Sociological Focus* 8(April):97–108.
Presser, Harriet
    1971   "The timing of the first birth, female roles and Black fertility."
            Milbank Memorial Fund Quarterly 49:329–361.
Rindfuss, Ronald R.
    1975   "Minority status and recent fertility trends." Center for Demography
            and Ecology, University of Wisconsin–Madison, Working Paper 75-
            21, July.
Rindfuss, Ronald R., and James A. Sweet
    1977   *Postwar Fertility Trends and Differentials in the United States.*
            New York: Academic Press.
Ritchey, P. Neal
    1975   "The effect of minority group status on fertility: A re-examination
            of concepts." *Population Studies* 29(July):249–257.
Roberts, Robert E., and Eun Sul Lee
    1974   "Minority group status and fertility revisited." *American Journal
            of Sociology* 80(September):503–523.
Ryder, Norman B.
    1973   "Recent trends and group differences in fertility." In Charles F.
            Westoff (ed.), *Toward the End of Growth.* Englewood Cliffs, New
            Jersey: Prentice-Hall.
Ryder, Norman B., and Charles F. Westoff.
    1971   *Reproduction in the United States, 1965.* Princeton, New Jersey:
            Princeton University Press.
Simirenko, Alex
    1964   *Pilgrims, Colonists, and Frontiersmen.* New York: The Free Press
            of Glencoe.
Slesinger, Doris P.
    1974   "The relationship of fertility to measures of metropolitan domi-
            nance: A new look." *Rural Sociology* 39(Fall):350–361.
Sly, David F.
    1970   "Minority-group status and fertility: An extension of Goldscheider
            and Uhlenberg." *American Journal of Sociology* 76(November):443–
            459.

Smith, T. Lynn
    1960   *Fundamentals of Population Study.* Chicago, Illinois: J. B. Lippin-
            cott.
Thomlinson, Ralph
    1965   *Population Dynamics.* New York: Random House.
Timms, Duncan
    1971   *The Urban Mosaic.* London: Cambridge University Press.
U.S. Bureau of the Census
    1973   Census of Population, 1970. Subject Reports, Final Report PC(2)-1B,
            Negro Population. Washington, D.C.: U.S. Government Printing
            Office.
Wagley, C., and M. Harris
    1959   *Minorities in the New World.* New York: Columbia University
            Press.
Westoff, Charles F., Robert Potter, Philip Sagi, and Elliot Mishler
    1961   *Family Growth in Metropolitan America.* Princeton, New Jersey:
            Princeton University Press.
Westoff, Charles F., and Norman B. Ryder
    1977   *The Contraceptive Revolution.* Princeton, New Jersey: Princeton
            University Press.
Whelpton, Pascal K., Arthur Campbell, and John Patterson
    1966   *Fertility and Family Planning in the United States.* Princeton, New
            Jersey: Princeton University Press.
Wilensky, Harold L.
    1965   "A second look at the traditional view of urbanism." Pp. 135–147
            in Roland L. Warren (ed.), *Perspectives on the American Community.*
            Chicago, Illinois: Rand McNally and Company.

9

A Fertility Reaction
to a Historical Event:
Southern White Birthrates
and the 1954 Desegregation Ruling[1]

RONALD R. RINDFUSS
JOHN SHELTON REED
CRAIG ST. JOHN

At a time in the 1950s when the overall U.S. birthrate was increasing sharply, the states of the South [2] displayed a markedly lower increase, thereby closing, even reversing, a longstanding regional difference in fertility. The most marked convergence between the entire South and the remainder of the country occurred between 1954 and 1955 (see Figure 9.1). This one sharp shift is the subject of this report; the long-range change also seen in Figure 9.1 is discussed elsewhere.[3]

[1] Supported in part by a grant from the Carolina Population Center of the University of North Carolina. We thank Judy Kovenock for assistance in programming. Originally published in *Science* 201 (14 July, 1978):178–180. Copyright 1978 by the American Association for the Advancement of Science. Reprinted by permission of *Science*.

[2] The "South" here is the "census South," which includes the 11 former Confederate states plus Delaware, Maryland, West Virginia, Kentucky, Oklahoma, and the District of Columbia.

[3] See R. R. Rindfuss, *Social Forces*, in press.

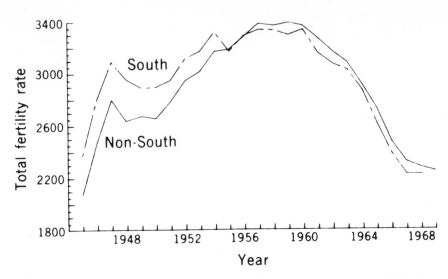

Figure 9.1   Total fertility rates of southern and non-southern women, 1945–1969. The total fertility rate is the number of children 1000 women of childbearing age would be predicted to give birth to in their lifetimes if the fertility rate of the base period remained unchanged. (Figure courtesy of *Social Forces*)

Because these fertility rates were computed from sample data from the 1960 and 1970 censuses, the shift in 1954–1955 was originally dismissed as being due to random variation. However, further inspection revealed that the same pattern exists in the total number of births actually registered. We examined reported vital registration data for whites and blacks. In the South between 1953 and 1954 the number of white births increased faster than in the nation as a whole (2.2% in the South, .8% nationally) but declined by .7% between 1954 and 1955 while the national figure was increasing by 1.9%. Between 1955 and 1956 the number of white births increased again in the South (by 2.2%), but more slowly than in the nation as a whole (the national increase was 2.6%). In 1955, 23 of the 32 non-southern states had more white births than in 1954, whereas only 4 of the 16 southern states did. The year before, 28 of the non-southern states and 14 of the southern states had shown increases. The pattern of black births was similar but less pronounced.

Aberrant behavior in the South in the year 1954 is likely to suggest its own explanation to those familiar with the recent history of the region. On May 17, 1954 the Supreme Court rendered its decision in *Brown* v. *Board of Education,* declaring public school segregation to be unconstitutional. It is clear that the court's unanimous decision struck at what many white southerners saw as the basis of their region's way of life and that it came as a shock to many southerners.[4] It seems reasonable, therefore, to entertain the conjecture that anomie and fear for the future led some southerners to put off having children who would otherwise have been conceived during this period.[5] First, the timing was right, roughly speaking: The effects of events in May and in the summer of 1954 would not show up in birth figures until 1955. Second, the slighter drop among blacks seems consistent with the hypothesis: Although black southerners also experienced uncertainty in the wake of the court's ruling (their traditional pattern of education was threatened, and undoubtedly they feared that violence might accompany desegregation), obviously the status and prerogatives of white southerners were more clearly threatened.

Table 9.1 shows the pattern of change in numbers of births in relation to the existence of segregated schools.[6] Of the 11 former Confederate states, all of which are included in almost any definition of the South, only 2—North Carolina and Florida—had an increase in white births between 1954 and 1955. (Nine of the 11 had had an increase the year before, and 9 had an increase the next year.) Six other states and the District of Columbia also required school segregation in 1954, but most of these had relatively small black populations and were less affected by the court's ruling. Three of these 6 states and the District of Columbia had fewer white births in 1955 than in 1954, and 3 had more. (In 1954 only the District of Columbia had fewer white births than in 1953. In 1956 only the District and Kentucky had fewer than in 1955.) Of the 31 other states, 22 had more white births in 1955 than

[4] White southern opposition to the decision hardly needs documenting: but it may be noted here that in a sample survey 2 years after the Court's ruling only 14% of white residents of the census South expressed support for school desegregation (see H. R. Hyman and P. B. Sheatsley, 1964).

[5] Psychological stress can trigger physiological subfecundity by blocking the release of the luteinizing hormone necessary for ovulation (L. Mastroianni, 1975). It can also reduce male potency. But we are not suggesting that the *Brown* decision had those effects.

We considered current events other than the court's decision as alternative explanations for the decline in southern fertility. These ranged from Hurricane Hazel to the possibility of a short-run economic downturn in the South. Upon investigation, none of these alternative explanations seemed plausible.

[6] This table is based on the absolute number of white births—in other words, on the numerator of a conventional fertility rate (the denominators are not available for individual states). This statistic is unsatisfactory in many applications (see, for example, M. Gomez, B. and J. Reynolds, 1973), but it is unlikely that the three regions' denominators changed appreciably (and differently) in the short time span involved.

TABLE 9.1

Direction of Change in Number of White Births between 1954 and 1955 in States with Dual School Systems and in the Other States

State group	Number of states with:	
	Increase	Decrease
Former Confederate states	2	9
Other dual-system states [a]	3	4
Remaining states	22	9

[a] The District of Columbia is included here.

in 1954; of the nine exceptions, 3—Pennsylvania, Indiana, and Kansas (the state in which the *Brown* case originated)—had a noticeable degree of school segregation at the local level.[7] (In 1954, 27 of the 31 had more white births than in 1953; in 1956, 22 had more white births than in 1955.)

We also compared 1954 and 1955 births grouped according to age of mother and to birth order of child. In every age group the ratio of the number of births in 1955 to the number of births in 1954 was less in the former Confederate states and in the other states with dual school systems than it was in the remainder of the country. The same is true for birth order, with one exception. Among all the groups of states there were declines from the number in 1954, in the number of second births in 1955 and the decline was slightly larger among the other states than in either group of dual-system states.

These differences between the states affected by the *Brown* v. *Board of Education* decision and those not affected by the decision do not in themselves, of course, establish a cause-and-effect relationship. Yet it is a striking coincidence and one that gets more striking when we look at month-by-month data.

The earliest one could possibly expect to see any effect the ruling might have on fertility would be in the early spring of 1955. Some couples who had not been practicing contraception may have begun to do so immediately after the Supreme Court decision. Some couples who had planned to stop using contraception in order to have a baby may have decided not to stop. In either case the effect on subsequent fertility

---

[7] Of the other 6, 5 were small states that exhibit considerable fluctuations in number of births from year to year: Idaho, Maine, North Dakota, Rhode Island, and Wyoming.

levels would be gradual because of the time required to conceive in the absence of deliberate contraception. Also, it can be assumed that these hypothetical decisions would not have been made the day after the Supreme Court's decision but that it took a while for the implications of the decision to sink in. Finally, after it became clear that segregation would continue for some time, that life would go on much as usual, that "all deliberate speed" could be very deliberate, and that southern politicians had some resources of their own to resist with—in other words, when it became clear that nothing much was going to change any time soon—our hypothetical couples would have resumed their normal fertility behavior, and the southern white birthrate would resume its increase. Thus, the major depression in southern white birthrates in reaction to the Supreme Court decision would be expected to occur in the late spring or early summer of 1955 and to terminate shortly thereafter.

In Figure 9.2 we have plotted for the three groups of states discussed above the number of white births in each month of 1955 expressed as a percentage of the number in the same month in 1954. This statistic, though crude, removes seasonal variation in birth rates (including variation due to differences in the number of days in a month) and any interaction of that variation with region.[8] In both sets of states with segregated schools we find a decrease in the number of white births that may have begun in late spring and early summer. In the summer both sets of states with segregated schools experienced lower fertility than the year before, but that is not the case in the remainder of the United States. By the end of fall this depression in number of births relative to the previous year was essentially over in both groups of dual-system states. The reduction was somewhat greater and lasted somewhat longer in the former Confederate states than in the other group, as would be expected.

The pattern of month-by-month variation within individual states further supports the evidence of Figure 9.2. In order to reduce chance variation, we examined only the 34 states that averaged more than 2000

[8] It has been suggested that the denominators for the data in Figure 9.2 be based on a 3-year average rather than on a single year. We have done this calculation; the differences between the dual-system states and the rest of the country are similar to those in Figure 9.2 but less pronounced. However, using a 3-year average increases the problems involved in numerator analysis (see Footnote 5). The 3-year average may conceal substantial and differential changes brought about by the substantial migration from the South. Using only the preceding year minimizes this effect. Also, the effect of the upward fertility trend of the early 1950s is less with a 1-year base than with a 3-year average.

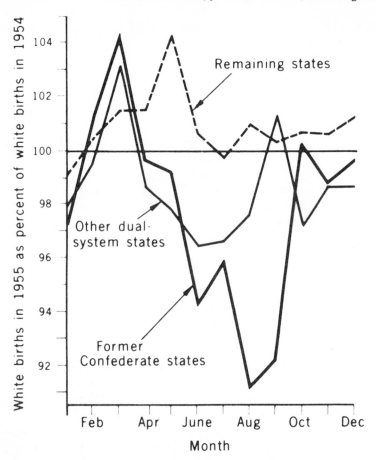

Figure 9.2 White births in each month of 1955 as a percentage of white births in the same months of 1954, in states with dual school systems and in the other states.

white births per month during this period. Of these, 16 were dual-system states. All but 2 of the 16 had fewer white births during the late spring and early summer of 1955 than in those periods in 1954. That was true of only 7 of the 18 unitary-system states, 6 of the 7 being states that border on one or more former Confederate states or other dual-system states.

In other words, we find the number of white births in the South to be lower than expected at almost the exact time we would predict, assuming that the *Brown* decision demoralized prospective parents enough to cause some who would otherwise have stopped contracepting to continue and to cause others who had not been contracepting to start using contraception. The deflection is short-lived: It is concentrated in a period of 3 or 4 months. It is not large: Southern white birthrates were reduced by something on the order of 5%.[9]

But even this small deflection is of considerable historical interest if one accepts our explanation of it. It may, in addition, have some implications beyond that—implications for the study of fertility trends elsewhere in the developed world and implications about the ability of social scientists to explain and predict such trends. Within the United States, for instance, since World War II there have been large, unprecedented, and unpredicted changes in fertility behavior, changes with significant consequences for many institutions in American society. The fact that these changes have been found within every social, economic, and racial group [10] suggests that they cannot be accounted for by changes in the composition of the population and that their explanation must be linked to historical events.

REFERENCES

Box, G. I. P., and G. C. Tiao
    1965   "A change in level of nonstationary time series." *Biometrika* 52: 181–192.
Glass, G. V.
    1968   "Analysis of data on the Connecticut speeding crackdown as a time series quasi-experiment." *Law and Society Review* 3:55—76.
Gomez B., Miguel, and Jack Reynolds
    1973   "Numerator analysis of fertility change in Costa Rica: A methodological examination." *Studies in Family Planning* 4(12):317–326.

[9] One should expect an effect like this not to be large. A deflection much greater than that observed would be, literally, incredible. The seasonally adjusted number of births in the former Confederate states for June, 1955 was slightly more than two standard deviations below the average number of births (seasonally adjusted) in those states for the previous 13 months. (June was chosen because it represents the approximate beginning of a substantial deflection. If August or September had been chosen, the difference would have been greater.) Alternatively, it is rather unlikely, if chance variation were the only factor at work, that the two groups of dual-system states would show declines for April, May, June, and July of 1955 (relative to the same months of the previous year) while the rest of the country experienced increases. Perhaps we should note that neither the Box-Tiao test (G. E. P. Box and G. C. Tiao, 1965) nor the variation proposed by Glass (G. V. Glass, 1968) is appropriate here, because we are predicting a temporary change rather than a permanent one.

[10] R. R. Rindfuss and J. A. Sweet, 1977.

Hyman, Herbert R., and Paul B. Sheatsley
    1964   "Attitudes toward desegregation." *Scientific American* 211(July):16–
            23.
Mastroianni, Luigi Jr.
    1975   "Fertility disorders." In Seymour L. Romney *et al.* (eds.), *Gyne-
            cology and Obstetrics: The Health Care of Women.* New York: Mc-
            Graw-Hill.
Rindfuss, Ronald R.
    1978   "Changing patterns of fertility in the South: A social–demographic
            examination." *Social Forces.* (in press)
Rindfuss, Ronald R., and James A. Sweet
    1977   *Postwar Fertility Trends and Differentials in the United States.* New
            York: Academic Press.

10

Indicators of Family
and Household Structure
of Racial and Ethnic Minorities
in the United States

JAMES A. SWEET

INTRODUCTION

One area of demography currently receiving increased attention is the study of familial processes and structures. A number of different subject areas fall under this rubric: studies of nuptiality, age at marriage, and assortative mating; studies of separation, divorce, and remarriage; studies of household size and composition and family living arrangements of the population; and studies of the various consequences or sequelae of the incidence and timing of these familial processes. (Some of this literature is reviewed in Sweet, 1977a.)

In this chapter I shall review some of the issues and concerns that have prompted the recent growth of interest in the demography of the family. I will then turn to an examination of a number of aspects of family and household structure of racial and ethnic minorities. Planned extensions of this work will be reviewed in the conclusion of this chapter.

Impetus to the study of household formation and structure has come from several sources.

The Demography of Racial and Ethnic Groups.

The Desire to Study the Effects of Household Structure on Measured Income Inequality

Although it has long been known that differences in family size and composition may affect the measured "inequality" of an income distribution, several studies have appeared that attempt to measure the magnitude of these effects and to adjust for differences in family composition (see Paglin, 1975; Plotnick and Skidmore, 1975; Rivlin, 1975). One of the reasons for this new emphasis is a recognition that there are wide variations from one country to another in the patterns of household composition and household formation. The recent experience in the United States and in other Western countries indicates that there can be rather abrupt changes in the pattern of family and household living arrangements. Kuznets (1976) provides a detailed discussion of these.

One issue that has received some attention in the literature is that one way disadvantaged persons may adapt to an inadequacy of economic resources is by modifying their household compositions (see Tienda, 1976). Rather than establishing a separate household, a young couple, young nonmarried adult, or elderly person or couple may share the household of a relative, thus taking advantage of "economies of scale" in providing housing services. The extent to which this practice occurs differentially among racial and ethnic minorities may vary depending on "cultural traditions" relating to kinship and on the accessibility of relatives as well as to the economic level of the group.

Differences in household composition can have an important effect on measured income inequality and on the relative economic well-being of racial and ethnic minorities as compared with the majority white population. In fact, among disadvantaged minorities the relative disadvantage may be seriously understated if families are larger and tend to have more adult earners within them (Sweet, 1973, Chap. 6).

Farley (1977) reviews the trends in inequality between blacks and whites from World War II to 1974. He notes that between 1969 and 1975 the median income of all black families (in constant dollars) fell although the median income of both major component family types—husband–wife and female-headed families—increased. However, during this period the proportion of families with female heads (whose median income is less than one-half that of husband–wife families) rose rapidly.

In an analysis of change in the overall distribution of family income, Treas and Walther (1977) found that within-group income inequality declined considerably since 1951 for all family types and for unrelated individuals. However, the degree of inequality for the aggregate income distribution remained virtually unchanged over the period. Family and household types with relatively low incomes have increased in relative frequency, counteracting the effect of the decline in dispersion of the income distribution within family types.

A number of recent social trends have affected the aggregate pattern of living arrangements:

1. The rapid decline in fertility beginning in 1957 and accelerating in the early 1970s has considerably reduced the average number of children per household and will continue to have this effect as the change accumulates through the life cycle.
2. In addition, historical fluctuations in fertility have affected the age composition of the population and, thus, the family composition distribution of the population.
3. There has been an abrupt rise in the rate of marital disruption and perhaps a very recent decline in the rate of remarriage.
4. The age at first marriage of both men and women has been increasing.
5. The living arrangements of single as well as separated, divorced, and widowed individuals have changed through time. There is a much greater propensity of individuals who are not married to form their own households and to live in one-person households or in small households that do not include a family grouping.

Each of these social trends may have occurred differentially in various racial and ethnic minorities.

The Concern with Understanding the Consequences of "Welfare Programs" on the Family

One of the major issues that has emerged in discussions of welfare reform has been the concern that the current as well as the proposed alternate welfare programs have a variety of effects on decisions determining family composition, that is, the decision to marry, to separate, to bear a child, or to form a separate household. Studies using data from the various income maintenance experimental programs (Hannan *et al.*, 1976, 1977a,b; Knudson *et al.*, 1977; Middleton and Haas, 1977) as well as research studies using both cross-sectional and longitudinal data (Hoffman and Holmes, 1976; Ross and Sawhill, 1975; Sawhill *et al.*, 1975) have attempted to investigate these various effects. To date the results are, to say the least, less than definitive. The issues, and the results of research, are reviewed in MacDonald and Sawhill, 1978.

One conclusion that has emerged from the planning and execution of these experimental income maintenance programs is that not only can the basic approach to income maintenance affect family decisions, but also even apparently minor administrative details of such programs can have considerable effects on the way in which individuals are sorted into households and families (Institute for Research on Poverty, 1977; Klein, 1971; MacDonald and Sawhill, 1978).

One of the most interesting studies to date is the one that uses data from the Seattle and Denver Income Maintenance Experiment (Hannan *et al.*, 1976). In that study, there are differences among the white, black, and Chicano populations in the response of family decisions to the experimental income maintenance program.

The Need to Assess Social Indicators of Family Structure and Process

The most immediate impetus for this paper derives from work in social indicators pertaining to the family. By a *social indicator* I mean, quite simply, a summary measure that indicates how the family circumstances of various groups compare, either across time or in different parts of the social structure. Several studies of social indicators of the family have appeared.

Ferriss (1970) has provided an excellent compilation of time series of family phenomena. His indicators are largely derived from published tabulations from the Current Population Reports of the U.S. Bureau of the Census and from certain other official publications, for example, those of the National Center for Health Statistics. Since he was concerned with measures of social change, his measures were limited to those indicators for which published data are available over a period of time. They are largely indicators for the total population and not for subgroups. The only subgroups for which much data are presented are age groups and white and nonwhite. Glick (1969) considers "family stability" as a social indicator with particular emphasis on identifying measures that indicate "desirable" versus "undesirable" social change. Farley and Hermalin (1971) focus on indicators of family stability in order to assess trends for the black and white populations. They compare the marital status distribution, the proportion of families with female heads, the household and family status distribution and illegitimacy, and the family living arrangements of young children. The rationale for their discussion of a variety of indicators of family stability can be seen in the following excerpt:

> These observations suggest that the marital status of adults, their living arrangements, and the type of households into which children are born and in which they are reared, all have a bearing on family stability. Thus, one might derive the following definition of stability: A stable family system is one in which adults marry and live with their spouses, in their own households and in which children are born into and raised in such a household.
>
> On several counts, however, such an overarching definition of family stability is not too useful. Data that would enable households in the United States to be classified as "stable" or "unstable" according to this composite definition are not available. Even if such a classification were available, it is possible that the trends of the separate components are not all alike and that some differ from the trend in the composite measure. This information would be lost by reliance on one composite measure. Lastly, insofar as stability has some effect on life chances, it is of theoretical and practical interest to determine which components of stability are most related to educational and occupational outcomes and to social and psychological variables deemed to influence these outcomes.
>
> For these reasons we concluded that it would be useful to analyze separately the various dimensions of stability [Farley and Hermalin, 1971:2].

Some of the commonly used social indicators are less than adequate, and some can be quite misleading. For example, we have now learned that measures of prevalence of separation and divorce within a population are a poor indicator of the incidence of marital disruption (for a general discussion, see Sweet, 1972; for a discussion of black–white differences, see Sweet and Bumpass, 1974). This is the case because prevalence measures confound differences in marital disruption, remarriage rates, age at marriage distributions, and age structure differences in a single measure.

Similarly, the prevalence of female family heads within a population or subgroup may be a deceptive indicator. The process by which two persons separate and create two households, one of which is a female-headed household, involves a whole chain of demographic events. An increase in the number of female-headed families may result from changes at any point in the process.

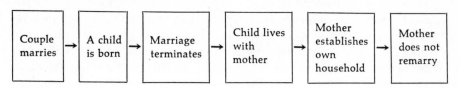

Female-headed families may also be created when an unmarried woman has a child (see also Cutright, 1973, 1974; Ross and Sawhill, 1975):

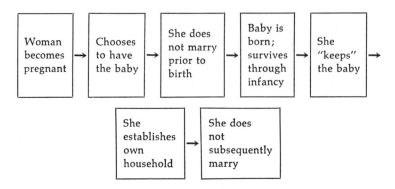

Yet neither of these processes, as I shall show later, is the modal path to female family headship—instead, it is widowhood. Thus, female family heads are not homogeneous with respect to the process by which they arrive in this status, with respect to the consequence of being in the status (e.g., not all female family heads have dependent children), or with respect to policy implications.

The Concern with Assessing the Consequences of the Incidence and Timing of Various Family Transitions

Duncan et al. (1972) address the question of family events as "career contingencies." There have been numerous studies of the effects of premarital pregnancy on marital disruption (for a review of the literature, see Sweet, 1977a:384). The effect of age at first marriage and age at first birth on the life chances of women and of young couples has also been studied by numerous investigators (see Sweet, 1977a:376–378).

A recent development of great significance for the study of the demography of family and household structure is the collection of longitudinal data on large samples of the population. We are now in a better position to understand the processes by which groups differ in household structure, whereas in the past we could only compare the structures themselves. Similarly, we could, in the past, observe the differential prevalence of family types among different economic or social categories or vice versa. Now we are in a position to understand better the social and economic determinants and consequences of family transitions (see Duncan and Morgan, 1976; Sweet, 1977a:397).

In this chapter, I present a number of indicators of family and household structure for racial and ethnic minority groups in the United States. These indicators have been selected primarily on the basis of their utility with respect to assessing the impact of variation among racial and ethnic groups in family and household structure on measured economic welfare and inequality. However, they also bear on other issues mentioned in the preceding discussion. The discussion will note the range of variability among ethnic groups and the strengths and weaknesses of these measures in saying something useful about family structure and process.[1]

DATA

Racial and Ethnic Groups

I have compiled data for 14 racial and ethnic groups (as defined by the U.S. Bureau of the Census in the 1970 Census). As a reference group I include:

1—Whites, excluding Spanish-surnamed whites (when using published materials, this group includes Spanish-surnamed whites).

Five "racial" minorities are identified:

2—Blacks
3—Chinese
4—Japanese
5—Filipinos
6—American Indians

Three Spanish-origin or descent groups are identified by responses to a direct question concerning the individual's origin or descent:

7—Mexican
8—Puerto Rican
9—Cuban

---

[1] The original version of this chapter included several other indicators, including: measures of prevalence of marriage, divorce, or separation, and remarriage; the living arrangements of children; and the living arrangements of the elderly. Copies of these tables and a discussion of them are available on request from the author at the Center for Demography, Social Science Building, University of Wisconsin, Madison, Wisconsin 53706.

As an alternative way of identifying the Mexican-origin population I
use:

10—Spanish-surnamed persons living in the five southwestern states.
In general, the figures for Mexican origin or descent and Spanish
surname are very similar. (For discussions of the identification of
this population, see Hernandez *et al.*, 1973.) We use Spanish
surnamed in addition to Mexican origin or descent because it is
available for earlier censuses and will permit measures of change.
The "origin or descent" question has been asked only in 1970.

11—Puerto Rico. I have included data on the population residing and
enumerated in the 1970 Census of Puerto Rico.

In addition, I have subdivided the black population into three components:

(*a*)—Those living in the rural South.
(*b*)—Those living in the urban South.
(*c*)—Those living outside the South.

The reason for this subdivision is that the previous literature suggests
that more "stable" black families reside in the rural South and least
"stable" families outside the South. The southern rural black population
is a predominantly nonfarm population. The rural farm black population
has virtually disappeared over the past several decades. When published
materials are utilized, the black population is not subdivided in this
manner.

Not all of the groups in this study are disadvantaged minority groups.
In fact, there is quite a wide range of variation in the socioeconomic
position of various groups. Median family income in 1969 varies from
$12,515 for Japanese Americans to $9961 for whites to $5832 for Ameri-
can Indians. In Puerto Rico it was only $3063.

Japanese	$12,515
Chinese	10,610
Whites (total)	9,961
Filipino	9,318
Cuban	8,529
Mexican	6,962
Puerto Rican	6,165
Black	6,067
American Indian	5,832
Puerto Rico	3,063

How do we classify married couples or families by ethnic status? With the exception of the Spanish-surname population,[2] there are several possible alternatives. In our earlier work on fertility (Rindfuss and Sweet, 1977), we chose to identify a couple as a member of an ethnic group if either husband or wife was a member. Thus, a couple consisting of a black husband and an Indian wife would fall in both the black and Indian universes. This procedure could be extended to households or families by including a person or family as a member of a group if any member of the household was a member.

The alternative is to use the ethnic status of the individual for that individual and the ethnic status of the household head for the household. In this chapter I have chosen this latter solution, largely to allow for computing convenience and to maximize comparability between the published census reports (which follow this practice) and our estimates made from the Public Use Samples.

Public Use Files

All data for this study derive from the 1970 Census of Population conducted in the United States and in Puerto Rico. I have used some information from the published census volumes but have relied primarily on the Public Use Sample tapes. Relatively little published information on family structure and composition is available for most of these ethnic minorities, with the exception of blacks. In order to supplement these published data, I have done a great deal of tabulation from the six separate 1% samples in the 1970 Census.

Sample Proportions

For the white population a 1/1000 sample has been used throughout. Because I use marriage data in some tables, the 5% state sample tape was used. For the two largest minority groups, Spanish surname and blacks, the full 1/100 sample from the 5% state file was used throughout. "Race" is available on all samples, so it was possible to use a 6/100 sample for the numerically smaller Indian, Chinese, Japanese, and Fili-

---

[2] Spanish-surname wives who did not have a Spanish surname at marriage acquired one at marriage. Similarly, their children are Spanish surnamed. In the census it is impossible to determine the separate ethnic identity of a woman and her husband based on the surname classification. It is, however, possible using the census question on Spanish origin or descent.

pino populations. However, when first marriage date and number of times married were required, only a 3/100 sample was possible. For Mexican Americans, Puerto Ricans in the United States, and Cubans, a 3/100 sample was used, since "origin or descent" is available only in the 5% sample. The data for Puerto Rico are available for a 1/100 sample.

By 1977 the results of the 1970 Census are somewhat outdated. In other work, I have used data from the March and June Current Population Surveys (CPS) to extend this work. Unfortunately, the CPS data may provide enough cases for whites, blacks, and Mexican American persons but not enough for the other groups considered here. In many instances, even the sample size for blacks and the Mexican American populations is not adequate.

FAMILY AND HOUSEHOLD INDICATORS

In the remainder of this chapter I consider indicators of the following aspects of family and household structure:

1. Age distribution
2. Family and household size
3. Population not living in families
4. Distribution of households by life-cycle stage
5. Female-headed families and children living in two-parent households
6. Families with nonnuclear family members
7. Living arrangements of certain categories of adults, including:
   a. Young unmarried persons
   b. Recently married couples
   c. Separated and divorced persons without children
   d. Separated and divorced mothers

Age Distribution

The age distribution of a population may have a considerable effect on its aggregate household and family composition. I present for later reference in Table 10.1 a summary of the age distribution of each of our populations.

1. High fertility populations such as American Indians, southern rural blacks, and persons of Spanish surname or Mexican origin have high proportions under 18.

TABLE 10.1

Age Distributions [a]

Racial–ethnic group	<18	18–44	45–64	65+	Total
White	33.1	35.0	21.3	10.6	100.0
Black	42.8	33.7	16.4	7.1	100.0
Spanish surname	46.3	35.8	13.4	4.6	100.0
Chinese	32.5	43.8	17.4	6.4	100.0
Japanese	29.3	42.7	20.1	7.9	100.0
Filipino	35.7	42.7	15.0	6.6	100.0
American Indian	45.4	35.2	13.4	6.0	100.0
Mexican	47.4	36.2	12.2	4.2	100.0
Puerto Rican	47.2	40.2	10.1	2.5	100.0
Cuban	32.4	39.2	21.6	6.7	100.0
Puerto Rico	43.6	34.7	14.9	6.8	100.0
Southern rural black	47.6	28.2	15.8	8.4	100.0
Southern urban black	41.9	33.4	16.9	7.8	100.0
Non-southern black	42.0	35.7	16.2	6.1	100.0

Source: Public Use Samples.

[a] In this and in all other tables derived from Public Use Samples, the white population excludes the white Spanish-surname population. In tables derived from published census sources, the white population includes the white Spanish-surname population. The Ns on which the percentages in this table and in all subsequent tables are based may be obtained by writing the author. They are omitted here for reasons of economy.

2. Some groups, such as Mexican Americans and Puerto Ricans (in the United States), have very low proportions of elderly persons, reflecting age patterns of immigration, the recency of immigration, and high fertility.

3. The low fraction of southern rural blacks at ages 18–44 probably results from out-migration.

Family and Household Size

In the census, most individuals are enumerated in households. The only individuals not in households are those living in group quarters, either as inmates of institutions or in other types of group quarters, such as college dormitories or rooming houses. The typical household consists of a family, that is, a number of related individuals sharing a common living unit. Not all households, however, involve families. A single individual living by him- or herself in an apartment or other housing unit would be regarded as a household, as would two or more unrelated individuals sharing a common living unit. Household size can vary from one group to another depending on such things as levels of fertility (determining the number of children in the average household), the age pattern of marriage, the age distribution of the population, levels of divorce and remarriage, and typical living patterns of the widowed elderly as well as of other unmarried individuals. I shall return to some of these issues in subsequent sections.

Average household size for whites in 1970 was slightly over three persons (Table 10.2). Black household size was about three and one-half persons per household, and Spanish-surname households had an average size of more than four persons. Other groups with household size exceeding four persons are Puerto Rico and southern rural blacks. Indian and Puerto Rican households are only slightly below four persons per household.

The overall average household size is a result of the average size of households of specific types and the distribution of households among the types. For my purposes, I have identified three types of households:

1. *Husband–wife families*—in which a married, spouse present, person is the head

TABLE 10.2

Mean Household Size

Racial–ethnic group	Husband–wife families	Other family households	Nonfamily households	Total
White	3.56	3.02	1.14	3.04
Black	4.28	4.05	1.18	3.54
Spanish surname	4.69	3.88	1.19	4.16
Japanese	3.79	3.13	1.19	3.18
Chinese	4.13	3.23	1.32	3.44
Filipino	4.37	3.68	1.39	3.66
American Indian	4.55	4.08	1.16	3.86
Mexican	4.81	3.96	1.20	4.24
Puerto Rican	4.30	3.83	1.16	3.79
Cuban	3.92	3.03	1.20	3.48
Puerto Rico	4.79	4.03	1.10	4.23
Southern rural black	4.97	4.65	1.14	4.30
Southern urban black	4.24	4.07	1.18	3.52
Non-southern black	4.07	3.88	1.19	3.33

Source: Public Use Samples.

2. *Other family households*—in which at least one other relative of the head is present (A large component of these households are female-headed families.)
3. *Nonfamily households*—in which no relative of the head is present (A large share of such households are one-person households.)

Husband–wife households are larger than the other household types. For whites, there are 3.56 persons in such households. This compares with 3.02 in other family households. Most racial and ethnic minorities have considerably larger family sizes. Apart from whites, Cuban (3.92) and Japanese (3.79) families are the smallest husband–wife families. The largest husband–wife family size is found for Mexican Americans (4.81), southern rural blacks (4.97), Puerto Ricans (4.79), and Indians (4.55).

Black husband–wife families are intermediate in size (4.28) and are even smaller outside the South (4.07). However, black families other than husband–wife families are quite large (4.05). Only Indian "other" families are larger (4.08). Southern rural black "other" families are especially large (4.65).

It is interesting that, although husband–wife families are larger for every group than other family households, the difference in average size is not great. For whites, the difference is about one-half of a person, and for blacks it is less than one-quarter of a person. For no group is the average difference as large as one person per household.

There is relatively little variation in the size of nonfamily households, with the one-person household the norm in every group. The lowest average size is 1.10 persons in Puerto Rico, and the largest size is found among Filipinos (1.36). Excluding Filipinos, the largest size is 1.21, found among Chinese.

Population Not Living in Families

Table 10.3 presents the proportion of each group living in nonfamily situations. This includes:

1. Persons living in family households but who themselves are not relatives of the household head. This would include lodgers, resident employees, and nonrelated friends of the family.
2. Persons living in nonfamily households. The majority of these are persons living alone in a one-person household. It also includes persons living with nonrelated "roomates," sharing an apartment or other dwelling units.
3. Persons living as "inmates" in group quarters. The inmate popula-

TABLE 10.3

Proportion of Total Population Living Outside of Families

Racial–ethnic group	Living in household—nonrelative	Nonfamily households			Group quarters		Total outside families
		One member	Two members	Three or more members	Inmate	Noninmate	
White	.5	5.6	1.0	.5	1.1	1.8	10.5
Black	1.2	5.3	1.2	.7	1.5	1.4	11.3
Spanish surname	.6	2.4	.6	.4	.7	.8	5.5
Chinese	1.1	4.8	1.6	2.0	.5	3.2	13.2
Japanese	.8	5.1	1.3	1.0	.5	1.8	10.5
Filipino	1.8	4.3	1.8	2.0	.5	5.3	15.7
American Indian	2.1	3.8	.9	.5	2.0	1.9	11.2
Mexican	.7	2.3	.6	.4	.7	1.0	5.7
Puerto Rican	.8	2.8	.6	.4	1.0	1.1	6.7
Cuban	.9	2.8	.8	.4	.4	.7	6.0
Puerto Rico	1.0	2.4	.3	.2	.4	.8	5.1
Southern rural black	.7	3.5	.6	.2	2.0	.7	7.7
Southern urban black	1.3	5.4	1.2	.8	1.1	1.6	12.4
Non-southern black	1.4	5.7	1.3	.8	1.7	1.4	12.3

Source: Public Use Samples.

tion includes persons in prisons, mental hospitals, other hospitals that typically involve long duration of residence, and old people's homes.

4. Persons living in other group quarters. The major components of these are:
   a. college students in dormitories
   b. military members living in barracks
   c. persons living in rooming houses with five or more residents not related to the household head

Overall, about 11% of all white and black individuals live outside of families. This proportion is closer to 5% for Spanish-surnamed persons, Puerto Ricans (living in both the mainland and in Puerto Rico), Cubans, and southern rural blacks, whereas for Filipinos and Chinese the proportion is higher (16 and 13%, respectively).

It is difficult to interpret the social meaning of a high or low proportion of a population living outside of family households. The largest component of this group is persons living alone in one-person households. Is this a "desirable" status or not? Single-person households have increased in numbers over recent decades in response to increasing affluence, growing employment, rising earnings of women, and perhaps an increased "taste" for privacy (Beresford and Rivlin, 1966). Indeed, living outside a household may increasingly become a regular concomitant of the routine life-cycle progression of individuals as they obtain their education, serve in the military, establish themselves in careers prior to marriage, and spend time between marriages in one-member households.

Demographically, the proportion of the population living outside of family households depends on the:

1. Age structure (Large numbers of elderly persons and large numbers of young adults would result in larger numbers of individuals in nonfamily households.)
2. Level of mortality resulting in widowhood (Widowhood also depends on the age difference between spouses, as well as on the level of mortality.)
3. Patterns of separation and divorce
4. Patterns of remarriage following separation or widowhood
5. The choice of living arrangements of persons in a nonmarried status

In later sections I will examine the living arrangements of one of the groups with the highest incidence of nonfamily living arrangements:

young, single adults. Living arrangements of the elderly are discussed in Sweet (1977b).

1. *Living in households, not related to head.* Among whites only one-half of 1% of the population are unrelated household members. This status is more common in each of the other groups considered here. Among the more disadvantaged groups such as Indians (2.1%), Filipinos (1.8%), and blacks (1.2% overall and 1.4% in the non-South), the proportions are higher. For Mexican Americans (or Spanish surname) and Puerto Ricans, however, the proportion is about the same as for whites.

2. The proportion of the total population *in one-person households* is very low among Mexican Americans (2.3%), persons in Puerto Rico (2.4%), and Puerto Ricans and Cubans (2.8% each). It is also quite low among blacks in the rural South. The proportion for whites (5.6%) and blacks (5.3% overall and 5.7% outside the South) are the highest. An additional 1.5% of the white population lives in two-or-more-person nonfamily households. This proportion varies from 5% for persons living in Puerto Rico to 3.8% for Filipinos.

3. *Group quarters.* Nearly 3% of the white population lives in group quarters, but only slightly more than 1% are inmates of institutions. Indians and blacks have larger proportions as inmates in institutions (2.0% and 1.5%, respectively). Chinese, Japanese, Filipinos, and persons living in Puerto Rico have very small proportions of inmates. The proportion of Mexican Americans who are inmates is also very low. The proportion in other group quarters is also quite variable, ranging from .7% for Cubans to 5.3% for Filipinos. As we shall see later, there are wide differences in the specific types of group quarters for different ethnic groups.

Distribution of Households by Life-Cycle Stages

An important aspect of the social structure is the distribution of a population by life-cycle stages. The life-cycle stage distribution of a population is dependent on, but distinct from, its age distribution, since it is affected by the whole series of family processes, including the distribution of age at marriage, the amount and spacing of childbearing, patterns of divorce and family dissolution, and the living arrangements of various groups within the population.

There are a variety of ways of classifying families by life-cycle stages, and I am not prepared to enter into a discussion of which way is the "best." I have chosen the classification presented in Table 10.4. The aim of this classification is to identify groups of households that have some qualitative difference from one another and are internally homogeneous with respect to family circumstances. There is also a concern for an ordering—that is, the ordered sequence of "stages" that typical individuals or families might proceed through as they age. However, for our purposes, I would emphasize the homogeneity within stages and the differentiation among them more than any inherent ordering or typical progression of individuals through the stages.

(1). I begin by identifying households headed by single never-married persons under the age of 30. These are typically one-person households and are usually transitional arrangements of persons who will leave the status by marriage within a short period of time.

(2)–(3). Households headed by single persons aged 30–44 and 45–59 are also typically one-person households but more commonly involve persons who will not subsequently marry—that is, they may be more "permanent" living units.

(4)–(6). I separate households headed by persons aged 60 and over (except the few with own children under 18). Typically, these are households in which the head is retired or is nearing retirement. These households are divided by marital status—married couple, formerly married (typically a widowed female), and never married (a very small group).

(7)–(9). Nonaged married couple households are divided into six categories—three with own children under the age of 18 and three without. Those with children are divided by age of youngest children:

(7) Youngest child under 6. These are families with the responsibility for at least one preschool aged child.

(8) Youngest child 6–11. These are households with at least one child of grade school age, but no younger child. A considerable child-care responsibility persists, but it is not typically of the same intensity as for younger children.

(9) Youngest child 12–17. These households have high school aged children present, but none younger.

The consumption needs and patterns of these three groups may also vary, although a classification involving numbers of children and the age of the oldest child might tap that dimension more adequately than does the present classification.

(10)–(12) Married couples with no children are divided by age of the wife:

(10) Childless couples with wife under 30 are typically in a temporary circumstance prior to the birth of their first child.

TABLE 10.4
Life–Cycle Stages—Households [a]

Categories	White	Black	Spanish surname	Chinese	Japanese	Filipino	Indian
Single [b,c]	*5.2*	*5.5*	*4.2*	*12.9*	*11.9*	*9.9*	*5.6*
14–29	2.4	2.2	1.9	6.9	5.2	4.7	2.8
30–44	1.3	1.8	1.3	4.0	3.9	3.1	1.6
45–59	1.5	1.5	1.0	2.0	2.8	2.1	1.2
Married couples [c]	*56.7*	*44.0*	*65.5*	*61.2*	*58.1*	*57.6*	*54.6*
No children,[d] wife <30	4.0	2.4	3.2	3.5	3.0	3.2	3.5
AYOC = 0–5	18.7	16.6	32.0	22.8	18.5	28.1	25.2
6–11	11.4	9.1	14.0	13.2	12.7	11.8	10.5
12–17	8.7	5.6	7.6	9.6	10.2	5.6	6.4
No children, wife 30–44	2.5	2.9	2.2	4.6	3.7	3.7	2.9
No children, wife 45–59	11.4	7.4	6.5	7.5	10.0	5.2	6.1
Formerly married [b,c]	*10.5*	*28.5*	*15.3*	*9.6*	*12.3*	*11.9*	*20.3*
<30, no children	.7	1.1	.7	.5	.7	1.1	1.0
30–44, no children	1.2	3.4	1.6	1.9	2.5	2.0	2.3
45–59, no children	4.1	7.9	3.5	3.5	3.8	2.8	5.2
AYOC = 0–5	1.4	7.2	4.1	1.1	1.5	3.0	5.6
6–11	1.5	5.2	3.2	1.2	2.2	1.8	3.7
12–17	1.6	3.7	2.2	1.4	1.6	1.2	2.5
Elderly—Aged 60+	*27.4*	*21.9*	*15.0*	*16.1*	*17.8*	*20.6*	*19.6*
MSP	13.9	8.4	7.4	8.2	9.8	10.0	8.4
Formerly married	11.5	12.2	6.6	6.3	6.8	5.9	9.9
Single	2.0	1.3	1.0	1.6	1.2	4.7	1.3
Total	100.0	100.0	100.0	100.0	100.0	100.0	100.0

(continued on next page)

| | | | | Blacks | | | |
Categories	Mexican	Puerto Rican	Cuban	Southern rural	Southern urban	Non-southern	Puerto Rico
Single [b,c]	4.9	5.8	6.2	2.7	4.9	6.9	4.1
14–29	2.4	3.0	1.7	.6	2.1	3.0	1.0
30–44	1.5	1.8	2.8	1.0	1.4	2.2	1.3
45–59	1.0	1.0	1.7	1.1	1.4	1.7	1.8
Married couples [c]	65.1	58.9	66.2	48.4	42.6	43.7	59.1
No children,[d] wife <30	3.4	4.2	2.9	1.6	2.4	2.5	2.7
AYOC = 0–5	32.9	28.0	22.0	19.3	16.0	16.3	25.4
6–11	13.9	11.8	16.4	11.0	8.7	8.8	12.0
12–17	7.2	6.3	10.2	7.0	5.4	5.3	9.6
No children, wife 30–44	2.2	3.4	4.2	2.0	2.8	3.3	2.4
No children, wife 45–59	5.5	5.2	10.5	7.5	7.3	7.5	7.0
Formerly married [b,c]	16.0	27.0	14.6	19.7	28.1	31.4	15.9
<30, no children	.8	1.0	.7	.5	1.1	1.3	.5
30–44, no children	1.8	2.6	2.6	1.5	3.2	4.2	1.5
45–59, no children	3.4	4.0	5.1	5.7	8.4	8.1	4.3
AYOC = 0–5	4.5	10.7	2.0	4.6	6.7	8.4	3.8
6–11	3.1	5.5	2.2	4.0	5.0	5.7	2.9
12–17	2.4	3.2	2.0	3.4	3.7	3.7	2.9
Elderly—Aged 60+	14.1	8.0	13.1	29.1	24.6	18.0	21.0
MSP	6.7	3.3	8.4	13.1	8.9	6.7	9.9
Formerly married	6.3	4.3	4.1	14.5	14.4	10.0	9.1
Single	1.1	.6	.6	1.5	1.3	1.3	2.0
Total	100.0	100.0	100.0	100.0	100.0	100.0	100.0

Source: Public Use Samples.
[a] Households are classified by characteristics of "head" of household. For explanation of categories, see text.
[b] Single includes only single persons without children; single persons with children are included with "formerly married."
[c] Excluding households headed by persons aged 60 and over.
[d] No own children under 18.

(11) Those with wife 30–44 are more likely to be permanently child-less couples, although it may include some couples who will go on to have children and others whose children have already left home.

(12) Those with wife 45–59 are more often persons whose children are 18 and over and who have already left home. This is the stage frequently referred to as the "empty nest stage," although it includes some whose "nest" includes some children aged 18 and over.

(13)–(18). The remaining stages are households headed by formerly married persons, divided according to the presence and ages of children and by age of the head, following the same patterns as for married couples. Never married persons with own children in the household are also included here.

There is great variability among racial and ethnic groups in the composition of households by family life-cycle stage (Table 10.4). Following are some of the more striking contrasts:

The proportion of all households with children of the head under 6 years of age:

White	20.1%
Black	23.8%
Spanish surname	36.2%
Puerto Rican	28.7%

The proportions of all households with any own children of head under 18 years of age:

White	43.3%
Black	47.4%
Spanish surname	63.1%
Puerto Rican	65.5%

The proportions of all households headed by persons over the age of 59:

White	27.4%
Black	21.9%
Spanish surname	15.0%
Puerto Rican	8.2%

The proportion of all households headed by nonaged married couples:

White	56.7%
Black	44.0%

Spanish surname   65.5%
Puerto Rican   58.9%

The proportions of households headed by nonaged formerly married individuals:

White   10.5%
Black   28.5%
Spanish surname   15.3%
Puerto Rican   27.0%

Female-Headed Families and Children in Two-Parent Households

Of all white families 9% are headed by females (Table 10.5). Of black families, 27% are headed by females. Indian families (18%) and Puerto Rican families in the United States (24%) also have high proportions of female-headed families. The proportions of Spanish-surname (and Mexican) families headed by women are higher than those of whites, although only slightly higher (13%). Relatively low proportions of the Chinese (7%), Filipino (9%), and Japanese (10%) are female headed. In Puerto Rico, 16% of all families are female headed.

The proportion of children in two-parent households is an indicator of the prevalence of marital disruption (and remarriage) looked at from the perspective of children rather than from the perspective of adults or marriages. One important fact about this measure is that the count of children living in two-parent households includes children living with "step-parents" as well as with both "natural" parents. It also includes a smaller group of children living with adoptive parents. It is not possible to estimate reliably from census data the proportion of children living with step-parents or adoptive parents (see, however, Sweet, 1974).

The lowest prevalence of children under 18 in two-parent households is found among blacks (57.3%). Other groups with low proportions are Puerto Ricans (66.5%), Indians (68.6%), and Puerto Ricans living in Puerto Rico (74.6%). Chinese and Japanese children have higher proportions living in two-parent families (90.1 and 89.3%, respectively) than do white children (86.8%).

The proportion of female-headed families with own children under 18 is a different sort of measure, one which complements our earlier measure of the proportion of families headed by women and of the proportion of children living with their mother but not in a two-parent family.

Among whites, 17% of the female-headed families have children under 6, and a total of 51% have children under 18. For most other groups,

TABLE 10.5

Female Headship Rates and Proportion of Children in Two-Parent Families

Racial–ethnic group	Proportion of families with female head	Proportion of children < 18 living in two-parent households [a]	Proportion of female-headed families with children	
			< 6	< 18
White	9.0	86.8	17.1	50.8
Black	27.4	57.3	30.8	66.3
Spanish surname	13.4	80.6	29.4	66.6
Chinese	6.7	90.1	12.5	48.5
Japanese	10.3	89.3	15.4	56.0
Filipino	8.6	83.3	39.1	68.8
American Indian	18.4	68.6	31.6	65.5
Mexican	13.4	80.2	30.5	67.6
Puerto Rican	24.1	66.5	44.4	80.7
Cuban	12.3	83.9	15.6	51.2
Puerto Rico	15.9	74.6	18.1	49.9

Source: U.S. Bureau of the Census, 1973a: Table 3; 1973g: Table 4; 1973h: Table 7; 1973e: Tables 3, 18, and 33; 1973f: Table 3; 1973b: Table 54; 1973c: Tables 18 and 126.

[a] Includes children living with step-parent.

the proportions are higher. Puerto Ricans (in the United States) have the highest proportions (44 and 81%, respectively) because of their youthful age structure. The proportions for Puerto Ricans living in Puerto Rico are more nearly like those of the white population in the United States (18 and 50%).

Blacks, Spanish surnamed (and Mexican), and American Indians all have approximately 30% of female-headed families with children under 6 and two-thirds with children under 18.

The proportion of all families with a female head observed in a cross section at a point in time is the result of a complex set of processes and circumstances. One way to get a clearer perspective on these processes is to examine the marital status distribution of female heads. We have reviewed the proportions of families headed by females in a previous section. Data in Table 10.6 show that we should not equate female family heads with persons in separated and divorced marital statuses. Among whites, only 39% of the female family heads are separated or divorced. Widows are the modal group. The marital status distribution varies quite widely. Nearly one-half of the black and Spanish-surname (or Mexican) female family heads are separated or divorced, whereas

TABLE 10.6

Marital Status of Female Family Heads

Racial–ethnic group	Married, spouse absent, other	Widowed	Divorced	Separated	Never married	Total
White	6.0	43.9	26.6	12.0	11.5	100.0
Black	5.0	30.8	15.9	32.0	16.4	100.0
Spanish surname	7.2	32.5	27.0	21.6	11.7	100.0
Chinese	10.9	50.1	20.3	5.1	13.6	100.0
Japanese	17.0	35.7	24.5	7.9	15.0	100.0
Filipino	31.2	22.8	20.3	8.4	17.3	100.0
American Indian	7.4	36.4	24.4	17.8	13.9	100.0
Mexican	7.5	32.9	25.2	21.4	13.0	100.0
Puerto Rican	5.4	14.3	17.2	48.6	14.5	100.0
Cuban	9.2	26.1	34.5	14.3	15.9	100.0
Puerto Rico	13.6	39.1	19.0	18.2	10.1	100.0
Southern rural black	5.2	48.9	10.1	21.3	14.5	100.0
Southern urban black	5.4	34.7	15.5	29.3	15.1	100.0
Non-southern black	4.6	23.8	17.5	36.5	17.7	100.0

Source: Public Use Samples.

this is true of less than one-quarter of the Chinese female family heads. Among Filipinos, Japanese, Chinese, and Cubans, a relatively large share of female family heads are married, spouse absent–other women. Widowhood accounts for more than one-half of the Chinese but less than one-fifth of the Filipino female family heads.

Of particular interest are differences among the three black groups. Widowhood accounts for almost 50% of the female family heads in the rural South but less than 25% of those living outside the South. Conversely, 54% of the non-southern female family heads are separated or divorced, but only 31% of those in the rural South are. The urban South is intermediate between the two other groups.

Nonnuclear Family Members

Next we turn our attention to the presence of adults in households of various types. Table 10.7 presents the average number of adults per household for each of three types of households. By *adults* we mean persons aged 18 and over. Among whites, husband–wife families include an average of 2.26 adults. This is smaller than any other group

TABLE 10.7

Average Number of Persons Aged 18 and Over per Household and Proportion of Households with Three or More Adults

	Mean number of adults			Households with three or more adults (%)[a]	
Racial–ethnic group	Husband–wife family	Other family	Non-family household	All households	Husband–wife family
White	2.26	1.85	1.13	16.2	20.1
Black	2.39	1.80	1.16	19.0	26.3
Spanish surname	2.41	1.88	1.16	23.6	27.4
Japanese	2.45	1.96	1.18	23.4	29.8
Chinese	2.55	2.15	1.31	27.7	33.6
Filipino	2.48	1.98	1.37	24.8	29.9
Indian	2.37	1.86	1.14	19.7	24.4
Mexican	2.42	1.90	1.18	23.9	27.8
Puerto Rican	2.30	1.54	1.14	17.1	22.2
Cuban	2.54	2.04	1.18	29.1	34.3
Puerto Rico	2.60	2.19	1.07	31.0	35.5
Southern rural black	2.54	2.13	1.11	27.3	33.4
Southern urban black	2.38	1.85	1.15	19.0	25.7
Non-southern black	2.34	1.67	1.17	16.6	24.3

Source: Public Use Samples.
[a] Persons aged 18 and over.

shown. The largest number of adults per husband–wife family are found for Chinese (2.55) and Cubans (2.54). Blacks have an average of 2.39 adults per husband–wife family.

Other white families have an average of 1.85 adults, only .4 adults fewer than husband–wife families. For most other groups, the number of adults per "other" family is higher than that for whites. The exceptions are blacks, with a slightly lower average number of adults (1.80), and Puerto Ricans, with only 1.54 adults per family. Particularly notable is that non-South black "other families" have a very small average size (1.67 adults). This reflects the high prevalence in the non-southern black population of female-headed families consisting of a separated or divorced mother and her children. The low number of adults per "other" family for Puerto Ricans undoubtedly reflects, in part at least, the fact that kin are spatially separated and that many Puerto Ricans would have to return to Puerto Rico in order to join a larger family unit. The same may also contribute to the relatively small size of the non-southern black families. The kin unit that they would join may be located in the South.

Table 10.8 focuses on the presence of "extraneous" adults (i.e., adults other than husband and wife) within husband–wife families. Two categories of "relatives" are distinguished—adult children of the couple and other relatives. Overall, 20% of white husband–wife families have another adult present. For blacks and Spanish-surname families and for families of most of the other groups, this proportion is about 30%.

In the most common situation, the adult is a child of the couple. Among white husband–wife families, only 7% have a related adult other than own children of the household heads. This is the lowest proportion of any group. The proportion is about two and one-half times higher for blacks (18%), and among southern rural blacks it is about one-quarter. High proportions are found for Filipinos (19%) and Cubans (23%). Mexican Americans, Chinese, Japanese, Indians, and Puerto Ricans all have proportions between 12 and 15%.

These tables on the presence of "extra" adults in families, particularly in husband-wife families, point to a particularly important issue with respect to the measurement of income inequality and economic welfare.

TABLE 10.8

Presence of Adult Relatives in Husband–Wife Families

	Proportion of all husband–wife families with:		
Racial–ethnic group	Any related adult	Own child aged 18+	Relative other than own child 18+
White	20.8	16.3	6.7
Black	30.4	19.2	17.5
Spanish surname	29.4	21.6	13.0
Chinese	34.4	25.0	14.2
Japanese	30.1	22.4	12.1
Filipino	31.2	17.8	19.3
American Indian	28.0	18.3	15.4
Mexican	29.8	22.2	12.7
Puerto Rican	24.6	15.4	12.3
Cuban	35.2	18.0	23.4
Puerto Rico	39.2	27.7	20.5
Southern rural black	40.1	25.8	25.1
Southern urban black	30.2	18.8	17.8
Non-southern black	27.2	17.2	14.5

Source: Public Use Samples.

Families with several adults may differ from families with two adults in several ways:

1. They may have more earners.
2. They do have more consumers, at least more adult consumers.
3. They may have more persons who are disabled or infirm.
4. Whatever the number of earners or persons unable to earn, they may represent an important type of demographic adaptation to economic need. That is, they may be in an extended household precisely because as separate households they would be unable to be economically viable, but by pooling resources and by taking advantage of economies of scale they may be more able to adapt to low earnings and/or disability or other financial hardship.

In regard to differences in the prevalence of adult children in the household, we have not recorded the extent to which the children are enrolled in school. To the extent that they are, the meaning of the differential prevalence may differ. For example, it is probable that a larger fraction of white than black children aged 18–24 are enrolled in school. However, of those enrolled, it is likely that a larger fraction of black students live at home. This is true for two reasons:

1. Black families are less able to finance children attending school and living away from home.
2. Black families tend to be concentrated in large urban areas, within convenient commuting distance of a variety of educational institutions.

Living Arrangements of Adults

The remainder of this chapter is devoted to a discussion of living arrangements of persons in specific life-cycle stages.

Young Adults

One life-cycle stage about which little has been written (see, however, Young, 1975) is the stage of young, unmarried adults. For our purposes, one interesting family indicator is the living arrangements of 18–24-year-old, never-married men and women.[3] The modal living arrange-

---

[3] We are aware of, but have chosen to ignore, the fact that persons in this age group–particularly disadvantaged minority males—are underenumerated in the census. The reason for ignoring it is that there is nothing we can do to "adjust" the data. The reason for mentioning it in a footnote is that it involves a potential bias. Persons omitted in the census enumeration would be disproportionately those

ment for such persons is that of living in the parental household. What proportion of such persons are living in their parental household? This proportion will depend on a large number of factors, including the prevalence of college attendance, the degree to which persons attending college are doing so within the local community, the extent of military service, the pattern of marriage ages that determines the age distribution of the never-married population aged 18–24, the employment and economic opportunities of young persons of a specific racial and ethnic group, and a variety of other factors.

For most groups, females are more likely to be living in the parental household than are males. It is tempting to suggest that this means that families are more apt to be protective of their female children than of their male children. However, it appears that the sex difference is due largely to a much higher incidence of men living in group quarters, particularly in armed forces group quarters. Women, however, tend to marry earlier than men for all groups considered here, and, consequently, the women in the sample of never-married persons aged 18–24 would tend to be younger than the men. Furthermore, the differences among groups in the prevalence of young unmarried adults living in the parental household would depend on the access to housing outside of the parental household, which would depend on the residential pattern of the group in question and on the nature of the available housing stock.

We shall look primarily at the pattern for females. A very high proportion of Mexican Americans (79%), Cubans (78%), and persons living in Puerto Rico (82%) are living in the parental household (Table 10.9). The proportion is extremely low for American Indians (54%). It is very similar for whites and blacks (63 and 65%). There are large differences among the three groups of blacks, with 80% of the men and women living in the parental household residing in the rural South. These differences can probably be explained primarily in terms of migration patterns and the available housing stock in the rural South.

Residence in group quarters is more common among young adults than among any other group. Table 10.10 shows the proportion of never-married persons 18–24 years of age who are living in group quarters. The proportion is generally higher among men than among women and varies widely from group to group: 25% of white and 21% of black single men live in group quarters. Very high fractions of Filipino, Indian, and Chinese men are found in group quarters, whereas

---

living outside of the parental household. Another problem with this age group is that there are many men who are omitted by virtue of being overseas in the armed forces.

TABLE 10.9

Percentage of Never-Married Persons Aged 18–24 Who Are
Living in Parental Households

Racial–ethnic group	Male	Female
White	59.4	62.9
Black	59.8	64.9
Spanish surname	71.4	78.7
Chinese	52.0	61.2
Japanese	59.9	59.3
Filipino	46.3	48.2
American Indian	53.2	53.5
Mexican	67.6	79.4
Puerto Rican	57.0	71.3
Cuban	71.0	78.0
Puerto Rico	79.2	82.3
Southern rural black	81.8	80.1
Southern urban black	52.9	59.3
Non-southern black	58.3	64.2
If foreign students are excluded:		
Chinese	59.3	67.4
Japanese	63.2	60.5
Filipino	48.6	51.0

Source: Public Use Samples.

only a small fraction of Spanish-surname (or Mexican) men are living in such locations. Similar ethnic differences are found for women, except that black women have a proportion much lower than white (8 versus 19%) and that Filipino women do not have an extremely high proportion in group quarters.

The remaining columns in Table 10.10 show the percentage of the total age group (not limited to never married) in specific types of group quarters. For men I show armed forces barracks, prisons and jails, and college dormitories. For women only college dormitories are shown.

Before describing group differences, I should point out that not all military personnel are enumerated in group quarters. Many military men live "off base" in apartments, and those men stationed overseas are not included. Nonetheless, these figures should indicate roughly the relative prevalence of membership in the armed forces.

Similarly, not all college students live in dormitories. Indeed, in 1970

TABLE 10.10

Population Aged 18–24 Living in Group Quarters

Racial–ethnic group	Percentage of never-married 18–24 year-olds in group quarters		Percentage of total 18–24			
			Male			Female
	Male	Female	In armed forces	In jails and prisons	In college dorms	In college dorms
White	24.2	19.0	7.4	.6	8.2	7.6
Black	20.6	8.4	7.0	4.0	3.5	4.1
Spanish surname	11.3	4.4	4.2	1.2	1.7	1.2
Chinese	23.2	16.0	2.4	.1	17.3	10.9
Japanese	18.5	14.4	5.1	.1	8.9	9.1
Filipino	34.8	16.0	25.7	.5	1.8	3.0
American Indian	26.8	15.1	9.8	3.2	4.3	4.5
Mexican	14.2	4.0	6.1	1.3	1.6	1.0
Puerto Rican	18.8	5.3	8.1	2.0	.8	.9
Cuban	11.6	5.8	2.2	.6	4.4	2.7
Puerto Rico	6.5	4.1	1.7	.6	.8	1.0
Southern rural black	15.9	5.7	2.6	10.7	3.2	3.8
Southern urban black	23.8	16.7	10.0	2.9	5.5	8.4
Non-southern black	19.8	7.5	7.8	3.9	3.0	3.3
If foreign students are excluded:						
Chinese	19.8	17.9	3.2	.1	13.7	8.5
Japanese	17.7	15.3	5.6	.1	7.9	9.6
Filipino	34.7	18.0	25.8	1.0	1.2	2.9

Source: Public Use Samples.

only 27% of the white male and 33% of the white female nonmarried college students [4] aged 18–24 were enumerated in dormitories. The probability of an enrolled person's living in a dormitory undoubtedly depends on several factors, including:

1. *Residence patterns*—Groups living in large urban areas have access to a diverse range of educational opportunities without leaving home. More dispersed and more rural groups do not.
2. *Affluence*—Groups that can afford it may be more likely to leave home to attend school than the less affluent.
3. *Emancipation from parental control*—Students not living in dormitories are not necessarily living at home. In groups exercising greater parental control, dormitory life may be preferred to apartments and other living arrangements.

In any event, our data are not intended to show prevalence of enrollment in higher education.

Among males, about 7–8% of whites, blacks, and Puerto Ricans are in military barracks. A lower fraction of Spanish surname (4%), Chinese (3%), Japanese (4%), and Cuban (2%) men are in barracks. Ten percent of American Indian men and 22% of Filipino men are in barracks. Evidently, a very large fraction of young Filipinos are in the armed forces.

As expected, the proportion of young black men and Indian men in prisons and jails is very high (4%) in contrast to whites (6%). Spanish-surname (Mexican) men have 1.2% in prisons and jails. The rates for Filipinos and Puerto Ricans are 1.7 and 2.0%, respectively.

Of white men, 8% are in college dorms. Less than 4% of blacks and 2% of Spanish-surname (Mexican) men are in college dorms. Very low proportions are also found for Puerto Ricans (less than 1%) and Filipinos. Over 20% of Chinese males and nearly 10% of Japanese males are in dormitories. The high proportion of Chinese in college dormitories also reflects, in part, the fact that Chinese foreign students are included in that category. In the panel at the bottom of Table 10.10, foreign students are excluded from the base.

For females, the ethnic differentials in the proportion in dormitories are quite similar to those for men. We would reemphasize that these data are not appropriate for an examination of differential rates of enrollment among groups or between the sexes within a group.

---

[4] By this I mean persons enrolled in college, excluding graduate school (i.e., those with less than 16 years of schooling completed).

Recently Married Couples

Most married couples establish an independent household at the time of marriage. However, for some couples this is not financially feasible. We have measured the proportion of couples who have been married for less than 5 years and who maintain a household of their own. This measure is an underestimate of the proportion of all couples who begin marriage in their own household, but it should give us a reasonable idea of the relative prevalence of doubling-up. The vast majority of couples not living in their own household are living in the household of the parents of one of the spouses.

Of the white couples, 96% are living in their own household. This compares with 90 and 91% of the black and Spanish-surname populations, respectively. Chinese and Japanese Americans have relatively high proportions with their own household (93 and 94%, respectively). A very high proportion is also found for Puerto Ricans in the United States. This could be explained in several ways, but certainly contributing to this high proportion is the fact that many of these Puerto Rican couples have parents who live in Puerto Rico rather than in the United States. The same would be true of Cubans, who also have a relatively high proportion in their own household. Lower than average proportions in households are found for Filipinos (86%) and American Indians (88%). Among the three groups of blacks, a very low proportion is found for southern rural blacks (80%), whereas for southern urban and non-southern blacks the proportions are 92 and 91%, respectively.

Separated and Divorced Persons with No Children

Another aspect of family and household structure is the living arrangements of persons who experience separation or divorce. To what extent do such persons form their own households and to what extent do they move into their parental household or live in other housing arrangements? We have selected for consideration the living arrangements of 25- to 44-year-old separated and divorced persons. In Table 10.11 we show the living arrangements of those persons with no children present. I shall not review the entire pattern, but I shall note some of the most significant differences. The proportion moving into the parental household is very high in Puerto Rico as well as among Spanish-surname persons. With these exceptions, between one-sixth and one-quarter of males live in the parental household. For most groups, the modal pattern is to form a nonfamily household—in most cases, a one-person household. Forty-nine percent of the whites, 38% of the blacks, and a relatively large fraction of all other groups (with the

TABLE 10.11

Living Arrangements of 25–44-Year-Old Separated and Divorced Persons

Racial–ethnic group	With no own children					
	Male			Female		
	Nonfamily households (%)	Child of head	Group quarters	Nonfamily households (%)	Child of head	Group quarters
White	48.8	24.9	8.7	47.3	17.3	2.8
Black	38.3	18.4	10.9	36.1	16.5	7.7
Spanish surname	43.1	26.6	7.5	48.7	23.3	5.0
Japanese	59.8	16.1	5.4	62.4	3.7	1.5
Chinese	50.6	15.2	2.5	46.3	19.5	7.3
Filipino	33.3	21.9	17.9	42.2	11.1	5.0
American Indian	27.4	22.3	29.2	34.7	17.4	
Mexican	34.0	24.4	15.2	26.2	23.5	4.0
Puerto Rican	42.6	13.5	12.5	35.2	11.4	1.5
Cuban	35.1	19.3	4.4	30.9	17.5	2.1
Puerto Rico	20.8	48.1	9.4	19.0	35.7	1.2
Southern rural black	20.9	31.9	20.4	14.8	37.5	7.0
Southern urban black	35.1	22.1	7.1	31.9	20.4	2.1
Non-southern black	42.8	14.1	11.7	41.5	11.4	3.2

Females with own children < 18 years of age

Racial–ethnic group	Family head (%)	Living in parental household (%)
White	86.9	11.2
Black	89.7	8.1
Spanish surname	86.7	10.4
Japanese	88.5	6.6
Chinese	87.3	11.1
Filipino	86.8	7.9
American Indian	86.9	11.0
Mexican	87.5	10.2
Puerto Rican	97.4	1.8
Cuban	86.0	9.8
Puerto Rico	72.3	25.2
Southern rural black	73.0	22.3
Southern urban black	87.6	9.5
Non-southern black	93.0	5.2

Source: Public Use Samples.

exception of American Indians, Filipinos, and Puerto Ricans) are in non-family households. Among females the same pattern tends to hold.

Separated and Divorced Women with Children

Table 10.11 also shows the living arrangements of 25- to 44-year-old separated and divorced women with own children under 18. For all groups, the modal pattern is to form one's own household. This is less true in Puerto Rico than it is in the United States, and it is even less typical in Puerto Rico than it is for Puerto Ricans living in the United States. The explanation for this undoubtedly lies in the fact that the parents of many Puerto Ricans in the United States are living in Puerto Rico. Hence, if they decide to live with parents they must return to Puerto Rico. For all other groups, the range in proportion who are family heads is from about 86% to about 90%. For all groups shown nearly all of those persons who are not living as family heads are living in their parental household.[5]

CONCLUSIONS

When I began work on this chapter I had intended that it be a discussion of the implications of racial and ethnic differences in family composition on measured income inequality. As I worked on it I gradually retreated from this goal toward the more modest one of documenting differences in family structure—differences that might have some implications for measured inequality and economic well-being.

It is clear from the analysis reported in this chapter that there is great diversity in family and household structure among the racial and ethnic groups considered. The diversity is not simply a difference between those minority groups that tend to be disadvantaged (blacks, Chicanos, and Indians) on the one hand and those that tend to be more affluent (whites, Chinese Americans, and Japanese Americans) on the other. Furthermore, although there are large black–white differences in family and household structure, these are not the only differences to be found. Frequently, blacks are found to be very similar to whites but quite different from Chicanos on one measure; on some other measure of family structure, blacks may tend to be similar to the Chicano popula-

---

[5] It is important to appreciate the fact that these figures refer to a cross section of the separated and divorced population. A higher proportion would be found in the parental household for a short period following separation while they are in the process of rearranging their lives.

tion but quite different from the white population. We have also noted diversity within the black population. A number of our measures show considerable difference among the southern urban, southern rural, and non-southern black populations. Also noteworthy are differences in family structure and living arrangements between the mainland Puerto Rican population and the population of Puerto Rico itself. Many of these differences, as well as differences among the three black populations, may be attributable in large part to the pattern of migration, particularly to the possibility of return migration in response to, or in conjunction with, a change in marital or family status.

Another conclusion emerges quite clearly from our examination of family and household structure. The processes determining the aggregate distribution of population by family and household structure are extremely complex.

I have suggested no way of making appropriately standardized comparisons of economic well-being and inequality using data such as that collected in the decennial census. I do, however, have a clearer sense of what the problem is. Not only do different populations differ in their age structure and in the size of the family units, but there are also important differences in the probability of various alternative living arrangements among any given age-by-marital status group (e.g., young, separated, and divorced adults and young never-married adults). There are also differences among the ethnic groups in both the number of children present per household and the number of adults present per household and per husband–wife family. Differences in the number of adults present is relevant both in terms of the consumption needs of the household and also in terms of the earnings potential of the household. The analysis, however, is complicated even further by the fact that the formation of an extended household unit may be a response to the economic difficulties experienced by the component adult members of that household in the absence of such a sharing arrangement. A significant fraction of these households with "extraneous" adult members probably involves households in which there is an aged or disabled person who may require more or less continuous supervision and care.

The analysis reported here has no time dimension to it. I have not reported on the degree to which these racial and ethnic differences in family composition and household structure observed in 1970 have been changing through time. Are these differences becoming more or less pronounced, or does our observation in 1970 reflect simply the continuation of the long-term pattern?

The analysis reported here has only scratched the surface of the possibility of analyzing these data to understand better family and household patterns within and among the racial and ethnic groups considered. Detailed analyses of socioeconomic differentials within ethnic groups would be possible and would certainly add to our understanding of these family patterns.

Neither have I considered with any care the demographic processes underlying these differences in household and family structure. I have not investigated age at first marriage patterns among the racial and ethnic groups, not have I looked at patterns of marital disruption or of remarriage. This is an important missing link in my analysis.

I have also (for lack of space) ignored the household situation of the elderly population, a group that represents a surprisingly large fraction of the total population of household heads. They represent a larger fraction of household heads than of the population because the elderly tend to live in very small household units, most frequently units with one widowed person or with two married, spouse-present persons.

Finally, from the perspective of monitoring and assessing social change, I would conclude that all of the diversity and all of the complexity underlying the sorting of individuals into families and households necessitates a whole array of social indicators rather than just a few. Average household size, the prevalence of female-headed households, and the average number of children per husband–wife family are important indicators, but in no sense do they tell the whole story.

REFERENCES

Beresford, John C., and Alice M. Rivlin
    1966   "Privacy, poverty and old age." *Demography* 3(1):247–258.
Cutright, Phillips
    1973   "Illegitimacy and income supplements." Pp. 90–138 in Studies in
                Public Welfare, No. 12, Part I–The Family, Poverty, and Welfare
                Programs: Factors Influencing Family Instability. Washington, D.C.:
                U.S. Government Printing Office.
    1974   "Components of change in the number of female family heads aged
                15–44: United States, 1940–1970." *Journal of Marriage and the Family* 36(4):714–721.
Duncan, Greg J., and James N. Morgan
    1976   "Young children and 'other' family members." Pp. 155–182 in G. J.
                Duncan and J. N. Morgan (eds.), *Five Thousand American Families:
                Patterns of Economic Progress*, Volume IV, Chapter 5. Ann Arbor,
                Michigan: Institute for Social Research, University of Michigan.
Duncan, Otis Dudley, David L. Featherman, and Beverly Duncan
    1972   *Socioeconomic Background and Achievement*. New York: Seminar Press.

Farley, Reynolds
  1977   "Trends in racial inequalities: Have the gains of the 1960s disap-
          peared in the 1970s?" *American Sociological Review* 42(2):189–208.
Farley, Reynolds, and Albert I. Hermalin
  1971   "Family stability: A comparison of trends between blacks and
          whites." *American Sociological Review* 36(1):1–17.
Ferriss, Abbott L.
  1970   *Indicators of Change in the American Family.* New York: Russell
          Sage.
Glick, Paul C.
  1969   "Marital stability as a social indicator." *Social Biology* 16(3):158–
          166.
Hannan, Michael T., Nancy B. Tuma, and Lyle P. Groeneveld
  1976   "The impact of income maintenance on the making and breaking of
          marital unions: Interim report." Research Memorandum 28. Menlo
          Park, California: Stanford Research Institute.
  1977a   "Income and marital events: Evidence from an income-maintenance
          experiment." *American Journal of Sociology* 82(6):1186–1211.
  1977b   "A model of the effect of income maintenance on rates of marital
          dissolution: Evidence from the Seattle and Denver income main-
          tenance experiments." Research Memorandum 44. Menlo Park,
          California: Stanford Research Institute.
Hernandez, Jose, Leo Estrada, and David Alvirez
  1973   "Census data and the problem of conceptually defining the Mexican
          American population." *Social Science Quarterly* (March):671–687.
Hoffman, Saul, and John Holmes
  1976   "Husbands, wives and divorce." Pp. 23–76 in G. J. Duncan and J. N.
          Morgan (eds.), *Five Thousand American Families: Patterns of Eco-
          nomic Progress*, Volume IV, Chapter 2. Ann Arbor, Michigan: Insti-
          tute for Social Research, University of Michigan.
Institute for Research on Poverty
  1977   "The effects of welfare reform alternatives on the family." A report
          for the U.S. Department of Health, Education and Welfare. Special
          Report Series 13. Madison, Wisconsin: Institute for Research on
          Poverty, University of Wisconsin.
Klein, William A.
  1971   "Familial relationships and economic well-being: Family unit rules
          for a negative income tax." *Harvard Journal on Legislation* (March):
          361–405.
Knudsen, Jon H., Robert A. Scott, and Arnold R. Shore
  1977   "Household composition." In H. W. Watts and A. Rees (eds.), *Ex-
          penditures, Health, and Social Behavior; and the Quality of the Evi-
          dence.* The New Jersey Income Maintenance Experiment, Volume 3.
          New York: Academic Press.
Kuznets, Simon S.
  1976   "Demographic aspects of the size distribution of income: An ex-
          ploratory essay." *Economic Development and Cultural Change* 25
          (1):1–94.
MacDonald, Maurice, and Isabel V. Sawhill
  1978   "Welfare policy and the family." *Public Policy* 26(1):89–119.

Middleton, Russell, and Linda Haas
    1977   "Marital dissolution and family interaction." In D. L. Bawden and
            W. S. Harrar (eds.), *The Rural Income Maintenance Experiment,
            Final Report.* Madison, Wisconsin: Institute for Research on Poverty,
            University of Wisconsin.
Paglin, Morton
    1975   "The measurement and trend of inequality: A basic revision."
            American Economic Review 65(4):598–609.
Plotnick, Robert D., and Felicity Skidmore
    1975   *Progress against Poverty.* New York: Academic Press.
Rindfuss, Ronald R., and James A. Sweet
    1977   *Postwar Fertility Trends and Differentials in the United States.* New
            York: Academic Press.
Rivlin, Alice M.
    1975   "Income distribution—Can economists help?" *American Economic
            Review* 65:1–15.
Ross, Heather L., and Isabel V. Sawhill
    1975   *Time of Transition: The Growth of Families Headed by Women.*
            Washington, D.C.: Urban Institute.
Sawhill, Isabel V., G. E. Peabody, C. A. Jones, and S. B. Caldwell.
    1975   "Income transfers and family structure." Urban Institute Paper
            979–03. Washington, D.C.: The Urban Institute.
Sweet, James A.
    1972   "Measurement of trends ond socioeconomic differentials in marital
            instability." CDE Working Paper 72-20. Madison, Wisconsin: Center
            for Demography and Ecology, University of Wisconsin.
    1973   *Women in the Labor Force.* New York: Seminar Press.
    1974   "The family living arrangements of children." CDE Working Paper
            74-28. Madison, Wisconsin: Center for Demography and Ecology,
            University of Wisconsin.
    1977a   "Demography and the family." *Annual Review of Sociology* 3:363–
            405.
    1977b   "Further indicators of family structure and process for racial and
            ethnic minorities." CDE Working Paper 77-30. Madison, Wisconsin:
            Center for Demography and Ecology, University of Wisconsin.
Sweet, James A., and Larry L. Bumpass
    1974   "Differentials in marital instability of the black population: 1970."
            Phylon 35(3):323–331.
Tienda, Marta
    1976   "Macro and micro contexts of age and economic dependency." Ph.D
            Dissertation, The University of Texas at Austin.
Treas, Judith, and Robin J. Walther
    1977   "Women's changing social roles and the distribution of family in-
            come." Paper presented at the annual meetings of the Population
            Association of America, St. Louis, April 21–23.
U.S. Bureau of the Census
    1973a   American Indians. Subject Report PC(2)–1F. Washington, D.C.: U.S.
            Government Printing Office.
    1973b   Census of 1970. Characteristics of the Population, Volume I. United

States Summary. Washington, D.C.: U.S. Government Printing Office.

1973c   Characteristics of the population, Part 53: Puerto Rico. Washington, D.C.: U.S. Government Printing Office.

1973d   Employment status and work experience. Subject Report PC(2)6A. Washington, D.C.: U.S. Government Printing Office.

1973e   Japanese, Chinese, and Filipinos in the United States. Subject Report PC(2)1G. Washington, D.C.: Government Printing Office.

1973f   Negro population. Subject Report PC(2)1B. Washington, D.C.: U.S. Government Printing Office.

1973g   Persons of Spanish Origin. Subject Report PC(2)1C. Washington, D.C.: Government Printing Office.

1973h   Persons of Spanish surname. Subject Report PC(2)1D. Washington, D.C.: U.S. Government Printing Office.

Young, Christabel M.

1975   "Factors associated with the timing and duration of the leaving-home stage of the family life cycle." *Population Studies* 29(1):61–73.

11

The Mortality of Spanish-Surnamed
Persons in Texas: 1969-1971[1]

BENJAMIN S. BRADSHAW
EDWIN FONNER, JR.

Differences among racial and ethnic groups in the United States in levels of mortality and causes of death may be considered as indicating to some extent the relative favorability of the life chances of those groups (Tumin, 1970:140). Similarly, differences among groups in income, education, labor force participation, occupation, marital status, fertility, and other achieved characteristics also reflect life chances. Cultural differences among racial and ethnic groups may also affect their mortality. Groups differ in such things as food preferences, definitions of illness, and responses to illness or the possible threat of it. However, it may be difficult or impossible to distinguish between effects of culture and effects of relative life chances on mortality and causes of death, since cultural differences may persist partly because of varying favor-

[1] The authors wish to thank the Texas Department of Health for providing the data on mortality that form the basis of this chapter and Professor Robert E. Roberts for his careful and helpful review.

ability of life chances among groups. Mortality patterns are also influenced genetically through the varying biological constitution of racial
and ethnic groups. The genetic influence in disease may be equally important as or more important than cultural and social influences. But the
relative importance of culture, environment, and heredity is poorly
understood (Damon, 1969).

The purpose of this chapter is to review available literature on Mexican American mortality and to describe and analyze certain differences
in the estimated mortality of Mexican Americans, as indicated by the
mortality of white persons of Spanish surname, and of other white
persons in Texas around 1970. (The designation "Mexican American"
will be used here to refer to residents of the United States of Mexican
birth or descent; there seems to be no generally accepted alternative.)
Comparable results are also presented for the nonwhite (Negro and
other races) population. In accomplishing these tasks, we do not propose to attribute mortality variation to specific environmental, social,
cultural, or genetic factors. Available data do not permit this. Rather,
the foregoing brief statement is meant as a setting in which to consider
mortality differentials between groups that have been frequently documented as having different social and economic characteristics. Such
consideration seems especially appropriate because so little is known
of Mexican American mortality and its relation to the sociocultural
matrix in which it occurs.

PREVIOUS INVESTIGATIONS

Unlike mortality studies of the general white and Negro populations,
analyses of the mortality of the Mexican American population (mainly
as operationally defined by Spanish surname) have appeared in few
publications. Probably the principal reason for this dearth has been the
lack of consistently defined death and population data. None of the
definitions employed for delineating the Mexican American population
are entirely satisfactory (Hernandez et al., 1973). Among those employed
to date, the only definition that might reasonably be used regularly to
identify Mexican American decedents with much expectation of consistency is through matching decedents' surnames with a standard list
of Spanish surnames. Virtually all of the few studies of Mexican American mortality employ this definition.

The earliest general studies of Mexican American mortality were
done by Ellis using, first, data for persons of Spanish surname from
Houston and, later, similar data from San Antonio (1959, 1962). He

found in both cities in 1949–1951 that male Spanish-surname mortality, adjusted for age, was only slightly higher than mortality of other white males, but mortality of Spanish-surname women was about 40–60% higher than that of other white women. The mortality differential between male and female Spanish-surname persons was much less than between other white males and females. Essentially similar results were reported by Roberts and Askew (1972) for Houston in 1950 and 1960.

Other major findings by Ellis (1959, 1962) were that age-adjusted death rates for malignant neoplasms and heart diseases for Spanish-surname males were lower than for other white males, but the opposite relationship was found for communicable diseases such as tuberculosis. (Among Spanish-surname males, tuberculosis was a more important cause of death than malignant neoplasms.) Spanish-surname females, however, had higher death rates than non-Spanish-surname women on virtually every cause, including heart diseases and cancers. In addition, like Spanish-surname males, they died relatively more frequently from communicable diseases. Moustafa and Weiss (1968) observed generally similar mortality differentials between persons of Spanish surname and other white persons in San Antonio in 1960, except that their observations were neither made on males and females separately nor were their reported rates standardized for age. Roberts et al., (1970) reported that cancer mortality among Spanish-surname males in Houston in 1960 was less than among other white males. The opposite relationship was reported for Spanish-surname females and other white females. Thus, for Houston in both 1950 and 1960 consistent observations were made that cancer differs in its importance as a cause of death in the Spanish-surname and other white male populations, being less important for the former.

Malignant neoplasm of the lung in the Mexican American and other white populations has been examined rather extensively in a series of articles (Buechley et al., 1957; Buell et al., 1968; Lee et al., 1976; Steiner, 1954). These studies, centered on California and Texas, have suggested what may be a concentration of high mortality due to cancer of the lung among birth cohorts of Mexican American women aged about 70 and older as of 1970 (Lee et al., 1976). At younger ages, however, death rates from that cause were less for both male and female Mexican Americans than for other whites and for blacks.

Studies of infant mortality of Mexican Americans have been confined to Houston (Burris and Bradshaw, 1974; Gee et al., 1976), California (State of California, 1973), and Texas (Teller and Clyburn, 1974). Data on infant mortality by surname are also routinely published for San Antonio (e.g., San Antonio Metropolitan Health District). Available information from California, based on matched birth and infant death records, indicates that there was very little difference in perinatal mortality of Spanish-surname and other white infants during the years 1965–1970. The Houston studies, also based on matched birth and death records for 1958–1960, showed that, despite probably less favorable social and economic circumstances, mortality of Spanish-surname infants closely resembled that of other white infants, particularly in the neonatal period. According to Gee *et al.* (1976:324),

> The unexpectedly low neonatal mortality among Spanish surname births appears to be attributable to their more favorable birth weight distribution and full-term gestation period. . . . On the other hand, the Spanish surname postneonatal mortality level is higher than that of Anglos, but still substantially lower than that of Blacks, which seems to reflect the influence of socioeconomic environment, nutrition, and access to health care.

Published data from San Antonio since 1949 reveal a convergence of Spanish-surname and other white infant mortality, mostly accounted for by a decline in postneonatal mortality of Spanish-surname infants (San Antonio Public Health Department and San Antonio Metropolitan Health District 1960–1969, 1971–1975). Similar trends for the state of Texas, 1964–1972, were reported by Teller and Clyburn (1974). Improving postneonatal mortality seems consistent with a generally rising level of living of the Mexican American population in these areas, since mortality during the second through eleventh months of life is more responsive to changes in environment than is mortality in the first month.

The results of previous studies provide a large amount of useful information. Most of them, however, are based on local, though large, Mexican American populations. Also, many of the studies employed data from 1950–1960. There are no general studies of Mexican American mortality that are derived from 1970s data for a large population. The results reported here will, we hope, help to provide needed information.

GENERAL CONSIDERATIONS

Unfortunately, this study also is limited to a single state, Texas, and to the white population designated as Spanish surname, which, for our purposes, provides the best definition of the Mexican American population. The problems of conceptually and operationally defining the Mexican American population are discussed extensively by Hernandez *et al.*

(1973). It is not appropriate to reconsider these problems here, but there are several that need to be discussed.

The true levels of Mexican American mortality cannot be precisely measured because the Mexican American population has never been precisely defined. Several operational definitions have been applied, but none are wholly satisfactory. The disadvantages with the Spanish-surname definition are that not all persons of Mexican descent have Spanish surnames and that some persons of Spanish surname are not of Mexican descent. Over time, because of intermarriage with persons of non-Spanish surname and of immigration of people of other nationalities with Spanish surnames, the Spanish-surname criterion presumably less and less clearly identifies the Mexican American population. One advantage of the Spanish-surname method is that it can be systematically applied to vital records. Statistics based on records so classified will be consistent with those from the census if the same list of surnames is employed. Furthermore, since there is commonly no question pertaining to national origin or descent on birth or death certificates, vital statistics for persons of Spanish surname provide our only estimates of mortality of a group that overlaps extensively with the population of Mexican origin or descent.

Our study area is confined to Texas in part simply because data from other states were not available in the necessary form. However, there are certain advantages to restricting the study to Texas. Aside from population size (about 1.6 million persons of Spanish surname), these advantages derive from the varying utility of Spanish surnames for identifying the Mexican American population. The population of Spanish surname in Texas appears to correspond best to the population of Mexican origin (composed of individuals who recorded themselves in the census as being of that origin or descent) among the five southwestern states where the Spanish surname criterion was applied (Arizona, California, Colorado, New Mexico, and Texas). In Texas, 85% of the Spanish-surname population was also of Mexican origin, and 87% of the Mexican-origin population was of Spanish surname. In the other four states combined, the corresponding figures were 64 and 80% (U.S. Bureau of the Census, 1973a). (These percentages refer to the female population only; similar data for males were not published.) As would be expected given these percentages, statistics on such characteristics as age, education, school enrollment, income, and cumulative fertility for the Spanish-surname and Mexican-origin populations in Texas are almost identical, more nearly so than in the other four southwestern states (U.S. Bureau of the Census, 1973a,b). Thus, the Spanish-surname criterion appears to identify the Mexican American population somewhat more efficiently in Texas than elsewhere, assuming Mexican origin to be the preferred definition. It is certainly the most "conservative" definition because it is based on self-identification.

Because of the uncertainties of definition, it is unknown whether the mortality of the Texas Spanish-surname population corresponds completely to the true Mexican American mortality either in Texas or elsewhere. However, it may be assumed, given the extent of overlap, that measures of mortality for the Spanish-surname population should provide reasonable estimates of the mortality of the Mexican-origin population, which must be considered an important segment of the (undefined) Mexican American population.

Finally, a comment should be made on the possible bias introduced by the effects of marriages (resulting in gain or loss of Spanish surnames) on the numerator and denominator data in death rates, especially of the female population. In cross-sectional (or period) rates such as those presented in this chapter, intermarriage would be of no importance. In a study of cohort mortality extending over several years, the effects of gain and loss of Spanish-surname persons through marriage might be rather extensive. The most recent discussion of intermarriage among persons of Spanish and non-Spanish surname is presented by Murguía and Frisbie (1977).

SOURCES AND QUALITY OF DATA

The data employed in computing the measures of mortality reported in this chapter originated from the United States 1970 Census of Population and from individual death records supplied by the Texas Department of Health. The mortality measures are based on the average number of deaths to Texas residents recorded in 1969 through 1971 and on age-specific census data unadjusted for coverage or reporting errors. No technique has been devised for preparing reliable coverage estimates for the population of Spanish ancestry (U.S. Bureau of the Census, 1974). Death rates for Mexican American males, particularly those aged 15–35, may be inflated somewhat more by underenumeration than comparable rates for other white males. The same is true for nonwhite males. For lack of clear guidelines, however, no attempt was made to adjust the population data.

The completeness of death registration of Mexican Americans as well as of other persons in Texas is also unknown. There is some suggestion that at least infant deaths may be underregistered in certain parts of Texas, particularly in the Mexico border region. We infer this from the unreasonably low infant mortality rates in that area, which are significantly lower than rates in the state as a whole (for a commentary on this subject, see Teller and Clyburn, 1974). At ages beyond infancy in that region and at all ages elsewhere in the state it seems unlikely that deaths of Mexican Americans should be reported differently from those of others. Probably death registration is more complete than the census enumeration, so that death rates reported here for Mexican Americans (as well as nonwhites) are biased slightly upward.

Assignment of cause of death may be somewhat less accurate for Mexican American descendents than for other white descendants. No direct evidence exists on this problem; however, the number of Spanish-surname decedents who were assigned "symptoms and ill-defined conditions" (ICDA codes 780–796) as a cause of death (3.4%) was a little larger than for other white persons (1.7%). The percentage of decedents assigned that category of causes is only a rough indicator of overall quality of cause-of-death diagnosis. If quality of diagnosis of cause of death is less satisfactory for persons of Spanish surname, the main effect is probably an inflation of such categories as cerebrovascular disease, ischemic heart disease, or other "popular" causes.

The accuracy of the manual coding of Spanish surnames on death certificates was investigated by utilizing data for Texas resident cancer deaths from the Texas Department of Health. This was done in the preparation of the article by Lee *et al.* (1976). Names of about 10,300 decedents that were coded by surname in the Department of Health were also independently coded in the University of Texas School of Public Health with the list of Spanish surnames employed by the U.S. Bureau of the Census. The degree of agreement with the original codes was greater than 99%. Therefore, we assume that there is reasonable consistency between the Spanish-surname coding employed for the death certificates and the census population statistics.

MEASURES OF MORTALITY

To eliminate effects of differing age distributions of the sex and ethnic groups, death rates for all causes of death combined and for several categories of primary cause were standardized by the direct method using age-specific death rates for 5-year age intervals. Standardized rates were prepared for broad age intervals as well as for all ages. Generally, as would be expected, there is little difference between the crude and standardized rates for broad age groups below the age of 45, but, for consistency, in some tables both sets of rates are shown for each group.

The 1970 Texas non-Spanish-surname white female population was selected as standard. This standard was chosen because it exhibited the lowest mortality on most causes of death common to all sex and ethnic categories, and, therefore, it presented a meaningful standard with which all other groups could be compared. The selection of a suitable standard population for aggregative mortality indexes has, of course, been a source of considerable discussion (e.g., Spiegelman and Marks, 1966). For most purposes, the age-adjusted rates are probably the best summary indexes for mortality comparisons. Such rates are not entirely satisfactory for comparing mortality among different groups; however, they at least yield "honest" comparisons (Keyfitz and Golini, 1975) that are readily understandable.

Some of the causes of death chosen for presentation in this chapter are very broad, and thus many interesting sex and ethnic differences in mortality by cause are not illustrated. The causes of death were chosen mainly on the basis of their general numerical importance, except for neoplasms of the lung, breast, and cervix uteri. The latter were included to illustrate well-known neoplasms that have long been recognized as varying among ethnic and socioeconomic groups. International disease classification codes specifying the causes discussed in this chapter are listed in the appendix. An important segment of mortality that will not be treated separately is mortality in infancy and early childhood. Mortality at those ages is complicated by a number of factors that deserve detailed attention in another work.

RESULTS

Differences by Sex and Age

Because of the low average age of the male and female Mexican American population, their overall crude death rates are about one-third lower than those of other white persons (Table 11.1). Much of the difference disappears or is reversed when the rates are adjusted for age. The age-adjusted death rates of white Spanish-surname and non-Spanish-surname males are virtually identical, and the white Spanish-surname female death rate exceeds that of other white women by about 19%. Crude and age-adjusted rates for nonwhite males and females were higher than those of their counterparts among the white Spanish-surname and non-Spanish-surname populations.

The difference between male and female age-adjusted death rates for all causes of death combined was relatively moderate for the Spanish-

TABLE 11.1

Crude and Age-Adjusted Death Rates per 100,000 Population for Broad Age Groups, by Sex and Ethnicity: Texas, 1969–1971 [a]

Age and ethnicity	Male		Female		Percentage difference, male from female
	Crude death rate	Adjusted death rate	Crude death rate	Adjusted death rate	
All ages					
White, Spanish surname	669.9	1255.5	467.9	862.6	45.6
White, other surname	991.9	1273.1	728.2	728.2	74.8
Nonwhite	1084.5	1477.0	780.1	988.7	49.4
Under 15					
White, Spanish surname	271.3	264.9	205.8	197.5	34.1
White, other surname	185.7	185.1	135.7	135.7	36.4
Nonwhite	318.6	320.1	238.6	237.8	34.6
15–29					
White, Spanish surname	256.0	267.3	76.9	79.1	237.9
White, other surname	155.5	155.6	67.4	67.4	130.9
Nonwhite	309.3	322.6	123.3	126.2	155.6
30–44					
White, Spanish surname	328.0	330.7	177.6	179.7	84.0
White, other surname	282.0	282.5	159.4	159.4	77.2
Nonwhite	696.8	703.5	378.7	382.5	83.9
45–64					
White, Spanish surname	1214.7	1282.3	765.9	813.8	57.6
White, other surname	1395.6	1415.4	628.9	628.9	125.1
Nonwhite	2073.0	2079.0	1371.7	1375.0	51.2
65 and over					
White, Spanish surname	6260.7	6941.0	4841.5	5154.4	34.7
White, other surname	6772.1	7337.5	4516.8	4516.8	62.4
Nonwhite	6339.0	6579.0	4584.0	4708.6	39.7

[a] Directly standardized on Texas non-Spanish-surname white female age distribution.

surname population, the rate for males being about 46% higher than that of females. The standardized rate for non-Spanish-surnamed white males exceeded that of females by about 75%. The smaller gap between the death rates of Spanish-surname males and females, as can be seen in Table 11.1, is at the expense of the females. The age-adjusted death rate for nonwhite males in Texas was almost 50% higher than for nonwhite females and more than double the rate for other white non-Spanish-surname females.

An examination of death rates by age provides better insight into mortality patterns than the summary measures just described. Spanish surname and other white males, whose overall age-adjusted death rates are nearly identical, have quite different death rates by age. Spanish-surname male mortality is substantially higher (56%) below the age of 30 but lower beyond the age of 45, when most deaths occur. Thus, the overall age-adjusted death rates for these two groups of males are similar despite dissimilar age-specific death rates. Mortality of Spanish-surname females, however, is higher than that of other white females at every age, the greatest difference being about 46% below the age of 15. With the exception of males over 65, nonwhite males and females had higher mortality than either of the two white groups at every age.

The difference in death rate by age between the sexes among the three ethnic groups was fairly uniform under 15 years of age and from 30–44 years of age. Under the age of 15, the mortality of males of all three groups was about 35% greater than female mortality and, at 30–44, about 80% greater. The most diversity appeared at young adulthood and at old age. In the 15–29 age group the age-adjusted death rate for Spanish-surnamed males (267.3) was 238% higher than that of Spanish-surnamed females (79.1). The excess of death rates of other white males (131%) and black males (156%) over the mortality of the respective female groups was also large but not nearly so great.

Some of the more striking sex and ethnic differences appear at the ages of 45 to 64. After diverging greatly from female death rates at ages 15 to 34 (a divergence undoubtedly increased by relatively greater under-enumeration of males), age-specific death rates of all males tended to converge with those of females. Whereas this convergence continues throughout the illustrated age span for Mexican Americans and non-whites, a new divergence almost equal to that at ages 15–34 appears for death rates of other white males and females aged 45–64. The difference is only partly made up at the age of 65 and over, and at that age the sex difference in mortality between such males and females is roughly twice that in the other two ethnic groups. As will be seen presently, this pattern is consistent with the different importance of certain causes of death among Anglo males and other males.

Differences by Causes of Death

Adjusted death rates (all ages) of all three groups of males are higher than those of females for every cause of death (of those causes for which males and females can be compared) except diabetes mellitus (Tables 11.2 and 11.3). The single greatest sex differential in age-adjusted rates by cause was in cancer of the bronchus, trachea, and lung among non-Spanish white and nonwhite males and females; the rates for males were over five times those of females. The death rate of Mexican American males from that cause (43.9 per 100,000) was 211% higher than that of Mexican American females. The next greatest sex difference by cause of death was in accidental and violent deaths among Mexican Americans and nonwhites, the rates for males being nearly four times those for females. Other differences in death rates by sex and cause of death for Mexican Americans and nonwhites were substantial for many causes but not nearly so dramatic as some of the differences between other white males and females. For example, the sex differential in mortality due to ischemic heart disease, a major cause of death, was under 55% for Mexican Americans and Negroes but over 100% for other white persons.

Within the two sex categories, several interesting contrasts are to be noted. First, there are several cause-of-death categories in which Mexican American and Negro males have much higher to moderately higher death rates than do other white males. The death rates of Spanish-surname males exceed those of other white males in infectious and parasitic diseases (by 212%), diabetes (by 119%), influenza (by 19%), and accidents and violence (by 29%). All these causes of death are among those that most likely could either be prevented or successfully managed. Furthermore, except for accidents and violence, they are relatively minor causes of death. Taken together, however, they make up about 21% of deaths that would have occurred to the Mexican American and nonwhite male populations had they had the age distribution of the standard population, that is, "expected deaths," but they comprise only about 14% of the deaths that would have occurred to other white males (Table 11.4).

As a group, these "preventable and manageable" causes of death are of relatively greater importance below the age of 45, although ultimately

TABLE 11.2

Crude and Age-Adjusted Death Rates per 100,000 Population by Ethnicity and Sex—Selected Causes of Death: Texas, 1969–1971 [a]

Cause of death: Ethnicity groupings	Male		Female		Difference, male from female (%)
	Crude death rate	Adjusted death rate	Crude death rate	Adjusted death rate	
All causes					
White, Spanish surname	669.9	1255.5	467.9	862.6	45.6
White, other surname	991.9	1273.1	728.2	728.2	74.8
Nonwhite	1084.4	1477.0	780.1	988.7	49.4
Infective and parasitic diseases					
White, Spanish surname	22.9	31.8	15.3	18.7	70.1
White, other surname	8.6	10.2	6.3	6.3	61.9
Nonwhite	19.2	22.1	12.0	12.7	74.0
Neoplasms, total					
White, Spanish surname	84.3	185.6	76.9	147.7	25.7
White, other surname	174.4	218.0	133.0	133.0	63.9
Nonwhite	162.8	238.9	117.1	152.4	56.8
Malignant neoplasms, trachea, bronchus, and lung					
White, Spanish surname	18.9	43.9	6.7	14.1	211.4
White, other surname	58.4	70.2	13.0	13.0	440.0
Nonwhite	44.2	63.4	8.6	11.3	461.1
Malignant neoplasms, breast [b]					
White, Spanish surname	—	—	11.0	19.5	—
White, other surname	—	—	24.5	24.5	—
Nonwhite	—	—	19.1	24.5	—
Malignant neoplasms, cervix uteri [b]					
White, Spanish surname	—	—	7.2	12.6	—
White, other surname	—	—	5.4	5.4	—
Nonwhite	—	—	11.9	15.2	—

TABLE 11.2 (Continued) [a]

Diabetes mellitus					
White, Spanish surname	16.3	34.3	25.1	53.0	— 35.3
White, other surname	11.8	15.7	16.2	16.2	— 3.1
Nonwhite	15.6	22.5	27.9	36.9	— 39.0
All circulatory diseases					
White, Spanish surname	240.1	582.2	178.1	407.6	42.8
White, other surname	501.8	682.8	395.8	395.8	72.5
Nonwhite	453.2	687.0	394.2	535.2	28.4
Ischemic heart disease					
White, Spanish surname	143.6	346.1	96.7	225.0	53.8
White, other surname	332.2	441.4	217.2	217.2	103.2
Nonwhite	252.4	382.7	198.8	271.8	40.8
Cerebrovascular disease					
White, Spanish surname	49.5	123.9	43.7	99.9	24.0
White, other surname	88.7	130.4	107.7	107.7	21.1
Nonwhite	107.6	165.6	116.7	159.4	3.9
Influenza and pneumonia					
White, Spanish surname	27.4	49.3	23.2	36.8	34.0
White, other surname	29.9	41.6	25.6	25.6	62.5
Nonwhite	42.7	54.0	26.6	30.7	75.9
Accidents and violence, total					
White, Spanish surname	123.8	149.3	31.6	37.6	297.1
White, other surname	108.6	115.8	47.6	47.6	143.3
Nonwhite	183.6	206.8	53.4	56.8	264.1
All other causes					
White, Spanish surname	155.1	223.0	117.7	161.2	38.3
White, other surname	156.8	189.0	103.7	103.7	82.3
Nonwhite	207.3	245.7	148.9	164.0	49.8

[a] Directly standardized on Texas non-Spanish-surname white female age distribution.
[b] Not calculated for males.

TABLE 11.3

Age-Adjusted Death Rates per 100,000 Population for Broad Age Groups by Sex and Ethnicity—Selected Causes of Death: Texas, 1969–1971 [a]

Cause of death: Ethnicity groupings	Male				Female			
	Under 30	30–44	45–64	65 and over	Under 30	30–44	45–64	65 and over
All causes								
White, Spanish surname	266.0	330.7	1282.3	6941.0	140.0	179.7	813.8	5154.4
White, other surname	170.7	282.5	1415.4	7337.5	102.5	159.4	628.9	4516.8
Nonwhite	321.3	703.4	2079.0	6579.0	183.5	382.5	1375.0	4708.6
Infectious and parasitic diseases								
White, Spanish surname	15.6	7.1	26.0	150.9	11.6	8.0	14.9	73.1
White, other surname	3.9	2.6	11.8	46.6	3.4	1.7	6.5	25.6
Nonwhite	11.1	13.0	27.3	74.0	9.1	6.3	16.7	30.3
Neoplasms, total								
White, Spanish surname	8.3	32.4	216.6	1136.7	7.4	48.3	235.4	748.5
White, other surname	8.4	42.8	320.0	1211.4	7.1	49.1	223.9	640.7
Nonwhite	6.4	59.6	440.5	1151.5	7.8	68.2	308.2	621.4
Malignant neoplasms, trachea and lung								
White, Spanish surname	c	4.9	53.1	277.9	c	2.2	20.4	82.3
White, other surname	c	11.6	134.3	345.6	c	5.8	29.6	49.5
Nonwhite	c	18.4	151.3	243.1	c	4.9	24.8	
Malignant neoplasms, breast [b]								
White, Spanish surname		—	—	—	c	13.2	42.0	72.3
White, other surname		—	—	—	c	14.3	55.9	87.3
Nonwhite		—	—	—	c	18.5	57.5	78.0
Malignant neoplasms, cervix uteri								
White, Spanish surname		—	—	—	c	8.0	28.1	42.3
White, other surname		—	—	—	c	5.0	9.8	20.3
Nonwhite		—	—	—	c	12.1	37.5	42.4
Diabetes mellitus								
White, Spanish surname	c	9.0	59.1	173.2	e	4.4	77.3	311.1
White, other surname	c	3.7	15.1	101.4	c	3.2	13.8	108.4
Nonwhite	1.0	10.5	36.4	108.7	1.3	9.7	72.0	168.3

TABLE 11.3 (Continued) [a]

All circulatory diseases								
White, Spanish surname	6.1	54.9	578.4	3911.4	3.9	30.9	284.4	2976.6
White, other surname	3.8	80.5	702.8	4531.3	3.0	27.9	217.0	3007.3
Nonwhite	10.2	170.1	964.9	3912.4	9.9	127.2	701.2	3142.3
Ischemic heart disease								
White, Spanish surname	1.1	30.4	374.1	2283.1	c	6.7	159.2	1663.1
White, other surname	c	55.8	530.2	2789.6	c	9.8	125.7	1652.7
Nonwhite	1.7	87.4	580.0	2129.2	1.3	45.1	363.5	1627.9
Cerebrovascular disease								
White, Spanish surname	1.5	10.6	95.4	884.9	1.1	10.3	62.5	737.8
White, other surname	1.1	8.1	65.3	1003.2	c	7.5	46.0	842.1
Nonwhite	2.6	33.4	195.2	1024.2	2.1	35.1	194.0	971.0
Influenza and pneumonia								
White, Spanish surname	14.6	4.1	27.9	310.1	12.6	7.3	17.4	224.0
White, other surname	6.5	4.1	26.0	281.5	5.5	4.0	13.4	169.6
Nonwhite	20.6	20.8	55.6	246.8	14.1	10.4	27.9	139.3
Accidents and violence, total								
White, Spanish surname	123.7	157.5	142.9	259.6	27.4	30.9	32.9	100.9
White, other surname	78.1	111.7	138.8	243.7	28.8	43.0	51.3	129.9
Nonwhite	153.9	315.1	245.5	197.6	44.4	66.2	55.8	98.1
All other causes								
White, Spanish surname	97.7	65.7	231.4	999.1	77.7	49.9	151.5	720.2
White, other surname	70.0	37.1	200.9	921.6	54.7	30.5	103.0	435.3
Nonwhite	118.1	114.3	308.8	888.0	96.9	94.5	193.2	508.9

[a] Directly standardized on Texas non-Spanish-surname white female age distribution.
[b] Not calculated for males.
[c] Less than one per 100,000.

TABLE 11.4

Percentage of Expected Deaths by General Classes of Causes of Death, by Ethnicity, Sex, and Age: Texas, 1969–1971

Causes of death: Ethnicity groupings	Male					Female				
	All ages	Under 30	30–44	45–64	65 and over	All ages	Under 30	30–44	45–64	65 and over
All causes										
White, Spanish surname	100.0	100.0	100.0	100.0	100.0	100.0	100.0	100.0	100.0	100.0
White, other	100.0	100.0	100.0	100.0	100.0	100.0	100.0	100.0	100.0	100.0
Nonwhite	100.0	100.0	100.0	100.0	100.0	100.0	100.0	100.0	100.0	100.0
"Preventable and manageable" causes										
White, Spanish surname	21.1	57.9	53.7	20.0	12.9	16.9	36.8	28.2	17.5	16.6
White, other	14.4	51.9	43.2	13.2	9.0	13.1	36.8	32.5	13.5	9.6
Nonwhite	20.7	58.1	51.1	17.5	9.5	13.9	37.5	24.2	12.5	9.3
Neoplasms and circulatory diseases, combined										
White, Spanish surname	61.1	5.4	26.4	62.0	72.7	64.2	8.1	44.1	63.9	72.3
White, other	70.7	7.1	43.6	72.3	78.8	72.6	9.8	48.3	70.1	80.8
Nonwhite	62.7	5.2	32.7	67.6	77.0	69.6	9.6	51.1	73.4	79.9
All other causes										
White, Spanish surname	17.8	36.7	19.9	18.0	14.0	18.9	55.1	27.7	18.6	13.9
White, other	14.9	41.0	13.2	14.5	12.5	14.3	53.4	19.2	16.4	9.6
Nonwhite	16.6	36.7	16.2	14.9	13.5	16.5	52.9	24.7	14.1	10.8

the death rates due to each of these causes is highest at the age of 65 and over. The death rates of Mexican American males due to the manageable causes are greater than those of other white males at every age, but they account for a greater percentage of expected mortality in the standard population below the age of 45. Higher death rates due to infectious diseases, diabetes, and accidents mainly account for the excess of Mexican American male mortality over Anglo male mortality under the age of 45.

Other causes of death, which are of greater numerical importance, are those less likely to be successfully prevented or managed—principally, neoplasms and circulatory diseases. These are predominantly diseases of middle and old age. The age-adjusted death rates due to both these causes for Mexican American males was about 15% less than those of other white males. Assuming standard age distributions, these two major causes accounted for 71% of the deaths to non-Spanish-surname males, compared to 61 and 63%, respectively, of the deaths to Spanish-surname and nonwhite males—a difference of about 8 to 10 percentage points. However, the nonwhite males' age-adjusted rates for these causes exceeded those of both Spanish-surnamed and other white males.

As may be seen in Table 11.3, age-adjusted death rates due to neoplasms and circulatory disease among non-Spanish-surname white males exceed those of Spanish-surname males in every broad age group beyond the age of 30. Only in the cerebrovascular disease category in middle age (45–64) is the Spanish-surname death rate higher than the other white male rate. It appears that it is the lower death rates due to these major chronic and degenerative diseases, which are often not amenable to prevention and management, that explain the favorable mortality of Mexican American males past the age of 45 with respect to other white males of that age.

Unlike Mexican American males, whose age-adjusted death rates are lower than those of other white males in the most important causes of death, the death rates for Mexican American females exceed those of other white females to some degree in both the broad classes of causes of death. The excess in the death rate due to neoplasms and circulatory diseases combined was only about 5%, however, whereas that of the less important preventable and manageable category was about 53%. Adjusted death rates for nonwhite females for these two categories of causes were, respectively, 30 and 43% higher than those of non-Spanish-surname women.

Overall, the neoplasms and circulatory diseases included 64% of the expected deaths given the age-specific death rates of Mexican American females, as compared with 73% of the deaths of other white females.

The percentage for nonwhite women was intermediate between these. The peak difference in rates by broad age groups was in ages 45–64, where the death rate of Mexican American women exceeded that of other white women by 18%. This was the locus of the peak difference for circulatory diseases (13%). For malignant neoplasms, however, the greatest difference occurred at ages 65 and over, where the death rate to Spanish-surname white women exceeded that of other white women by 17%. At that age, there was virtually no difference between the two ethnic groups with respect to deaths from all circulatory diseases, but within that category Spanish-surname women had a lower death rate due to cerebrovascular disease (about 12% below that of other white women).

DISCUSSION AND CONCLUSION

Are these results consistent with those reviewed earlier (that were obtained mainly from local city populations)? Generally our results are consistent. However, problems of comparability with respect to area and time of the 1970 Texas population and earlier study populations preclude any estimation of trends in Mexican American mortality. Data such as those from San Antonio 1950–1970 show that in that city death rates (all causes, both sexes combined) of Mexican Americans and other whites have tended to converge. Probably a similar covergence has occurred at the state level. It seems reasonable to suppose also that the major differences in cause of death reported here for Texas and by Ellis and others existed at the state level at least as far back as 1950.

There are obvious limitations to this study. For example, there is the problem of definition of the Mexican American population. We do not know precisely in what ways mortality of persons of Spanish surname differs from the mortality of the Mexican American population, if it differs at all. Despite this limitation, it is clear that in Texas there remain important differences in mortality by cause of death of white persons of Spanish surname (most of whom are of Mexican origin) and other white persons and nonwhites (most of whom are Negro). The geographic limitation is in some ways more bothersome than the definitional limitation. Assuming that our measures of mortality for the Spanish-surname population are reasonable estimates of the mortality of the Texas Mexican-origin population (as identified in the census), what generalizations can we make to other areas of the United States?

It seems likely that the levels of mortality, expressed as rates, are probably not generalizable, except insofar as the Mexican origin population outside Texas resembles the Texas population in ways that would affect mortality (e.g., in those social, cultural, and economic characteristics that affect life chances). Certain characteristics of the cause of death structure, on the other hand, may be generalizable. On the basis of findings for Texas, we can hypothesize that the Mexican-origin population (and presumably the broader Mexican American population) tends to have lower mortality due to certain causes (such as cancer and circulatory diseases). Obviously, studies elsewhere are needed.

We cannot conclude from this type of analysis whether the ethnic differences in mortality in Texas by cause are due to hereditary proclivities toward relative resistance or unresistance to diseases or to environment and level of living. The studies by Lee *et al.* (1976) of cancer mortality of Mexican Americans suggest that these relationships are indeed complex and possibly unstable, at least for that major cause of death. We may, however, make some reasonable conjectures about possible future trends in Mexican American mortality. Mortality of Spanish-surname males may be reduced significantly below that of other white males, in the absence of major population changes due to selective migration in either group, especially the former. There is essentially no difference in their overall mortality and that of other white males. If preventable and manageable causes of death in Spanish-surname males are reduced, then such a consequence would almost inevitably occur, assuming a persistence of lower mortality due to neoplasms and circulatory diseases. Changes in level of living, resulting from upward social mobility of that population, that affect access to routine health care (especially for management of diseases such as diabetes and prevention of communicable diseases) and that more broadly affect the environment in which the population works and lives may contribute to this. However, deaths due to cancer and circulatory diseases would undoubtedly become relatively more prevalent, if only because more people would survive to be at risk of these causes. That is, those individuals who did not die due to preventable causes would be at risk of dying of other causes.

In general, the same conclusions probably apply to Spanish-surname females. At present there are only modest differences between the death rates of Spanish-surname females due to neoplasms and circulatory diseases, and, if the preventable causes are reduced in importance, then there should be convergence in the death rates of Spanish-surname and other white females.

Appendix 11

Cause of Death Categories and Corresponding ICDA Classifications [a]

Primary cause of death	ICDA four-digit code
Infective and parasitic diseases	000 −136
Neoplasms, total	140.0−239.9
Malignant neoplasms, trachea, bronchus, and lung	162.0−162.1
Malignant neoplasms, breast	174
Malignant neoplasms, cervix uteri	180
Diabetes mellitus	250
All circulatory diseases	390 −458.9
Ischemic heart disease	410.0−414.9
Cerebrovascular disease	430.0−438.9
Influenza and pneumonia	470 −486
Accidents and violence, total	800 −999.9

[a] U.S. National Center for Health Statistics, 1965. The International Classification of Disease, Adapted for Use in the United States, Volume 1, Eighth Revision. Washington, D.C.: Government Printing Office.

REFERENCES

Buechley, Robert, John E. Dunn, Jr., George Linden, and Lester Breslow
    1957   "Excess lung-cancer mortality rates among Mexican women in California." *Cancer* 10:63−66.

Buell, Philip E., Winifred M. Mendez, and John E. Dunn, Jr.
    1968   "Cancer of the lung among Mexican immigrant women in California." *Cancer* 22:186−192.

Burris, Janet, and Benjamin S. Bradshaw
    1974   Black, Mexican-American and Anglo Infants in Houston, Texas, 1958−1960. Paper read at the annual meeting of the American Public Health Association, New Orleans, October 24.

Damon, Albert
    1969   "Race, ethnic group, and disease." *Social Biology* 16:69−80.

Ellis, John M.
    1959   "Mortality differences for a Spanish-surname population group." *Southwestern Social Science Quarterly* 39:314−321.

    1962   "Spanish-surname mortality differences in San Antonio, Texas." *Journal of Health and Human Behavior* 3:125−217.

Gee, Susan C., Eun Sul Lee, and Ronald N. Forthofer
    1976   "Ethnic differentials in neonatal and postneonatal mortality: A birth cohort analysis by a binary variable multiple regression method." *Social Biology* 23:317−325.

Hernandez, Jose, Leo Estrada, and David Alvirez
    1973   "Census data and the problem of conceptually defining the Mexican American population." *Social Science Quarterly* 53(4):671–687.

Keyfitz, Nathan, and Antonio Golini
    1975   "Mortality comparisons: The male–female ratio." *Genus* 31(1–4):1–34.

Lee, Eun Sul, Robert E. Roberts, and Darwin R. Labarthe
    1976   "Excess and deficit lung cancer mortality in three ethnic\groups in Texas." *Cancer* 38:2551–2556.

Moustafa, A. T., and G. Weiss
    1968   "Health Status and Practices of Mexican Americans." Mexican-American Study Project, Advance Report 11, Graduate School of Business Administration. University of California, Los Angeles.

Murguía, Edward, and W. Parker Frisbie
    1977   "Trends in Mexican American intermarriage: Recent findings in perspective." *Social Science Quarterly* 58(3):374–389.

Roberts, Robert E., and Cornelius Askew
    1972   "A consideration of mortality in three subcultures." *Health Service Reports* 87(3):262–270.

Roberts, Robert E., George W. McBee, and Dorothy J. Schneider
    1970   A Research Note on Mortality From Malignant Neoplasms Among Chicanos, Blacks, and Anglos. Paper presented at the Tenth International Cancer Congress, Houston, Texas, May 22–29.

San Antonio Metropolitan Health District
    N.D.   Vital Statistics 1960–1969, Bexar County and City of San Antonio.
    N.D.   Vital Statistics 1971–1975, Bexar County and City of San Antonio.

San Antonio Public Health Department
    N.D.   Ten Years of Vital Statistics, 1949–1958.

Spiegelman, Mortimer, and Herbert H. Marks
    1966   "Empirical testing of standards for the age adjustment of death rates by the direct method." *Human Biology* 38(3):280–292.

State of California, Department of Public Health, Bureau of Maternal and Child Health
    1973   Impact of Medi-Cal on Perinatal Mortality in California.

Steiner, P. E.
    1954   *Cancer: Race and Geography.* Baltimore, Maryland: Williams and Wilkins.

Teller, Charles H., and Steve Clyburn
    1974   "Trends in infant mortality." *Texas Business Review* 48(10):240–246.

Tumin, Melvin M.
    1970   *Readings on Social Stratification.* Englewood Cliffs, New Jersey: Prentice-Hall.

U.S. Bureau of the Census
    1973a   Census of Population: 1970, Subject Reports PC(2)-IC, Persons of Spanish Origin. Washington, D.C.: U.S. Government Printing Office.
    1973b   Census of Population: 1970, Subject Reports PC(2)-ID, Persons of Spanish Surname. Washington, D.C.: U.S. Government Printing Office.

1974   Census of Population and Housing: 1970, Evaluation and Research
           Program PHC(E)-4, Estimates of Coverage of Population by Sex,
           Race, and Age: Demographic Analysis. Washington, D.C.: U.S.
           Government Printing Office.
U.S. National Center for Health Statistics
    1965   The International Classification of Disease, Adapted for Use in the
           United States, Volume 1, Eighth Revision. Washington, D.C.: U.S.
           Government Printing Office.

12

Application of an Indirect Technique to Study Group Differentials in Infant Mortality

ALBERTO PALLONI

INTRODUCTION

The United States has a fairly complete vital statistics registration system that generally allows reliable inferences to be drawn from annual figures of certain vital events. Serious shortcomings, however, may exist in the registration of births and deaths for some racial–ethnic groups. Of particular importance are any errors occurring in reports of the number of births and the number of children dying before attaining their first birthdays during a calendar year period. Errors in one or both of these quantities will bias the measure of infant mortality (upward or downward, depending on the particular type of error affecting the official figures). These errors may be quite systematic for certain ethnic groups for a host of reasons that will be considered later. The important point to note now is that, above and beyond the biases affecting the measure of infant mortality for the particular group in question, there will in all likelihood be *larger* biases associated with measures of differ-

The Demography of Racial and Ethnic Groups.

ential infant mortality among different ethnic groups. (The reference here is to relative rather than absolute error.) This is important, since infant mortality rates have long been used as "indicators" of the general health conditions affecting a group. Whether or not infant mortality rates are the most appropriate measures of such conditions is a moot issue at this juncture, since proponents and critics alike have failed to come up with other more reasonable alternatives. Furthermore, infant mortality rates continue to be used as rough indicators of general health conditions. Regardless of their validity, they may be biased owing to inaccurate reports on infant deaths. This is the issue that will be addressed in this chapter.

AN EXAMPLE: MORTALITY
AMONG MEXICAN AMERICANS

In a study of trends in infant mortality in the state of Texas, Teller and Clyburn (Teller and Clyburn, 1974) report that several areas show higher neonatal mortality for the black and Anglo populations than for the Mexican American population.[1] In Table 12.1 are displayed the values of neonatal, postneonatal, and infant mortality rates for the Anglo, Spanish-surname, and black populations in nonmetropolitan state economic areas. In four of these units, the Spanish-surname population shows lower infant mortality rates than the Anglo population. In the rest of the units, the differences between the Anglo and the Spanish-surname population are no more than one-half of the differences between the Anglo and the black population. The figures for metropolitan state economic areas (not shown here) reveal essentially the same pattern and, in some cases, do so even more acutely than in nonmetropolitan state economic areas. It is apparent that at least in four and with a high probability in all nonmetropolitan state economic areas, the infant mortality rates for the Spanish-surname population may be seriously underestimated. It is likely that underreported neonatal deaths are the major factor affecting the relatively low values in infant mortality rates. Some demographers have thought that the low values of neonatal death rates among the Spanish-surname population may not be due to errors but, rather, to factors such as differential adequacy of health care. Thus, better prenatal care among the Anglo population may increase the chances that pregnancy will end in a live birth even though the chance of

[1] By Mexican American I mean the population with Spanish surnames. The problems of definition entailed are quite complicated but do not affect my argument.

surviving the first few days of life are very slim. By contrast, among the Spanish-surname population the pregnancies that result in a live birth are more likely to survive the first few days, since the weakest or less fit among them come to an end before a live birth occurs. This state of affairs is imputed to a lower quality of prenatal health care.

An alternative explanation would attribute the low values of neonatal and infant mortality rates either to errors in registration or to random errors affecting the rates, or to both. The existence of errors in registration are likely to be the major factor contributing to the observed results. These errors could originate in two sources:

1. Underregistration of deaths (or inflation of births) by mothers of Mexican nationality who cross the border to register their birth in this country in order to obtain United States citizenship for the child that, in turn, facilitates their possibilities of obtaining legal residence. These mothers may return to Mexico and never report the death of the child if it ever takes place.
2. Underregistration of deaths by Mexican American mothers who voluntarily conceal the death of the child in order to avoid official sanctions if they are not in possession of a permit making them legal residents or in order simply to bypass the economic and social costs of a traditional burial.[2]

The extent of the underregistration of infant deaths may be assessed indirectly by assuming that there exists a certain predetermined relationship between neonatal and postneonatal deaths for the population in question. If it is assumed that postneonatal deaths are correctly reported (a very unlikely situation), a predicted value for the neonatal mortality rate may be obtained and may be compared with the observed one. Since such a predetermined relationship has not been defined for the Spanish-surname population, we could use as a substitute the relationship already established for the black population, which may present conditions similar to the Spanish-surname population.[3] The relationship between neonatal and postneonatal deaths for the black population was estimated for the years 1952–1967 by J. Sullivan (1972) by fitting a regression line. It should be mentioned, incidentally, that the estimated relationship for

[2] The practice of concealing infant deaths and, in general, deaths occurring at other ages as well is not an uncommon practice among people living in isolated places. But it is also a fairly established practice among groups in which burial procedures are fairly elaborate and relatively expensive for low-income families. Death concealment takes place in these instances as a measure of avoiding shame and other social sanctions.

[3] This is not an entirely accurate argument. It has been reported that black Americans show excessive neonatal deaths, in part due to genetic factors (see, for instance, Stockwell, 1962).

TABLE 12.1
Texas Infant Mortality Rates by Ethnic Group and State Economic Area (Nonmetropolitan), 1970–1972 Mean

	Mortality rate								
	Neonatal			Postneonatal			Infant		
	Anglo	Spanish surname	Black	Anglo	Spanish surname	Black	Anglo	Spanish surname	Black
Post Oak	17.8	18.7	19.0	4.0	9.9	15.7	21.8	28.7	34.7
Northern High Plains	18.1	20.5	34.3	4.0	9.3	15.2	22.1	29.8	49.5
Southern Blackland	19.1	15.7	15.6	4.5	12.0	10.4	23.6	27.8	25.9
Rolling Plains	15.5	16.9	32.7	5.7	11.5	12.6	21.2	28.4	45.3
Southern High Plains	15.8	16.7	27.3	5.2	9.4	15.1	21.0	26.1	42.4
Western Edwards	17.3	17.9	9.9	5.3	8.5	.0	22.6	26.4	39.9
Trans Pecos	22.1	13.0	—a	3.3	8.4	—a	25.4	21.4	—a
Southeast Sandy Lands	16.1	17.7	14.9	4.4	4.4	11.4	21.2	22.1	26.3
Northeast Sandy Lands	15.5	20.7	19.0	3.7	12.9	10.9	19.2	33.6	29.9
Coast Prairie	15.4	13.9	21.5	3.3	9.3	10.2	18.7	23.2	31.7
North Central Texas	16.4	14.3	41.4	4.3	6.5	14.8	20.8	30.9	56.2
Northeast Rio Grande	13.6	14.8	38.6	3.9	8.2	.0	17.5	23.1	38.6
Northern Blackland	13.8	13.9	25.6	4.1	7.9	10.8	17.9	21.8	36.4
Eastern Edwards	15.4	13.8	37.4	3.7	8.1	8.6	19.4	21.2	46.0
Lower Rio Grande	16.7	12.4	—a	7.1	7.1	—a	23.8	19.4	—a
Southwest Rio Grande	14.8	14.8	15.5	5.0	3.9	7.8	19.8	18.7	23.3

Source: Teller and Clyburn (1974, Table 2), p. 242.
a Base is less than 100 live births.

the white population for the years 1935–1945 is very similar to the one prevailing for the black population.

The results of applying Sullivan's regression equation to the data presented in Table 12.1 are displayed in Table 12.2. The last column of this table shows the ratio of the observed infant mortality rate and the expected infant mortality rate, which was calculated by adding the observed postneonatal death rate to the neonatal death rate predicted by the regression equation. In all but one case the observed infant mortality rate underestimates the expected one. The extent of the underestimation—disregarding the case of Southeast Sandy Lands, where there also seems to be a heavy downward bias on the figures for postnatal deaths—varies from a high of 30% to a low of 3% and has an average (unweighted) level of 18%. It is not surprising that those state economic areas where underestimation is larger are closer to the Mexican border. This is to be expected if the arguments given earlier to account for *observed* infant mortality differentials have any validity.

One should not forget that these figures are hypothetical, since they depend on the validity of the assumption that black and Mexican Ameri-

TABLE 12.2

Texas Spanish-Surname Population: Observed and Expected Neonatal Deaths, by State Economic Area

	Observed	Expected	Ratio observed to expected infant mortality rate
Post Oak	18.7	21.98	.90
Northern High Plains	20.5	21.47	.97
Southern Blackland	15.7	23.74	.78
Rolling Plains	16.9	23.32	.82
Southern High Plains	16.7	21.56	.85
Western Edwards	17.9	20.80	.90
Trans Pecos	13.0	20.71	.74
Southeast Sandy Lands	17.7	17.36	1.02
Northeast Sandy Lands	20.7	24.54	.90
Coast Prairie	13.9	21.47	.75
North Central Texas	14.3	27.52	.70
Northeast Rio Grande	14.8	20.54	.80
Northern Blackland	13.9	20.29	.77
Eastern Edwards	13.8	20.46	.74
Lower Rio Grande	12.4	19.62	.73
Southwest Rio Grande	14.8	16.94	.90

Source: Table 12.1.

can populations are characterized by virtually identical relationships between postneonatal and neonatal mortality rates. Furthermore, it has been assumed that postneonatal rates are roughly correct. This may be an inaccurate assumption, but, if so, it would certainly be the case that the final effect will be to *bias downward* the extent of the estimated underregistration. We could, in this sense, consider figures in Table 12.2 as lower bounds for the values of infant mortality in nonmetropolitan state economic areas.

A rather different way of proceeding is to determine an expected value for the infant mortality rate by utilizing a sequence of known mortality rates and some assumptions regarding the pattern of mortality to which the population is exposed. Here, as elsewhere, we need to start by assuming the correct values of some mortality parameters. In this case, we assume that the value of a set of age-specific death rates are known. Deviations from this assumption can, of course, vitiate our conclusions. Since there is no reason to assume that underregistration of male infant deaths is more or less severe than underregistration of female infant deaths, we can utilize the population of either sex and subsequently generalize our conclusions to the whole population. For this purpose, I have taken the female Mexican American death rates for Texas as of 1970. These rates are shown in Table 12.3 for three age groups. In Column 2 of the same table are displayed the values of infant mortality consistent with each age-specific death rate if the underlying pattern of mortality were model West of the Coale–Demeny families (Coale and Demeny, 1966). Finally, the last row shows the observed value of infant mortality and the mean of the values in Column 2. With the exception of the second age group, all other age-specific death rates are compatible with a mortality function characterized by an infant mortality rate in excess of 20.10 per thousand births.

Variation in the consistent infant mortality rates calculated in Table 12.3 may be due to several factors. Among these, certainly the most important is the noncorrespondence between the hypothetical and the true underlying mortality model. Thus, for instance, the change between the consistent mortality rate for the next to last and last age-specific death rates may be due to an excess of adult mortality in the female Mexican American population relative to the mortality rates in model West. Similarly, the exception in the second age group may be produced by excessively low mortality in late childhood and early adolescence. On the other hand, we cannot exclude the possibility that the observed irregularities are due to systematic errors in population counts and in death reporting. The most likely situation is one in which death rates above the age of 16 are understated because of failure to report deaths.

TABLE 12.3

Death Rate for Texan Mexican American Females: 1970

Age group	Age-specific death rates	Consistent infant mortality
1– 4	.0011	.0223
5–14	.0004	.0154
15–24	.0012	.0201
25–34	.0020	.0203
35–44	.0052	.0320

Observed infant mortality   .0182

Average value of infant mortality   .0220

Source: Coale and Demeny, 1966; Rodriguez, 1975:60, Table 8b.

If this were the case, the levels of infant mortality consistent with model West are lower bounds for the "true" ones. Taking the average value in Column 2 of Table 12.3 as the value of infant mortality corresponding to the mortality experience of the entire population, we can now determine an estimate of the amount of error involved in the observed figure for the infant mortality rate. The ratio of the latter to the former is .83, implying an error of .17. Notice that this is approximately the average error in infant mortality estimated before, using a totally different procedure (see Table 12.2).

In summary, the two procedures I have utilized show that in non-metropolitan state economic areas and in Texas as a whole the Mexican American infant mortality rate, on the average, seems to be in error by about 17%. Obviously, figures subject to errors of this magnitude can be utilized neither to perform any serious analysis of the mortality conditions of this ethnic group nor to establish any type of conclusion about past and future differentials in the mortality condition of this (the Mexican American) and other ethnic groups.

The Use of Indirect Techniques

Techniques are available to estimate indirectly infant and childhood mortality. They are "indirect" in the sense that they neither rely on information about deaths occurring during the particular calendar year of interest nor rest on any reports whatsoever about the number of births in that same year. Instead, they require information on certain parameters that provide sufficient knowledge about the history of mortality to which the children of ever-married females have been exposed during the past and are experiencing at the time of the census. In particular, one needs to know the proportion of children ever born who have died by the time of the census or survey. Answers to two questions are usually necessary to provide such a quantity: one about the number of children ever born and the other about the number of children who have died. The proportion of deaths to children ever born is not, however, sufficient to provide an estimate of infant or childhood mortality. For that purpose, one needs to know something about the fertility history of ever-married women. Information on fertility histories can, in turn, be obtained through two indicators: One is the number of children ever born to females in various age groups and the other is the age distribution (or any parameter summarizing it) of children surviving. In order to derive the fertility history from the number of children ever born, it is necessary to make the assumption that fertility has remained constant during the past. Alternatively, if information on the age structure of children surviving is available, no assumption whatsoever about the character of the fertility history is required. With these two pieces of information—the proportion of deaths to children ever born and data on the fertility function or the age distribution of children surviving—it becomes possible to estimate the conditions of mortality to which the children born to these mothers have been exposed. In short, the procedure consists of estimating a quantity M depending on the fertility schedule or, if available, the age structure of children surviving, by which the proportion of children dead has to be inflated (deflated) to be equal to the probability of dying before a certain age i_a, which depends on the mother's age group. That is, for every age group of mothers we have the following equality:

$$\hat{q}(i_a) = M_a(D/B)_a \, , \tag{1}$$

where $q(i_a)$ is the estimated probability of dying before age i_a, M_a is the "multiplier" for the age group of mothers a, and $(D/B)_a$ is the proportion of children dead for mothers in the age group a.

It has been verified elsewhere [4] that the ages i_a, which work the best from an estimation point of view, are 1 for the age group 15–19, 2 for the age group 20–24, 3 for the age group 25–29, 5 for the age group 30–34, and 10, 15, and 20 for the next three age groups. This correspondence between ages i_a and the age group of females is an empirical one, and it simply expresses the fact that a certain age group of females provides optimum information about the cumulative mortality up to a

---

[4] For a more comprehensive review of the techniques described here, see Brass and Coale, 1968. See also Preston and Palloni, 1978.

certain age. In what follows, I will assume that M_a has been calculated exactly by using knowledge of the age distribution of surviving children so as to avoid additional assumptions about the fertility schedule.

Are there any real advantages to be gained by using such indirect techniques intsead of using defective vital statistics? The reader may reason that if omission of deaths is a systematic phenomenon it *should affect both types of estimates*, the direct and the indirect, and, hence, there is no reason to believe that any of them enjoys special advantage over the other. This is not so in most "real world" situations. In fact, if females tend to conceal selectively a proportion of infant deaths, particularly neonatal deaths, the *infant mortality rate* will tend to be affected in equal magnitude. However, if the same type of omission occurs when reporting the *total number* of deaths to children ever born during the past, the estimated infant mortality rate will be biased by a factor of smaller magnitude, simply because not all deceased children died when they were infants. This assertion, however, needs to be qualified by explaining and defining some types of omission or concealment of infant deaths that can take place when a group of mothers are being interviewed and asked about their pregnancy histories.

There are two types of death omission that we will consider. First, we will assume that mothers conceal only infant deaths that have taken place in the immediately preceding year. This implies that infant deaths occurring before that, even though they may have been concealed at the time of the occurrence, are disclosed to the interviewer (or forgotten together with the birth itself, with the ensuing result of introducing only slight changes in the quantity D/B). It is well known that concealment of deaths is made easier if the person who died has lived for only a short period of time. In fact, it is a complicated matter to conceal from authorities and from the community the burial of an adult, but it is easier to carry out so-called "shoe-box" burials of infants. On the other hand, infants who died in the distant past, even if concealed at the time of the occurrence, may be included in the mother's recollection or, equally beneficial for our purposes, completely forgotten.

The second type of concealment is an extension of the former. We consider here the case in which mothers omit not only the infant deaths that took place the preceding year but also all infant deaths that occurred during their reproductive lives. What will be shown in the next sections is that the error in the estimate of infant mortality obtained by using the indirect technique will be smaller than the original error of omission, and, hence, it will assume a smaller magnitude than the error obtained by using vital statistics figures on infant deaths.

Omission of Infant Deaths Occurring the Preceding Year

If a female of age a declares only a proportion h_a of the infant deaths occurring during the preceding year, then the cumulative proportion of deceased children observed by the researcher will differ from the true one by a factor approximately equal to

$$k(1 - h_a)F_a(1 - {}_1L_0^s),\tag{2}$$

where k is the ratio of the probability of dying before age x in the true, underlying mortality function [5] to the probability of dying before age x in the standard mortality function, F_a is the average proportion of children ever born who were born during the preceding years to females now in the age group a, and ${}_1L_0^s$, is the number of person-years lived in the age interval 0–1 in the standard mortality function.

It is clear that the change in the cumulative proportion of children for a fixed value of h_a will be larger if F_a increases and if k is large (that is, if mortality is high). These remarks amount to saying that, the larger the proportion of children born during the preceding year and the worse the mortality conditions, the more serious the (absolute) error due to under-reporting of infant deaths. As a consequence, one should expect the following regularities:

1. For a given proportion of omitted infant deaths and a given fertility and mortality schedule,[6] the older the female the less the error on D/B. This occurs simply because, for older females, children born during the year preceding the interview is only a small fraction of children ever born.

2. For a given proportion of omitted infant deaths and a given mortality schedule, the younger the age at which childbearing begins, the less the error in D/B. This is because an early fertility start implies an older distribution of children ever born.

3. For a given proportion of omitted infant deaths and a given fertility schedule, the higher the mortality the larger the error on D/B. This occurs due to increases in the risk of infant deaths. Numerically, it is simply the result of an increased value of k.

In order to show graphically the operation of these regularities, Table 12.4 has been prepared. In this table are displayed the absolute magni-

---

[5] Mortality functions pertaining to each of the four models created by Coale and Demeny can be represented as follows:

$$q(x) = kq_s(x),$$

where the subscript s denotes the standard selected, usually level 11 in each model, and k is a proportionality factor approximately constant for all ages below 25.

[6] By mortality schedule we understand any particular life-table among those in the Coale–Demeny family.

tude of the error incurred in the calculation of the quantity D/B when h_a assumes values of .95 and .75, which are equivalent, respectively, to a 5 and a 25% omission of the preceding year's infant deaths. These figures, for three age groups of females, were calculated for four different populations obtained by combining high and low levels of mortality with early and late patterns of fertility.[7] In Table 12.4 I have also displayed the ratios of the observed (affected by error) and the true values of the quantities D/B. It is seen in all cases that the percentage of error affecting D/B is always less than the value of $(1 - h_a)$; this pattern is more salient the older the female and the earlier the fertility schedule.

An increase in mortality brings about a significant increase in the absolute amount of error associated with the observed value of D/B; these increases are more significant the later the fertility pattern and the younger the female. The behavior of the ratios of observed to true values of the proportion of child deaths is analogous to the behavior of the absolute errors. There is one exception to this: Variations in mortality levels appear not to have any influence. This is simply due to the fact

TABLE 12.4

Errors in the Proportion of Deaths in Children Ever Born: Hypothetical Simulations Subject to Various Errors $(1 - h_a)$, Three Age Groups

Population [a]		$h_a = .95$			$h_a = .75$		
		15–19	25–29	35–39	15–19	25–29	35–39
A	Absolute error	.0021	.0004	.0001	.0107	.0019	.0009
	ratios [b]	.996	.996	.999	.827	.980	.992
B	Absolute error	.0010	.0002	.0001	.0051	.0009	.0003
	ratios	.987	.998	.999	.940	.991	.998
C	Absolute error	.0063	.0011	.0002	.0314	.0056	.0025
	ratios	.963	.996	.999	.817	.980	.993
D	Absolute error	.0030	.0005	.0002	.0151	.0027	.0008
	ratios	.987	.998	.992	.934	.992	.997

[a] Population A has low mortality (level 17, model West) and late fertility; Population B has low mortality and early fertility; Population C has high mortality (level 7, model West) and late fertility; Population D has high mortality and early fertility.
[b] These are the ratios of "observed" (including errors) to true values D/B.

[7] For more details on the simulation process, see Palloni, 1977.

that, when mortality changes, the true value of D/B increases or decreases proportionately by the same factor as does the calculated or observed value D/B. In fact, those ratios should be approximately equal to the ratio that would obtain had the standard mortality function been combined with the given fertility schedule. That is:

$$\frac{(D/B)_s - F_a(1 - {}_1L_0')(1 - h_a)}{(D/B)_s},\tag{3}$$

where the symbols are defined as before and the subscript s refers to the standard mortality function.

The errors in D/B are reflected in errors affecting the estimates of the probabilities of dying before certain ages. For small changes in D/B, the error in $q(i_a)$ is approximately given by $M_a\Delta(D/B)_a$, where M_a is defined eras before and $\Delta(D/B)_a$ is the absolute error in $(D/B)_a$.

For every age group of females, the changes in $(D/B)_a$ will produce changes in $q(i_a)$ and, consequently, in the value of infant mortality that is consistent with $q(i_a)$ (under the assumption that a certain mortality model holds true). The full impact of the initial error in $(D/B)_a$ on infant mortality is shown in Table 12.5. In each case, I have calculated the ratio of the true to the estimated values of infant mortality. The reader may note that Table 12.5 provides the same numbers (except for aproximation errors) as does Table 12.4. This is simply the result both of assuming that the mortality functions are proportionate to each other and of using the *correct* multiplier M_a. In fact, the equality $kq_s(x) = q(x)$ ensures that the ratios of calculated and true proportions D/B and calculated and true infant mortality rates will be approximately equal *if*

TABLE 12.5

Ratios of Estimated and True Value of Infant Mortality: Four Populations Combining High and Low Mortality and Early and Late Fertility

	Population							
	A		B		C		D	
Age group	$h = .95$	$h = .75$	$h = .95$	$h = .75$	$h = .95$	$h = .75$	$h = .95$	$h = .75$
15–19	.966	.827	.987	.910	.963	.816	.987	.936
25–29	.996	.981	.999	.992	.996	.982	.998	.999
35–39	1.000	.999	1.000	.999	.999	.992	.991	.996

Source: Table 12.4 and Palloni (1977).

the quantity M_a is estimated correctly by removing the effects of random errors. This was the procedure followed to construct Table 12.5 so as to show only the *effects of error in D/B suppressing other sources of error that could be operating.*

We have already noticed that the indirect technique reduces the original error created by omission of a certain fraction of infants and that the amount of reduction varies according to age group of mother, fertility pattern, and mortality level. This "reduction effect" can be better illustrated by calculating the minimum proportion of infant deaths that have to be omitted in order to produce a given percentage of error in the estimated infant mortality rates. Table 12.6 was constructed accordingly. It is seen in Population A, for instance, that if the researcher estimates infant mortality on the basis of the information provided by females aged 15–19, an omission of 7.3% of infant deaths will be required to produce a 5% error in the infant mortality estimate. Likewise, if the researcher prefers to utilize the information provided by females aged 25–29, the required percentage of omission is nearly 10 times larger, 70.1. Finally, if the researcher finds it convenient to use the information provided by females aged 35–39, there is no way of producing an error as large as 5%; in fact, the maximum possible error for females in this age group is approximately given by

$$\frac{100 \times kF_{35-39}(1 - {}_1L_a^s)}{(D/B)_{35-39}} = 1.36\%, \tag{4}$$

obtained by setting h_a to a value of zero.

The maximum possible errors in each population and for every age group are shown in Table 12.7. Of course, Table 12.6 and Table 12.7 are essentially already contained in Tables 12.4 and 12.5, and, hence, even if providing more detail, they allow us to arrive at nothing more than the same relations obtained before. Populations with an early fertility pattern more easily absorb the errors in omission than do populations with late fertility patterns, whereas changes in mortality level make no significant contributions except to alter the values of absolute error for the estimates of infant mortality. On the other hand, females with an older age distribution of children ever born provide information that is remarkably robust with respect to the type of omission we have been studying.

Omission of Infant Deaths That Have Occurred in the Past

This type of error, of course, will have more serious consequences than the one previously analyzed. However, it will still be the case that the indirect technique produces estimates of infant mortality contain-

TABLE 12.6

Minimum Percentage of Infant Deaths Omission to Produce a 5 and 25% Error in the Estimated Value of Infant Mortality Rate

	Population							
	A		B		C		D	
Age group	.05	.25	.05	.25	.05	.25	.05	.25
15–19	7.3	36.2	19.00	96.9	6.8	34.1	19.4	96.9
25–29	70.1	x^a	x^a	x^a	62.4	x^a	x^a	x^a
35–39	x^a	x^a	x^a	x^a	x^a	x^a	x^a	x^a

^{a} x indicates that the calculated value of h_a is less than 0.

ing less error than those obtained by directly manipulating the information contained in the vital statistics. The *net relative effect* on the final estimate of infant mortality will, as before, be more or less independent of mortality level but will be strongly affected by the fertility pattern and the age of the female.

The quantity expressing the difference between observed and true proportions of deaths among children ever born is given by

$$h_a \int_0^{a-(\alpha+1)} \int_0^1 f[a - (x + t)]q(x) \, dx \, dt,$$

where $f(a)$ denotes the probability that a female of a given age will have a child at exact age a and t is a variable representing the interval of time since the birth took place; finally, x denotes the age of the child. Using some approximations, we can express the ratio of the calculated to the true proportions of children dead as

$$1 - \frac{(1 - {_1}L_0{^s})(1 - h_a)}{(D/B)_s},$$

where $(D/B)_s$ is, as always, the proportion of deaths to children ever born if a particular fertility schedule holds in combination with standard mortality. Values for Expression (6) are displayed in Table 12.8. This table shows again that errors in omission have less impact the earlier the fertility pattern and the older the female. Compared with errors shown in Table 12.5, these errors appear to be larger, as expected. Thus, for instance, for the age group 15–19, where the absolute magnitude of the error is more considerable, a 5% omission of those infant deaths that occurred during the preceding year produces an error in the final infant mortality estimate amounting to 1–2% less than that generated

TABLE 12.7

Maximum Percentage Error in Infant Mortality Rates for Various Populations and for Three Age Groups of Females

Age group	Population			
	A	B	C	D
15–19	31.0	25.9	73.4	25.8
25–29	8.1	3.5	7.9	3.4
35–39	1.4	.86	1.3	.84

by an omission of 5% of all infant deaths that took place during the reproductive life of the mother and between 7% and 14% less when the proportion of omitted death is .25. However, it is important to notice that the final proportionate errors are here again less than the original proportionate error of omission.

Final Remarks: The Advantages of Using Indirect Techniques

From the preceding analysis, certain tentative conclusions seem in order. In the first place, the indirect technique examined here produces a reduction effect in the proportionate size of the error in infant mortality estimates when omission of infant deaths takes place. Second, this reduction effect is considerably greater for older age groups of females. This suggests that the researcher will be better off utilizing the information provided by older age groups or, perhaps, a combination of age groups. Third, the reduction effects are larger if the pattern of fertility is early rather than late. This is a fortunate circumstance, since most of the

TABLE 12.8

Ratios of Calculated to True Proportions of Deaths to Ever-Born Children When Omission of Infant Deaths Extends to All Years Before the Survey or Census: Two Populations and Three Age Groups of Mothers

Age group	Population with early fertility		Population with late fertility	
	$h = .95$	$h = .75$	$h = .95$	$h = .75$
15–19	.968	.840	.955	.777
25–29	.977	.885	.973	.867
35–39	.980	.900	.979	.895

groups for which this technique is of value are characterized by relatively early age at marriage.

The types of errors considered here are extremes. The first type of error may be an exaggeration of what really occurs in that mothers reporting information on their reproductive histories are likely to omit not only the deaths occurring in the preceding year but also some or all of those that took place in the more distant past. The second type of error exaggerates in the other direction, magnifying rather than reducing the potential error. In fact, it is very unlikely that females will forget or conceal a fraction of all infant deaths without at the same time forgetting about the corresponding births and thus minimizing the net impact of the error. In practice, it would seem that errors falling somewhere between these two extremes are most likely to occur.

It should be noted, however, that the indirect technique is also subject to errors, some of which are systematic, and others random, in character. Thus, the prediction of the value M_n, the "multiplier," is subject to errors created by one or another fitting procedure that attempts to determine M as a function of known parameters either describing the age distribution of children surviving, as advocated here, or the age distribution of children ever born, as in the well-known Brass technique (Brass and Coale, 1968). Furthermore, the determination of M presupposes knowledge of the mortality pattern underlying the population under study. This is an optimistic requirement (especially for human groups for which adequate statistical information is lacking). Finally, and of less importance, these indirect techniques may be affected by errors in some of the given parameters, mean age of surviving children, or other parameters indexing the fertility schedule.

Barring the effects of such problems, we could, as a final step in the analysis, study the data presented before in Tables 12.1 and 12.2 and estimate how much better off the researcher would be if he or she had used the indirect technique rather than the vital statistics figures. Table 12.2 shows that the error due to omission of Mexican American infant deaths in nonmetropolitan state economic areas in Texas may be anywhere between .30 and .03, depending on the state economic area considered (I have excluded Southeast Sandy Lands for reasons explained before), with an average very near .20. Under these conditions, simple arithmetic operations performed on data from Table 12.1 show that the average relative error in the difference between the Anglo and Mexican American infant mortality rates reaches a value as high as 50% of the true differential.

The same proportion of omission in the reporting of infant deaths—

that is, on the average, .20—would produce much lower errors had we used the indirect technique. In fact, from Table 12.5 we can derive by straightforward interpolation that, under the worst conditions, the percentage error in the infant mortality rate of an average state economic area would be .15 (obtained with $h = .80$, females in the age group 15–19 and Population C). Utilizing the best strategy available, that is, females in the age group 35–39, the researcher would incur an error never exceeding .09. This implies that the maximum error in the estimate of the difference between Anglo and Mexican American infant mortality rates could reach on the average a value of .40 and could be, in all likelihood, as low as 20%. These last figures represent, respectively, a reduction of 20 and 60% in the bias associated with the measure of infant mortality differentials between the Spanish-surname and the Anglo populations.

The advantages offered by the application of indirect techniques seem well worth the extra effort of obtaining additional information from surveys or even from the census itself in order to eliminate differentials in coverage errors for different racial–ethnic groups.

REFERENCES

Brass, William, Ansley J. Coale, Paul Demeny, Don Heisel, Frank Lorimer, Anatole Romaniuk, and Ettienne Van de Walle
  1968   *The Demography of Tropical Africa.* Princeton, New Jersey: Princeton University Press.
Coale, Ansley J., and Paul Demeny
  1966   *Regional Model Life Tables and Stable Populations.* Princeton, New Jersey: Princeton University Press.
Palloni, Alberto
  1977   "Estimating infant and childhood mortality from data on children surviving." Unpublished Ph.D. dissertation. Seattle, Washington: Center for Studies in Demography and Ecology, University of Washington.
Preston, Samuel H., and Alberto Palloni
  1978   "Fine-tuning brass type mortality estimates with information on the ages of surviving children." United Nations Population Bulletin. (forthcoming)
Rodriguez, Romeo
  1970   "Mortality experiences of Chicanos, Blacks and Anglos, Texas, 1970." Austin, Texas: Population Research Center, University of Texas.
Stockwell, Edward
  1962   "Infant mortality and socioeconomic status: A changing relationship." *Milbank Memorial Fund Quarterly* 40:101–111.

Sullivan, Jeremiah
    1972   "A review of Taiwanese infant and child mortality statistics, 1961–
              1968." Taipei, Taiwan: Population Papers, The Institute of Econom-
              ics, Academia Sinica.
Teller, Charles H., and Steve Clyburn
    1974   "Trends in infant mortality." *Texas Business Review* 48(10):240–246.

13

Mortality Differences
by Race and Sex:
Consequences for Families

GORDON F. SUTTON

From an ecological perspective, the social organization of the human community provides the adaptive mechanism by which human populations survive. Organizational arrangements are conditioned by both biological and social features of populations, including mortality. Families, it has been maintained, have been organized around sex and age features of the human organism, and these are related to sustenance-producing processes. Thus, mortality conditions within families play a significant role in influencing family living arrangements and, in turn, life chances in both present and later generations. Just as high levels of mortality have been observed in relation to high levels of fertility and as sex ratios that depart seriously from unity have reflected certain marriage practices and sex-selective infanticide, so group differences in mortality may be studied with regard to their social consequences.

Group differences in mortality between the white and nonwhite population in the United States are the subject of this chapter. The

The Demography of Racial and Ethnic Groups.

risks of death among married males are of principal interest. However, the consequences of these deaths for family members are partly a function of sex differences in mortality, so sex differentials are introduced. I outline a procedure for evaluating color differentials in the effects upon surviving family members of the deaths of married men during their working lifetimes. These differentials are seen to be different from and larger than the differences between the mortality rates of white and nonwhite men. Moreover, the basis upon which the differentials are computed lends itself to the measurement of economic impacts that may be considered in formulating social policy.

MEASURING DIFFERENTIALS BY RACE

There is a problem of meaning in the measurement of mortality differentials. This is evident in a number of studies that show that not only are sex differentials in mortality in the United States subject to variation as a function of the way in which mortality differentials are measured but also that differentials in survivorship rates comprise yet a different set of values that are not readily derived from corresponding mortality rates (Keyfitz and Golini, 1975; Sheps, 1958, 1959).

A comparison of mortality versus survivorship rates is illustrated by an example from Sheps. Referring to data from one of her papers (here reproduced as Table 13.1), she notes:

> Ninety-five and one-tenth percent of newborn girls, as compared to 92.1 percent of boys were expected to live to age forty, so that there would be 3 percent more women than men alive at this age. One could also say that since 4.9 percent of the girls and 7.9 percent of the boys would die before the age of forty, mortality of males was 61 percent higher than that of females. The two statements are both correct . . . [1958:1–2].

Recent observations on the decline of mortality to quite low levels in modern societies have led to increasing interest in studies of morbidity as indicators of the health and well-being of modern populations. With regard to aggregate effects noted by Fuchs, useful measures of the economic value of a change in the death rate over time can be computed, but, "Because death rates at productive ages are as low as they are, it is becoming increasingly difficult to show large economic returns to reductions in mortality [Fuchs, 1965:11]."

Measures of the costs of mortality in society have been of two kinds: (a) measures of aggregate losses to the society; and (b) measures of loss to individual families computed for purposes of establishing compensation claims for survivors. On the matter of losses experienced by families

TABLE 13.1

Pecentages of White Males and Females Surviving and Dying between Birth and Age 40

	Male	Female	Difference (2) − (1)	Survivor's ratio (2) ÷ (1)	Death ratio (1) ÷ (2)
	(1)	(2)	(3)	(4)	(5)
Survivors	92.1	95.1	3.0	1.03	—
Deaths	7.9	4.9	3.0	—	1.61

Source: Table adapted from Sheps, 1958:1210–1214.

with regard to the deaths of their members, a sizeable literature exists. Less attention has been paid, however, to the economic losses borne by *classes of families* taken in aggregate terms (for an exception, see Weisbrod and Hansen, 1968). If, indeed, mortality rates are so low as to be insensitive to analytical tools applied to their study, there is nevertheless continuing interest in group differences in mortality within the society (Kitagawa and Hauser, 1973). Moreover, even Fuchs seems to have changed his views in his recent book *Who Shall Live?* (1974).

As we look at race and color differentials in mortality, what is it that we wish to determine? The impact of mortality may be assessed by computing ratios (race-specific mortality rates), as shown in Table 13.2. Having removed the effect of age composition, we can compare these "risks," finding a nonwhite to white ratio of 1.01 in 1969, down from 1.06 in 1960. This would perhaps be sufficient if we had not already become enmeshed in social policy questions and issues that demand more from us than, say, the rate of change of ratios (Sutton, 1971).

Moreover, as Keyfitz and Golini point out (1975), the age-adjusted rates, although sensitive to the rate of loss of life in the compared populations, are quite indifferent to the ages at which these losses occur. Regarding sex differentials, they suggest the following possibility:

$$I_e^f = \frac{\Sigma p_x^f \ell_x^f u_x^m}{\Sigma p_x^f \ell_x^f u_x^f},$$

where

I_e^f = Index of loss of expected years of life among women.

p_x^f = Number of females of age x.

ℓ_x^f = Expectation of female life among those aged x.

$u_x^{f(m)}$ = Age-specific death rates for females (males).

TABLE 13.2
Ratios of Nonwhite to White Mortality Rates:
United States, 1969 and 1960

Age	Year	
	1969	1960
All ages [a]	1.01	1.06
15–19	1.54	1.40
20–24	1.96	1.79
25–29	2.62	2.44
30–34	3.05	2.70
35–39	2.86	2.61
40–44	2.50	2.34
45–49	2.14	2.00
50–54	1.90	1.92
55–59	1.73	1.72
60–64	1.62	1.74

[a] Includes ages from under 1 through 85 and over.
Source: U.S. National Center for Health Statistics, 1973,
      Table 3.

Still leaving something of an enigma for interpretation, this formula
weights death differentially as to *age* of occurrence, placing greater
weight upon those occurring early in the prospective life span. Hence,
the weighting of deaths by the forgone remaining lifetimes aggregated
across subpopulations reveals different comparisons with the total
population than those suggested by the comparisons of mortality rates.

Again we need to ascertain what it is that we are trying to measure.
The answer that guides the argument in this chapter accepts the premise
from Fuchs that the magnitude of the difference in mortality rates by
color has (a) been a familiar figure in public health statistics for many
years; and (b) is not subject to exotic movements or properties, possibly
excepting findings in recent investigations directed at identification and
interpretation of differentials in causes of death (Preston *et al.* (1972).
This answer proposes to discover the social and economic cost differentials by color as these are measured among surviving family members.
This is a return to Dublin and Lotka's (1930) notion of the "money value
of the man." It does not purport to measure emotional strains and
suffering but, rather, to look at changes in income, level of living, and
others of the more tangible features of family life.

When one's focus is on the survival of the population, certainly an
ecologically important idea, the Keyfitz and Golini index of loss of
expected years of life is a step in the right direction but one that perhaps

does not go quite far enough. The formula is appealing as a measure of attrition in the population of the years of lifetimes remaining rather than merely as the measure of undifferentiated lives themselves. Yet, although the measure deals with survivorship rather than mortality, it does not embrace surviving dependent persons whose lives are implicated in a family organization that may be changed in a fundamental way upon the death of certain members (such as the male head).

Clearly, differentials in mortality by race can be assumed to reflect something of the race differentials in the impact of mortality upon surviving family members. But there may also be differences that have important consequences. Changes in the one kind of measure may not necessarily parallel changes in the other, and it can be shown that the measurement of the effects of color differentials in mortality upon relative well-being within compared populations becomes too complex a matter to attempt through direct analysis.

If widowhood were a more common experience among nonwhite women than among white, this difference could emerge not merely because of differences in mortality and in the risk of marriage in the two populations but also because of the *sex differential in mortality by color.* Given that nonwhite women are more likely to become widowed during ages prior to 65 and that they are likely to spend more years as widows in the working years than are white women, the mortality sex differential that favors women over men might be assumed to be more pronounced among nonwhite than among whites. Also, nonwhite men might be expected to be *worse off* relative to their wives than white men relative to theirs. The actual mortality ratios entailed in this comparison show the opposite. How can nonwhite women have a larger sex differential in mortality in their productive lifetimes if nonwhite women (*a*) are less likely to get married than are whites; (*b*) have mortality by age more like their opposite sex than white females in relation to their opposites; and (*c*) expect, looking forward from age 14 to age 65, to spend more years as widows than white women? I shall only say at this point that the sex differential can play a role, but it appears that the absolute magnitude of the difference between the color groups, specifically between the female components, is of sufficient size to override the effects of the sex differential that appears to work in the reverse direction.

MORTALITY IN THE PRODUCTIVE AGES

The timing of loss of life in the human lifetime has important consequences for population survival and for the well-being of members of population components. Should every birth lead to a lifetime ended uniformly at the beginning of a "fixed retirement age," the productive capacity of the population would be at a maximum with regard to the social–biological process. Newborn humans must spend, it may be agreed, a sizeable portion of their lifetimes in socialization, during which time they incur net social and economic costs to the society and, for the economic side at least, to their families. If this "investment period" is followed by a period of productive work during which the individual contributes to the society at least what he took and takes out and if life concludes at the point at which this productive lifetime closes, then the investment made by society in this individual is returned.

Conversely, if individuals born into the society or into some component of the society live only to the age at which they are about to begin to make positive contributions to the economy (or if they tend to vastly outlive their productive years), then the investment on the part of the society in these lives is considerably reduced as to net lifetime returns. Indeed, such a hypothetical society would seem bound to vanish. If life expectations fail to accord with the productive capabilities of the population or if this should be true for some component of the population (as expressed in dependency ratios), we may properly expect this state of affairs to increase the risk of population failure. Yet, such burdening conditions may also be considered to bear upon the families or upon other organizational features of the society that play important roles in the maintenance of the society and, therefore, may adversely affect the prospects for well-being among the members of the society or some specific component of it.

METHOD

The present chapter is mainly concerned with showing the way in which measures of color differentials in mortality might differ among married males from measures of the effects of differentials in mortality upon survivors. The literature on mortality differentials is ostensibly at hand. Measuring the effects of mortality upon survivors needs a little explaining. The procedures used here are outlined in the following. (Readers with interest in further details are referred to other publication, specifically Sutton, 1977.)

Given the nature of the system of collection of vital statistics in the United States, it is not feasible to attempt to study widowhood by looking at vital records, since information is not collected, at least directly, on this topic. The resource I used instead was the June, 1971 Current Population Survey (CPS) microdata file (U.S. Bureau of the Census, 1971). That survey contained marital and fertility histories for women, from which I constructed an "experience period"—from July, 1961 to June, 1971—from which to draw observations about changes occurring in the population. The marital life status table—a multiple increment-decrement table devised by Shoen and Nelson—was very nicely suited to address the problem at hand (Schoen, 1975; Schoen and Nelson, 1974). I modified the Schoen–Nelson program to accommodate the observations taken from the June CPS, and, for mortality among the women in the synthetic tables, I created a set of female mortality rates for 1970 adjusted with marital status-specific mortality rates from 1960 and population underenumeration corrections for 1970.

Oversimplifying the matter somewhat, the CPS survey was used to provide transition probabilities by age, color, and marital status among marital status classes. Beginning with an arbitrary 100,000 women of each color at exactly the age of 14 (from birth), we immediately subject these to risks of (a) marriage; and (b) death appropriate to their age. For those who survive that first year, we do it again for the next age interval, and so forth. For women who marry, we introduce them into a "married" table in which they become subject to risks of (a) divorce; (b) widowing; and (c) death. If a woman becomes widowed, she is entered into yet another table where she becomes subject to the risks of (a) marriage; or (b) death. There is yet another table for widowed women.

The process described has two absorption states, only one of which—death—is constantly at hand. The other state is the 65th birth anniversary, at which point the woman has survived the "working years of life." The process seems analytically complicated. However, the L_x and T_x columns and the 1_x columns can be read to extract the fruit of the process—the numbers of person-years of experience in the various marital statuses during the 51-year run of the table and the numbers of person-episodes of marital status change for each marital status transition possibility. As an added feature, we can look at how these numbers evolve with regard to specific ages.

The matter of paternal orphanhood entails a data problem similar to that for widows. I used the retrospective fertility data in the same CPS to provide the basis for transition probabilities of women to the child-present condition by age, keeping track of the births so that the imputed child's age, along with the mother's, can be used in the characterization of women at any point in the 51-year lifetimes. Actually, the children are, as it were, characteristics of the women in this analysis; a woman accumulates child-years of life in each year of her own life in each marital status up to what are now three absorption states: (a) death of mother; (b) mother's exit at age 65; and (c) child's exit at age 18. As an added feature in the input, I introduced age-specific child mortality decrements that were applied to the estimates of child-years of life generated in the system; therefore, this is really a fourth absorption state, although it does not appear in the process as a direct contingency.

What is obtained in dealing with these births are estimates of child-years of life generated in the female marital life status tables—in which the females are viewed as mothers—and years of paternal orphaned life that can be related to the total and then used in the computation of the color differentials. There are a number of things to worry about in making the kinds of estimates I have prepared for this study, and this is especially the case for these orphans. Family living arrangements are not taken into account in the retrospective histories, so the questions of mortality burden, which are to some degree problematic with regard to widows, are even more so with regard to these orphans.

COLOR DIFFERENTIALS IN MORTALITY
AND IN THE EFFECTS OF MORTALITY
UPON SURVIVING FAMILY MEMBERS

Table 13.2 contains ratios of white to nonwhite mortality rates by age. By inspection, we note that the age-adjusted values for all ages, 1.04 in 1969 and 1.06 in 1960, are substantially below the age-specific values shown for the 15–64 age interval in the table. Clearly, there are important differences in the age distribution at death for these two populations, a difference illustrated in the accompanying Figure 13.1. Not only are there striking differences between these populations in this distribution, but, because mortality risks are dramatically greater at the older ages, when a color parity emerges, the age-adjusted figure is seriously misleading with regard to the force of mortality during the working ages.

Moving to more sharply drawn comparisons, we see in Table 13.3 that the majority of the age-specific ratios that relate nonwhite married male to white married male mortality are *lower* than the combined-sexes comparison in the preceding table but that the age-adjusted value calculated for the working age of 15–64 is much larger. This table seems to suggest that the comparative position of nonwhite married males in relation to their white counterparts is better than that for all nonwhites in the working ages.

Going one step further, Table 13.4 shows the values for widowings for white and nonwhite populations. The values in this table are extracted from estimates prepared in connection with the construction of

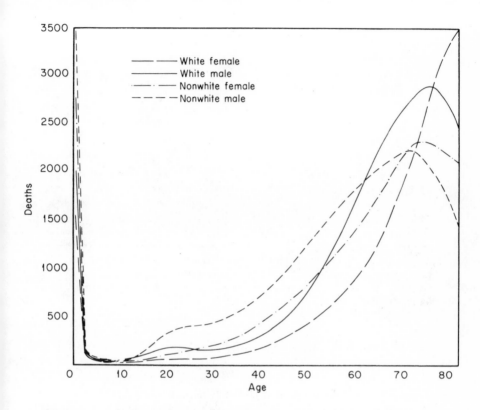

Figure 13.1 Number dying in year, by age (graph of life-table function). *Source:* U.S. National Center for Health Statistics, 1970.

the Schoen–Nelson (1974) marital life status tables from retrospective survey data for the 1961-1971 period. Since these estimators are basically derived from survey data, the marital life process construction procedure has only minor effects upon the results.

Note that the age-of-spouse entries in the far-right column are merely suggestive of the appropriate comparisons that might be made with preceding tables: With age data grouped in 5-year intervals, the assumption that men are about 5 years older than their spouses is perhaps not a bad one. In any case, the comparison of values in this table with those in the first two tables shows larger color differentials with respect to widowing. Note that although a direct comparison might be made of mortality rates for married males with widowings per 1000 married women, in which the numbers should be more comparable, my choice of presentation features a measurement of risk expressed in terms of L_x

TABLE 13.3

Mortality Rates for Married Males by Color: 1970 [a]

Age	White	Nonwhite	(2) ÷ (1)
	(1)	(2)	
Ages 15–64 [b]	6.15	8.91	1.45
15–19	1.44	2.73	1.90
20–24	1.36	2.90	2.13
25–29	1.36	3.21	2.35
30–34	1.33	3.25	2.44
35–39	2.72	5.36	1.97
40–44	2.69	5.50	2.04
45–49	7.38	11.45	1.55
50–54	7.21	11.03	1.53
55–59	15.04	18.80	1.25
60–64	23.48	25.92	1.10

Source: Computed from vital statistics and census sources. See Sutton, 1977.

[a] Rates adjusted for underenumeration in the census.

[b] Age-adjusted rates, by the unweighted average age-specific mortality rates of the distribution of white and nonwhite married males in 1970.

TABLE 13.4

Widowings per 1000 Years of Married Life of Women, by Color: 1961–1971

Age at widowing	White	Nonwhite	(2) ÷ (1)	Approximate age at death of spouse
	(1)	(2)	(3)	(4)
Total ages, 14–64	9.04	14.87	1.64	20–69
14	.00	.00	—	—
15–19	2.84	3.88	1.37	20–24
20–24	1.12	4.09	3.65	25–29
25–29	1.31	3.41	2.60	30–34
30–34	1.83	4.24	2.32	35–39
35–39	3.35	6.38	1.90	40–44
40–44	5.55	6.82	1.23	45–49
45–49	8.50	17.68	2.08	50–54
50–54	13.36	24.71	1.85	55–59
55–59	22.40	29.02	1.30	60–64
60–64	32.13	53.80	1.67	65–69

Source: Sutton (1977) and tabulations of CPS (1971).

values, that is, the number of person-years of married life in the respective populations during each of the age intervals. The resultant values should depart from the widowing–married rate differentials to the degree to which there are differences in duration of marriage (see Sutton, 1971). The differentials as I have computed them in Table 13.4 are somewhat larger than the widowings per 1000 married rate differentials.

Extending the view of differences in marriage durations, I show in Table 13.5 the duration of widowhood relative to marriage; again, a more pronounced differential is found. These results may be partly a function of the condition noted in the previous table; if there are differences in marital status durations that make the widowing per 1000 married years color-differences larger, then the duration of widowhood itself may account in part for where that nonmarried time is spent.

Turning to a consideration of the effects of mortality upon survivors, we see in Table 13.6 the degree to which loss of life among nonwhite male parents compares with that among white counterparts in its effect upon the next generation. Paternal orphans, those children bereaved through the death of the male parent, show substantially larger differentials than those for widows, as based upon estimates of duration of orphanhood expressed as a proportion of child lifetimes.

In recent years—up to 1975, at least—several facts seem to urge our close attention to the effects of mortality upon survivors, particularly with regard to race and color differentials. One factor is the sex disparity

TABLE 13.5

Person-Years of Widowed Life per 1000 Years of Married Life: Marital Life Status Tables for American Women, 1961–1971

Women in the ages:	White	Nonwhite	(2) ÷ (1)
	(1)	(2)	
Total ages, 14–64	70	133	1.90
14–19	1	2	2.00
20–24	1	4	4.00
25–29	2	7	3.50
30–34	4	15	3.75
35–39	7	24	3.43
40–44	13	36	2.77
45–49	27	64	2.37
50–54	50	120	2.40
55–59	94	186	1.98
60–64	172	320	1.86

Source: See Table 13.4 footnote.

TABLE 13.6
Years of Paternal Orphanhood under 18 per 1000 Child-Years of Dependency [a]

	Total	In marital unions	Ratio of nonwhite to white values	
			Total	In marital unions
Children under 18 years				
White	16.09	17.12	3.05	3.34
Nonwhite	49.13	57.15		
Children under 12 years				
White	8.93	9.41	3.82	4.16
Nonwhite	34.14	39.12		
Children under 6 years				
White	5.15	5.39	4.29	4.63
Nonwhite	22.10	24.98		

Source: See table 13.4 footnote.
[a] Adjusted for child mortality.

in mortality that favors females over males and that has continued to increase. In the 1950s and 1960s, we saw mortality among men remain unchanged while female mortality rates continued to decline. In the late 1960s and early 1970s, rates for both sexes declined significantly, but, again, females gained more than did males (Metropolitan Life, 1977a). By 1975, life expectation for males was 68.5 years, whereas it was 76.4 years for females. A result of this development has been to increase the chances that a married woman will be widowed during her lifetime, as well as to increase the chances that children who lose a parent will be paternally orphaned before they reach their 18th anniversary of birth. Moreover, if a woman has a son who is 20 years her junior in age, she has a 1 in 4 chance of outliving him (Metropolitan Life, 1977a).

What about the color differentials in life expectations? Between 1969–1971 and 1975, nonwhite expectations of life at birth gained by 3 years. (Metropolitan Life, 1977b). This rapid rise contrasts with slower movements in previous decades and with a slight decline for nonwhite males during the 1960–1970 decade. And the sex differential is also present in that improvements have favored females for both the 1960–1970 decade and for the present period of rapid increase in nonwhite life expectations. For both white and nonwhite populations, the specter of a rising widowhood rate and a growing paternally orphaned population is present.

CONCLUSION AND SUMMARY

Color differentials in mortality are commonly studied with an eye to group differences in health conditions and well-being in the population. Another aspect of color differentials in mortality is that concerned with the consequences of premature death of adult males upon surviving and dependent family members. Measures of widowhood and paternal orphanhood for differentials are computed and are shown to exceed the values of mortality differentials as to the extent of the disadvantage of the nonwhite population. The color differentials are influenced by sex differentials in mortality by color but do not predominate in the outcomes. Although such demographic measures illuminate the matter at hand, the next steps in the study of the burden of mortality upon survivors is the calculation of measures of economic loss and color differentials in such losses for use in the consideration of national social policy.

REFERENCES

Dublin, Louis I., and Alfred J. Lotka
  1930   *The Money Value of a Man.* New York: The Ronald Press.
Fuchs, Victor
  1965   Some Economic Aspects of Mortality in the United States. (Unpublished; mimeographed)
  1974   *Who Shall Live?* New York: Basic Books.
Keyfitz, Nathan, and Antonio Golini
  1975   "Mortality comparisons: The male–female ratio." *Genus* 31(1–4):1–34.
Kitagawa, Evelyn M., and Philip M. Hauser
  1973   Differential Mortality in the United States. Cambridge, Massachusetts: Harvard University Press.
Metropolitan Life Insurance Company
  1977a   "Current patterns of dependency." *Statistical Bulletin* (January):10–11.
  1977b   "Expectation of life among non-whites." *Statistical Bulletin* (March): 5–7.
Preston, Samuel H., Nathan Keyfitz, and Robert Schoen
  1972   *Causes of Death.* New York: Seminar Press.
Schoen, Robert
  1975   "Constructing increment–decrement life tables." *Demography* 12:313–324. (See also author's correction notice, *Demography* 12:571.)
Schoen, Robert, and Verne E. Nelson
  1974   "Marriage, divorce, and mortality: A life table analysis." *Demography* 11:267–290.

Sheps, Mindel C.

1958   "Shall we count the living or the dead?" *New England Journal of Medicine* 259:1210–1214.

1959   "An examination of some methods of comparing several rates or proportions." *Biometrics* 15:87–97.

Sutton, Gordon F.

1971   "Assessing mortality and morbidity disadvantages of the black population of the United States." *Social Biology* 18:369–383.

1977   "Measuring the effects of race differentials in mortality upon surviving family members." *Demography* 14:419–430.

U.S. Bureau of the Census

1971   June, 1971 Current Population Survey. Microdata file copy at Madison, Wisconsin: Center for Demography and Ecology, University of Wisconsin.

U.S. National Center for Health Statistics

N.D.   Vital Statistics of the United States, Volume II, No. 5. Rockville, Maryland: Department of Health, Education and Welfare.

1973   "Mortality trends: Age, color, and sex: United States, 1950–69." Vital and Health Statistics, Series 20, No. 15.

Weisbrod, Burton A., and W. Lee Hansen

1968   "An income–net worth approach to measuring economic welfare." *American Economic Review* 58:1315–1329.

Subject Index